Worst Enemy

The Reagan Imprint: Ideas in American Foreign Policy from the
Collapse of Communism to the War on Terror

From Troy to Entebbe: Special Operations in Ancient
and Modern Times

In Athena's Camp: Preparing for Conflict in the Information Age

Networks and Netwars: The Future of Terror, Crime,
and Militancy

Worst Enemy

THE RELUCTANT TRANSFORMATION
OF THE AMERICAN MILITARY

John Arquilla

Ivan R. Dee

CHICAGO 2008

www.ivanrdee.com

Library of Congress Cataloging-in-Publication Data:
Arquilla, John.
  Worst enemy : the reluctant transformation of the American military /
John Arquilla.
      p. cm.
  Includes bibliographical references and index.
  ISBN-13: 978-1-56663-750-3 (cloth : alk. paper)
  1. United States—Armed Forces—Reorganization. 2. Military doctrine—
United States. 3. Strategy. I. Title.
  UA23.A725 2008
  355.30973—dc22   2007038597

For David Ronfeldt
visionary, colleague, friend

Contents

Preface

FOR SEVERAL YEARS NOW, the United States has been spending about as much on its military as the rest of the world combined, a trend that shows no signs of abating. These have been war years, and the American people have been exhorted to accept the fact that a new mode of terror-styled conflict has emerged, and that it will persist indefinitely. Given the huge financial commitments and psychological demands being made upon Americans, it would seem there are no more important questions to ask now than "What kind of military is needed to win the war on terror and future conflicts?" and "How should American armed forces be employed?" This book offers some answers.

To some degree these questions have been raised in political and military circles, and they are increasingly being considered by the general public too. But so far they are questions that have proven difficult to answer; and they have sparked a sharp, often bitter debate within the American defense community: a war of ideas about the idea of war has unfolded. Traditionalists, a category that includes most of the senior military and civilian leadership and much of the mid-level officer corps, hold to the

notion that existing weapons systems, organizational structures, and battle doctrines retain much of their value. This
underpins their view that changes should be introduced only
in the most careful, deliberate, and incremental fashion, to
mitigate risk and hedge against a possible resurgence of old-
fashioned conventional warfare. But the traditionalists do
acknowledge the need to improve our ability to cope with irregular threats, such as those posed by terror networks and
insurgents. So they support calls for a greater emphasis on
special operations forces and the additional elements (perhaps
covert) required for countering such adversaries.

On the other side of the "war over war," those who perceive
a need for major military reforms believe that incremental
changes alone will not be enough to master the challenges that
have emerged over the past decade. Instead they seek what former defense secretary Donald Rumsfeld liked to call "military
transformation," the development of a new array of tools and
practices designed to change military affairs drastically. From
armed forces made up of relatively few heavy armored divisions, carrier battle groups, and wings of attack aircraft, they
would shift our military structure to far more numerous but in-
dividually much smaller units of action—on land, at sea, and in
the air. While those who favor major reforms are a minority,
drawn from the ranks of both civilian defense analysts and military officers at all levels, they are nonetheless a significant one.

The loss of Donald Rumsfeld as a "product champion" who
favored major change has already been exploited by traditionalists. In the wake of his dismissal, they have managed to soft-
pedal discussion of transforming the military. The best example
of this exploitation is the manner in which the debacle in Iraq
has been used to shore up support for our old ways and to
pillory those in favor of major change. This has been done
skillfully—and by many traditionalists sincerely—in the form
of the critique that we went to war in Iraq with "too few troops
on the ground." This view has been widely embraced by both

liberals and conservatives, and is perhaps the single most dangerous thrust to the heart of the military reform movement.

In this book the reader will find Rumsfeld an elusive, complex character, right on the big issues about military innovation, tragically wrong about both the idea of invading Iraq and the manner in which the campaign there was conducted. It is especially ironic that this great advocate of nimble, networked field operations acceded to military bureaucratic pressures to mount a classical "shock and awe" aerial bombing campaign and a traditional massed armored thrust up Mesopotamia.

Beyond a desire to explicate the issues underlying military reform, the nature of the intervention in Iraq, and the role of Rumsfeld, I have also been driven by a concern that our conception of twenty-first-century warfare has become blurred and confused. At the most abstract level, our adherence to a military philosophy of overwhelming force—the so-called Powell Doctrine—seems exceptionally ill-suited to our time, guaranteeing staggering expenditures, major collateral damage inflicted upon innocents, and growing global resentment of the United States.

In terms of more specific strategic ideas, the situation is just as discouraging. The army remains tied to organizational structures that keep it big and balky, allowing it to be tied down—some use the term "broken"—by just a few thousand terrorists and insurgents. The navy's concept of operations is, if anything, even more curious. Its intention is to be able to fight with the fleet close to hostile shores, despite the facts that our ships will burn to the waterline if hit and that our potential foes are coming into possession of highly effective anti-ship missiles, torpedoes, and "brilliant" mines. The air force remains devoted to a strategic bombing doctrine that has seldom worked—if ever—since the dawn of airpower a century ago. The Marines have almost completely lost touch with their roots in support of naval campaigns; and the Special Operations Command has grown so greatly in size and heavy with bureaucratic structure that it threatens to become just another conventional service. In short, we seem to have become our own worst enemy.

From the outset of his tenure as secretary of defense, Rumsfeld was well aware of virtually all these contradictory impulses. He strove hard to bring about change but failed, despite six years during which he enjoyed full presidential support. Beyond demonstrating that even an activist commander-in-chief and an iron-willed secretary are small cogs in the machinery of big defense, their failure to effect needed reforms speaks to the larger issue of inherent military resistance to change. In this respect the current leadership of our armed forces still marches in step with those who have come before them. Their predecessors and counterparts, both from our own and from other strategic cultures, have always been suspicious of changes that might undermine military effectiveness. What they have seldom appreciated, however, is that there are times when resistance to change engenders an even greater risk of catastrophe. In fact, in most eras military affairs fall into this latter category. The historical record suggests that stodgy resistance to innovation has almost always caused far more problems than it has prevented.

In our present era of conflict, we are once again relying heavily on well-worn conventional military means in the fight against networked terrorists and insurgents. We are also continuing to spend almost all our defense allocations on weapons systems that are growing ever less relevant to the future of warfare. Thus we find ourselves in something of a double bind: our huge conventional military punches itself out against elusive networks while our potential nation-state adversaries leapfrog ahead of us by crafting radically new concepts of operations and investing in innovative types of weapons systems. Unless we rekindle our own defense debate and confront these issues in a flinty-eyed manner, we are fated to fail against the networks and to confront other nations in future conflicts with an exorbitantly expensive but increasingly outmoded military.

Acknowledgments

IT IS COMMON for professors to confess how much they learn from their students, but this admission takes on a special meaning when one teaches at a military graduate school in wartime. The officers who come through all have remarkable, often searing experiences to share, and are bursting with ideas that have been waiting for just such a period of introspection to set them loose. I am humbled by their courage and commitment, and grateful to all who have come along over the years to help shape my thoughts. Special thanks are owed to Lt. Amber Hopeman, USN, for sharing her views on the future of the navy, and Maj. Ken Burgess, USA, for his insights into army reform. Lt. Cdr. David "EGON" Norton, USN, and Maj. Ivan "Lizard" Kanapathy, USMC—two great fighter pilots—tutored me on some of the fine points of aerial combat in the twenty-first century. Maj. Jeff Bracco, USA, gave me a real education about the potential for creating "one-gun" artillery batteries.

Army majors Cameron Sellers, Greg Reck, and Matt Zahn helped a great deal with their reflections on "influence operations." Maj. Sam Brasfield, USA, shared his thoughts about the many different ways to take airborne operations "beyond the parachute." Army majors Wayne Lacey, Todd Clark, and Pete Hopewell always had interesting, stimulating opinions on many topics. More than a dozen other officer students had insightful things to say about the military potential of airships, large and small, with air force majors Phil Acquaro, Mack Bessemer, and Chad Riden providing especially extensive comments. Majors Bret Hyla, USMC, and Jason Colbert, USA, offered special insights on this topic as well. Army Maj. Dennis Wille explained to me why "ground pounders" had come to rely so much on satellites for intelligence and communications. Indian army colonels Rajan "Ravi" Ravindran and Ulhas Kirpekar have kept me abreast of their country's many remarkable military developments.

Among my academic colleagues at the Naval Postgraduate School, I am particularly grateful for ongoing discussions about military reform and innovation with Doug Borer, Peter Denning, Sue Higgins, Wayne Hughes, Ira Lewis, Bob O'Connell, Nancy Roberts, Hy Rothstein, and Kalev Sepp. A special debt of gratitude is owed Gordon McCormick for fostering and sustaining such a lively intellectual environment.

My RAND Corporation colleague David Ronfeldt, to whom this book is dedicated, has exerted a continuing influence on my views for many years, and still does. Michael Wilson too has been a fountainhead of ideas. I am also indebted to John Kao and Ned Desmond, who have urged me, on and off for a long time, to write this book. Ivan Dee has once again edited with exceptional deftness, and Sherry Pennell has assisted in many ways, from administrative to conceptual matters.

Dick O'Neill and other members of the Highlands Forum have been kind enough, over the past dozen years, to hear and comment on my ideas. The Del Mesa Carmel Library Association has provided another wonderful venue for testing my ideas, and I am grateful to its members for their warm embrace. Finally, the late Art Cebrowski served as a remarkable sounding board for my thoughts over the years, as I sometimes did for his. He is sorely missed.

J. A.

Monterey, California
January 2008

We have the problem fully worked out. But the chain of reasoning was as clear two hundred and fifty years ago as it is now; why then was it so long in being worked out? Partly, no doubt, because old traditions . . . had hold of and confused men's minds; chiefly because men are too indolent to seek out the foundation truths of the situation in their day, and develop the true theory of action from its base up.
—Alfred Thayer Mahan, *The Influence of Sea Power upon History* (1890)

It is not that generals and admirals are incompetent, but that the task has passed beyond their competence. Their limitations are due not to a congenital stupidity—as a disillusioned public is apt to assume—but to the growth of science, which has upset the foundations of their technique. They are like men who cling to their huts in an earthquake. The only way of salvation would be to get out in the open—to survey the problems in complete detachment and from the widest point of view. But a scientific habit of thought is the least thing that military education and training have fostered.
—B. H. Liddell Hart, *Europe at Arms* (1937)

The topic today is an adversary that poses a threat, a serious threat, to the security of the United States of America. . . . It stifles free thought and crushes new ideas. . . . It's the Pentagon bureaucracy. Not the people, but the processes. Not the civilians, but the systems. Not the men and women in uniform, but the uniformity of thought and action that we too often impose on them.
—Donald Rumsfeld, a speech at the Pentagon (September 10, 2001)

Worst Enemy

CHAPTER ONE

Stability, Change, and the Art of War

ARMED CONFLICTS are, among other things, time portals. They showcase traditional practices that allow us to view the powerful pull of past ways of war, and at the same time they feature innovative weapons and concepts of operations that afford us glimpses of emerging tactics, strategies, and military doctrines. For those who develop skills at this sort of "time traveling," the dividends can be considerable, helping inform decisions about when or whether to make important changes. For those who don't learn to mine the military past and present in this manner, the costs can be huge, with dangerously outmoded practices remaining in use and innovative new ones being tragically ignored.

The "war on terror" that President George W. Bush declared in the wake of the September 11, 2001, attacks on the United States—history's first protracted conflict between nations on one side and networks on the other—provides a perfect example of a conflict in which past and future aspects of the art of war are on clear display. The central dynamic has been that U.S. armed forces, for the most part massed in World War II–style formations capable of delivering heavy firepower, have had great trouble finding and fighting the enemy's small, dispersed, but coordinated bands, which have only grown stronger in the years since 9/11. This is a global struggle between largely tradition-bound nations and innovation-oriented networks, with both the past and future of conflict apparent.

Whether in Afghanistan, Iraq, or elsewhere around the world, terrorists and insurgents have in recent years foreshadowed the further rise of the still embryonic concept of network-based warfare (or "netwar," for short), offering us a preview of the likely form these conflicts will take. Meanwhile U.S. military operations have remained all too backward-looking, too redolent of the past: slow, balky, and almost totally lacking a capacity for employing surprise. A few shining exceptions do suggest that we are at least aware of the future ways of war. These include the networked offensive undertaken by just a few hundred of our commandos in Afghanistan late in 2001, and the small, secret operations undertaken with surrogate forces and other allies in places like the Sahara Desert, where we brought an end to the al Parra terrorist group in 2005. But these few exceptions prove that our vision—and that of many other advanced powers—remains profoundly in thrall to the past, as it has been, in our case, since at least the mid-nineteenth century.

Visions of what was and what will be in warfare have often clashed on the battlefield. In the Civil War (1861–1865)—still America's bloodiest conflict ever, with well over 600,000 soldiers killed—both sides clung to half-century-old Napoleonic notions of massed forces at the "decisive point" and frontal attacks. Union and Confederate generals ordered foolish frontal assaults time and again—Pickett's Charge was emblematic—despite their full awareness of the increasing range and lethality of rifles capable of inflicting horrific casualties. Both armies in this war insisted on massing in one spot, or in just a few, despite the rise of railroads capable of widely distributing the many hundreds of thousands of troops each side had under arms at the height of the war across a theater of operations as big as Western Europe. The process might have been neatly orchestrated by telegraph. Even though the future of warfare was on nearly full display with these new weapons, means of transport, and information systems, few on either side seemed to grasp their implications at the time, or for at least fifty years afterward.

The result was that few strategic lessons were learned from the Civil War, by Americans or others, and the dead hand of Napoleon continued to guide events during World War I (1914–1918). In this conflict the shadow of set-piece battles of the preceding century continued to loom large over the plans of the combatants, impelling them to mount their attacks with closely massed infantry. Now this time-honored practice ran headlong into maturing new weapons of war that were far more deadly than the rifle: machine guns, mortars, and high-explosive field artillery. These emerging tools of wars to come decimated those who employed the battle practices of the past. And millions on both sides were slaughtered for want of innovation in the face of radical change. Tanks, planes, radios, and looser fighting formations—tools and organizational forms still in their infancy—were also on display during World War I, foreshadowing what was to come a generation later when the Axis Powers made their lunge for global domination. Even when the near future is not yet ready to determine the outcome of an ongoing conflict, the way ahead for the next war may often be seen with considerable clarity.

In World War II (1939–1945), innovation-oriented fascist forces used tanks, planes, and new types of mobile military units to bowl over the concentrations of machine guns and field artillery that by then represented the received wisdom in military affairs. The Maginot Line in Western Europe, the totem of those who thought they had learned the enduring lessons of World War I, was swiftly and hopelessly outflanked, even penetrated in spots. In this case a vision of conflict drawn from even the near past—from the weapons that had caused so much slaughter less than three decades earlier—was overwhelmed by the maturing heralds of modern maneuver warfare.

This same conflict also provided a vision of the longer-term future, as jets and cruise and ballistic missiles made their debut, all three the creations of German scientists. But the danger of fixating on the future was also highlighted, for these weapons were in far too embryonic a state to shape the outcome of the war. As the historian Richard Overy has put it, by overemphasizing the production of these "wonder weapons" at the cost of fielding more tanks and propeller-driven aircraft, the Germans tried to win a war of the 1940s "with the weapons of the 1950s." The Americans avoided this sort of mistake. Even though they succeeded in conjuring the nuclear genie out of the Manhattan Project—whose lead scientist, J. Robert Oppenheimer, would become the zeitgeist of apocalyptic strategic thought—they concentrated on the mass production of tanks, planes, ships, and guns.

In the wake of World War II, it seemed to U.S. military leaders that all the tools and practices that could possibly be needed for waging any sort of conflict, at any level of intensity, had come into their own. Tanks, jets, missiles, aircraft carriers, and atomic weapons, and the communications systems to provide for skillfully commanding and controlling them, together formed the basis for a hoped-for Pax Americana. But this myth was almost immediately shattered. In the Korean War (1950–1953), poorly armed Communist forces, including Chinese formations employing Mao Zedong's "People's War" concepts, held their own by grasping at a key element of the future of war: the rise of irregular swarming tactics, undertaken by countless small bands of fighters aiming to overwhelm U.S. ground units. Once again, it seemed, a piece of the future was showing enough strength to withstand forces guided by the best lessons of even the very recent past. The Korean War ended with a military stalemate and an edgy cease-fire, both of which persist to this day.

American military leaders seem not to have been fazed by the outcome in Korea, and in U.S. conflicts over the past half-century successive generations of generals and admirals have continued to behave as though the paradigm of modern mechanized warfare, crafted in response to the fascist threat and considered vital for containing Communist expansion during the cold war, remained the most relevant model. It should not surprise us, therefore, that U.S. forces were used in a fundamentally traditional manner during the main years of our involvement in Vietnam (1965–1972), a time when army Gen. William Westmoreland's basic strategic equation was "Mobility plus firepower equals attrition."

The debacle in Vietnam was followed a decade later by a failed intervention in the Lebanese civil war, where a successful suicide bombing of a U.S. Marine barracks in 1983 unraveled U.S. strategy and hinted at the rise of suicide terrorism as an emerging form of war. Ten years later a chaotic firefight in Mogadishu against irregular forces drove American troops out of Somalia, yet another benighted country, where they had come with the intention of doing good. Fast-forward one more decade, to 2003, and the modern maneuver warfare technique, along with "shock and awe" aerial bombing, was on display yet again, this time in Iraq. But the results were similarly disheartening, as the by-now-hoary conventional tactics of the U.S. military did little to suppress the rise of a loose-jointed, largely leaderless insurgency. Our aging way of war had run head-on into a future organizational concept—the fighting network. While still in an early stage of development, it was already extremely potent.

Since World War II the record of the U.S. military in trying to replicate its successful methods of the 1940s has been spotty. Against the reverses already noted, one can count the successful small interventions in Grenada (1983) and Panama (1989), and the larger Operation Desert Storm (1991). But in Grenada a massive American force confronted only a few hundred armed Cuban "construction workers." In Panama the opposition posed by Manuel Noriega's "dignity battalions" was even lighter, and U.S. forces benefited from having long-established bases in that country. As to Desert Storm, Saddam Hussein was easily expelled from Kuwait by a coalition of more than thirty nations, which enjoyed complete air and naval mastery. The only striking success of the past sixty years was the special-forces invasion of Afghanistan in late 2001, waged in a manner radically different from all that had come before, a real sneak preview of future possibilities.

Any reasonable assessment of our combat record since 1945 should leave one with a sense that the U.S. military has consistently enjoyed great manpower and material resources but has shown little awareness of emerging combat trends. Its gaze has remained too fixed on what has worked in the past. It has failed to understand that the travails of the present, and of the past half-century, have grown out of an unwillingness or inability to consider the kinds of conflicts to come.

It would be unfair to single out *American* military leaders for such criticism: they march in a long, unbroken historical line of generals and admirals who have been reluctant—sometimes with good reason—to retool their forces or change their operational concepts radically. War is the most dangerous of all human enterprises, the stakes often being as high as national survival or the world system itself. Military organizations cannot adopt innovations as freely as commercial enterprises do with their product lines, or other nonmilitary organizations do with their practices. To "take a flyer," expecting failure and hoping it will be counterbalanced by a few successes, is simply not a good idea.

Still, the failure to embrace change, especially when others are successfully doing so, may engender risks and consequences just as dire. This built-in tension has characterized the dynamics of military affairs from time immemorial, with some strategists finding the right balance between stability and change, and many others falling by the wayside. Knowing more about the origins of this enduring dilemma, and how successful militaries have coped with it, will help us understand American efforts to comprehend the future of conflict, which can often be glimpsed only "through a glass, darkly." Examples from the past at least have the benefit of greater clarity. As we try to look ahead, we first do a bit of looking back.

*

Recognizably professional military organizations first appeared in Egypt and Mesopotamia several millennia ago. They have been with us ever since, their general purpose being to secure the needs of life, whether represented by the water and food sources of these ancient river civilizations or in our more sophisticated modern preoccupations with the allocation of goods and concepts of self-governance. For whatever reasons they arose, armed forces remained because there was almost always fighting to be done. Writing forty years ago, Will and Ariel Durant found this to be one of the central truths that emerged from their exhaustive study of civilization. "In the last 3,421 years of recorded history," they noted, "only 268 have seen no war." The past four decades have added not a single year to the total of peaceful ones; the near-term future seems to hold only the prospect of continued conflict.

For most of the long years of our bloody past, and into the war-torn present, military organizations have also fought a war of ideas, with battle lines drawn between the powerful pull of tradition and the allure of innovation. Both causes have had their share of champions; each side has had its innings. Those who draw comfort and strength from tradition believe that war is a complex, perilous undertaking whose inherent risks and high costs demand that the closest attention be paid to identifying and mastering those practices that may actually work in battle. On those occasions when seemingly immutable "principles of war" are distilled from experience, they are reverently passed from one generation of soldiery to the next. The partisans of innovation, on the other hand, are more highly motivated by the view that armed conflict is prone to change. The very nature of war and the urgent need to win impels combatants to find and field better weapons, and to embrace new fighting formations that can confront the enemy in surprising ways.

This tension between honoring existing military tools and practices versus introducing new ones has been consistently sharp for five millennia. The debates are apparent, whether we examine the ancient Akkadian approach to controlling Mesopotamia by building a great fortress at the point where the Tigris and Euphrates flowed just fifteen miles apart, or in our own time by trying to parse the U.S. military's plans, in recent years, for winning the Battle of Baghdad on virtually the same ground. Seen in historical context, the acrid ongoing debates in the American defense community over military transformation comprise just the latest chapter in a long, ongoing historical saga.

If the U.S. Army today is torn between keeping some of its beloved heavy tank brigades or replacing them with nimbler, lighter strike forces, this sort of problem differs little from the doctrinal debates in ancient Rome over whether legionaries should discard their body armor so as to improve their mobility on the march. In the Roman situation, the emperor Gratian, who ruled in the latter half of the fourth century C.E., chose in favor of unarmored infantry, which soon left his men prey to hordes of barbarian horse archers. As Edward Gibbon noted, "the Goths, the Huns and the Alani . . . excelled in the management of missile weapons; they easily overwhelmed the naked and trembling legions." Here is a clear example of the grave risks associated with change, which have profoundly influenced the military imagination.

If there is a built-in bias toward stability in military affairs, it is nevertheless possible to see many kinds of changes that have recurred throughout history. For example, the single massed force of the Greek phalanx gave way to the much more flexible formation of the Roman legions, the latter distinguished by having some sixty small maniples (from the Latin for "handfuls") of one hundred soldiers each (a "century," led by a centurion), which could be arrayed in many ways. This large/small organizational theme has stayed with us. Just look at the massed waves of infantry of World War I that gave way, in the last year of the conflict, to the small groups of "storm troops" the Germans created—which almost gave them victory. The great military historian Lynn Montross first noted this similarity between ancient and modern forms, observing that "the armies of 1918 were bringing up to date the ancient tactical duel between the legion and phalanx!" This duel seems to be playing out once again in the war against terrorists, where large formations from advanced militaries have attempted to engage "handfuls" of dispersed terrorists using infiltration tactics. Given that the legion won out over the phalanx, and storm-troop infiltration tactics were clearly superior to massed ground assaults—indeed, they have been the benchmark for infantry combat for the past ninety years—perhaps we should ponder more seriously the value of fielding smaller units.

Change in military affairs can take a variety of forms, and debates over the pace of change can be just as sharp as those over whether to pursue a new course at all. Since antiquity, the major question of change has been whether to make incremental modifications or to pursue major shifts. Nearly 2,500 years ago, for example, the leaders of Athens argued bitterly about how to deal with the threat posed by the Persian Empire. Herodotus recounts that Themistocles believed that only a fundamental shift of Athenian power toward the sea could secure Greece from invasion. He therefore argued the case for building a navy; but his opponents in council resisted being "chained to the oar." Instead they preferred to emphasize greater numbers of heavy infantry, since the first Persian attack had been thwarted by these *hoplites* at Marathon. In the end, Themistocles prevailed—just barely—arguing that only sea power could prevent the Persians from coming into Greece at all. He reasoned that a bigger army might well prevail in pitched battles on Greek soil, but that it would do little or nothing to eliminate the threat of repeated future incursions. Themistocles turned out to be right, and the Greek naval victory at Salamis that he made possible ensured not only the independence of Greece but also the rise of the West.

In more modern times the American naval theorist Alfred Thayer Mahan was particularly inspired by the Roman strategic choice for change, seeing in Rome's quantum shift to sea power during the Punic Wars clear lessons for U.S. naval policy in the decades before World War I. His writings deeply influenced such leaders as President Theodore Roosevelt, creator of America's "Great White Fleet." But ideas can be easily and widely diffused; and Mahan's notions also inspired the rise of the Japanese and German navies—the latter sparking a bitter antagonism with Britain, the leading maritime power of the day, and contributing to the outbreak of World War I in 1914. Like the examples from ancient times, these great shifts toward sea power by the United States, Germany, and Japan were instances not just of choosing to change but of embarking on fundamental alterations to the form of their military power.

The German case proves especially interesting. Germany's head of state, Kaiser Wilhelm II, was an ardent navalist who insisted that copies of Mahan's *The Influence of Sea Power upon History* be placed in all his warships. His leading admiral, Alfred von Tirpitz, remained in office for two decades and oversaw a naval expansion that the German legislature consistently funded generously. Tirpitz settled on the idea of transforming the German navy into a force that would look mostly like its British counterpart, because he believed that the best way to confront battleships was with battleships. He ruled against building a submarine-centered fleet because of these vessels' limited range. As he put it, "I refused to throw away money on submarines so long as they could only cruise in home waters." Apparently he gave too little thought to accelerating the development of submarines which, even though he neglected them, came close to winning World War I.

Instead a beautifully built High Seas Fleet of dreadnoughts emerged, a bit less than two-thirds the size of the Royal Navy's Grand Fleet. But Britain was not at all deterred from going to war by the existence of Tirpitz's "risk fleet," which, as matters turned out, the German naval leader was extremely reluctant to risk in battle. The High Seas Fleet fought only one major action with its dreadnoughts, winning a tactical victory at Jutland. But it suffered such serious losses in the battle that it could not resume the struggle for naval mastery. Thus the High Seas Fleet remained only "in being" for the rest of the war. It was a fleet that stayed in port, and when the kaiser finally ordered his admirals out to fight again in 1918, their crews mutinied.

Amazingly, Tirpitz's error was immediately repeated, as Germany began World War II in 1939 with scarcely more U-boats than it had had in 1914. In a convincing demonstration of the constraining power of "strategic culture," Adolf Hitler and his naval advisers hewed to the same path followed by their Wilhelmine predecessors and decided to build a battleship fleet. Although smaller, it would, they thought, be technologically superior to the Royal Navy, whose own battle line was still replete with many of the same dreadnoughts that had performed so indifferently at Jutland. In the sea war that ensued, Hitler's battleships went down one by one while his U-boats nearly brought Britain to its knees.

This German experience at sea over the course of two world wars should demonstrate the powerful attraction of imitation over innovation—imitation not only of the adversary but perhaps also of one's earlier choices—and its potentially grave costs. This "German lesson" was somehow learned by the Russians who, when they became a serious seagoing power during the cold war, chose not to imitate the structure of the new leader, the United States Navy. Instead they concentrated on building submarines designed to interdict the NATO alliance's all-important "sea lines of communication" (SLOCs) in the event of a major European conflict. From what has been learned since the end of the cold war about Russian armaments, capabilities, and intentions, it should be considered a great stroke of good fortune that the continued American emphasis on large surface ships—aircraft carriers being the successors to dreadnought battleships—was not put to the ultimate test.

Today it seems that the People's Republic of China has determined to go to sea in a similarly innovative fashion, but in a manner somewhat imitative of the Russian approach, eschewing the American "battle group" mentality in naval affairs in favor of submarines and other stealthy weapons.*

Thus, while a powerful impetus may often drive change in imitative directions, there is also much evidence of a willingness to take innovative approaches, or to follow the path of an innovative challenger, rather than choosing to imitate a conventional-minded "leader." Concepts become still more complex when one considers change not only in terms of the tools of war but also in its "practices."

*

In addition to technology, equally careful consideration must be given to practice—strategy, tactics, and doctrine. The ancient Romans, for example, closely followed the design of a shipwrecked Carthaginian "trireme" (the term refers most likely to having three men to an oar) that washed up on an Italian shore at a time when the Senate was debating whether to

---

*A detailed discussion of China's approach to becoming a sea power may be found in Chapter 3.

create a real Roman navy. So far, so imitative. But the Romans had no seafaring tradition; they were infantrymen at heart. Thus, while they used the Punic ship model the gods had sent them—and built a very large fleet along these lines—instead of trying to match Carthaginian ship maneuvers and ramming techniques, the Romans innovated in the area of practices. They realized that their best chance would be to give sea battles a flavor of land warfare; so Roman engineers conjured up a *corvus* ("crow"), something that looked like a mast with an iron beak that could be swung around, lazy Susan style. Whenever a Roman vessel came close enough to the enemy, the "crow" would be turned as needed and let loose, its metal beak fastening on to the opposing deck. Soldiers would then run across the narrow, now horizontally deployed gangplank on the back of the crow, and board the enemy vessel. The *corvus* allowed the Romans to achieve their aim of engaging in an infantry fight at sea, and they soon wrested naval mastery from the Carthaginians, a determining factor in the outcome of the Punic Wars.

Roman naval innovations featured both technological and doctrinal aspects in almost equal shares; but sometimes change occurs almost entirely in the realm of practice. An excellent example of this was provided by sixteenth- and seventeenth-century Swedish military leaders, who first showed a full appreciation of how smoothbore muskets could be used in battle by infantry. The Swedes made only incremental improvements to the weapon's short range and poor accuracy; their great contribution was to recognize the value of massing their musketeers close together and having them volley all at once at their targets. This maximized their effectiveness and created what the historian Michael Roberts first termed a "military revolution" in one of his lectures at Oxford more than fifty years ago. He used this phrasing because the value of massed volley fire was immediately appreciated and soon thereafter imitated by many others. The average European field army quickly grew tenfold in size, maneuvers became far more complex, and the overall impact of warfare on society was felt with an exceptional new keenness.

The Dutch adopted this Swedish practice, adding an important twist of their own: drill, the formal practice of such evolutions as deploying from the march to a firing line, keeping order during a flanking movement, or shifting from defense to attack. As the historian William McNeill has observed of the Dutch, "they discovered that long hours of repeated drill made armies more efficient in battle. Drill also imparted a remarkable esprit de corps to the rank and file, even when the soldiers were recruited from the lowest ranks of society." Lest the value of volley fire and drill be understated, it should be noted that both the Swedes and Dutch were few in numbers, yet both these small nations rose to great power in the seventeenth century. The Dutch had a navy that also relied heavily on drill, which helped "embed information" in their military organization.

Notions of massing and drilling came to dominate strategic thought in all leading states, and for the most part have persisted ever since. Nowhere was this more apparent than in seventeenth-century England. Oliver Cromwell, the great Lord Protector, first came to appreciate the power of mass and the value of drill—to which he added a dash of his own religious zealotry—during the English civil war, when he created England's New Model Army. At the same time, in a series of sea wars with the Dutch, English naval leaders (then called "generals-at-sea") were learning to appreciate the benefits of well-drilled ships sailing virtually bow-to-stern in line ("close hauled") in order to maximize the effects of their concerted fire. In 1691 the close-order line of battle and massed cannonades were enshrined in the Royal Navy's famous (and famously restrictive) Fighting Instructions.

Beyond England, where notions of mass and drill became staples of military and naval thought, Frederick the Great of Prussia grew to be the best-known virtuoso of these practices in

land warfare during the following century. In a series of conflicts in which his forces were almost always outnumbered,
Frederick led his small nation successfully (if exhaustedly) to
great-power status. Many others soon tried to emulate him, including George Washington, who went so far as to hire a Pruss-
ian drillmaster, the Baron von Steuben. At the close of the
eighteenth century, Napoleon Bonaparte rose to make France's
statement about the importance of mass. His conscripted
forces, which used their numbers to great advantage, were
known as the *levée en masse*. Three million Frenchmen were
drafted between 1792 and 1815. One million of them died, in
part because of Bonaparte's stubborn adherence to massed
frontal assaults in an age in which firepower—from smoothbore
to the emerging rifled infantry weapons and on to artillery—was
making important advances in range, accuracy, and lethality.

This trend would deepen and broaden throughout the nineteenth century, and into the twentieth, with increasingly powerful consequences for military affairs. As the killing power of
rifled infantry weapons* and field artillery grew steadily
throughout the nineteenth century, new questions about the
need to reform military practices arose, especially in the wake
of increasingly costly frontal assaults on well-defended positions in the American Civil War, the Franco-Prussian War
(1870–1871), and the Anglo-Boer War (1899–1902). In each of
these conflicts, accurate defensive fire caused heavy attrition
among attackers. At least one thoughtful observer, Ivan Bloch,
could see the portent of catastrophe for massed, drill-driven
armies. Bloch was a banker who had done logistics work for
the tsar during one of Russia's wars against the Ottoman Empire. He later immigrated to France (becoming Jean de Bloch)
and spent much of his energy in identifying and interpreting
the many strategic implications of the industrial age.

---

*The circular grooving of the rifle's barrel imparts spin to bullets and makes them
more likely to stay on aim. As does the spiral on a well-thrown football.

But Bloch was not a professional soldier, so his radical ideas about changes in the conduct of warfare were for the most part dismissed. Military leaders of the time viewed Bloch's challenge to their core beliefs, and the increasingly troubling results of recent conflicts, as a set of problems that could be solved only by Napoleonic means—that is, with more mass, better drill, and the added ingredient of "confidence." An iconic figure in the pantheon of traditional strategic thought, revered and re-ferred to by virtually all the leading militaries around the world, was the French army colonel Charles Ardant du Picq. His *Battle Studies* became their Bible. When he spoke of the co-hering benefits of drill, his tone grew mystical: "Unity alone produces fighters." He saw confidence in a similarly metaphys-ical light, affirming that "we are naked against iron, naked against lead, which cannot miss at close range. Let us advance in any case, resolutely. Our adversary will not stand."

Du Picq fell in battle during the Franco-Prussian War, a con-flict that his beloved military lost disastrously. But his death seemed only to scatter the seeds of his thought, as armies of all the great powers reaffirmed their faith in the ability of well-drilled, massed forces—and their unconquerable spirit—to overcome even the deadliest fire. This faith was eventually re-inforced by a great military, the Japanese army, which seemed to exhibit all the traits du Picq described. Just a decade before World War I erupted, Japanese infantry were able to mount successful frontal assaults in their war against the Russians in the Far East. For traditionalists, here was proof positive that mass and drill still worked. But the reality of the situation was a bit more complex, for in this conflict the Japanese actually used small-unit infiltration tactics, much like those the Ger-mans would finally employ in 1918. Most militaries looked past this subtlety, content to point at last to an example of a suc-cessful infantry offensive, even in the face of artillery and ma-chine guns. The Russo-Japanese War (1904–1905) also featured the triumph of a massed, well-ordered line of battleships, which obliterated the Russian fleet at Tsushima. It was fought one hundred years after Trafalgar, but Japanese Admiral Togo commanded with a Nelsonian brio that seemed to confirm the case against radical change in naval affairs as well. On land and at sea, the mantra of mass thus continued to dominate the doctrines of the leading militaries, guaranteeing ruin when methods at least a century out of date were relied upon in the intensely destructive European war that came soon after.

The hecatomb of World War I at least opened a line of counterargument to military traditionalism. In the 1920s and 1930s, for example, German officers built a new blitzkrieg armored-maneuver doctrine on the foundations of small-unit storm-troop tactics. The U.S. Marines and navy learned from the Allied disaster at Gallipoli and revitalized amphibious warfare. Airpower theorists of almost all the leading nations created a wholly original body of strategic thought about aerial bombardment.

But these dramatic doctrinal advances were offset by persistent traditionalist views. Almost alone among the great powers, the Germans saw that land warfare would soon shift from static attritional battles to fluid, mobile engagements; and their creation of armored ("panzer") divisions, working in close cooperation with attack aircraft, was not imitated by others until well after the panzers' initial successes in Poland and France. Naval leaders of all the great powers, despite growing inner doubts, remained sufficiently in thrall to their traditional faith in the massed firepower of the line of battleships, and so failed to appreciate that the aircraft carrier had become the new capital ship. Among air enthusiasts, advocates of mass bombing generally dominated the debate, leading to a neglect (save in the German case) of the valuable role that close-support attack aircraft could (and would) come to play.

World War II turned out to be a conflict in which both the innovators and the traditionalists held sway at different times, sometimes in the very same places. For example, mobile

maneuver warfare was often featured—on land, at sea, and in
or from the air—but massive attritional struggles were engaged
in just about as often, with the Russo-German conflict, the
largest-scale military campaign in history, featuring much of
both. The Battle of France in 1940 might have been a masterpiece of armored maneuver warfare, but its sequel in the summer of 1944 began with nearly two months of bloody,
stalemated attrition in Normandy, and concluded in similar
fashion—after a brief period of mobility—with Allied armies
bogged down in the Low Countries and along the approaches
to Germany. Even in the Pacific War, the initial six months of
lightning conquests by Japanese carrier strike and amphibious
forces gave way to prolonged attritional struggles, ranging from
Guadalcanal to the fighting in Southeast Asia and China, and
on to the final American "island-hopping" invasion of Okinawa.

This alternating pattern of mobile and static operations was
repeated in Korea, where a first year of skillful maneuver gave
way to something that looked like World War I. But after Korea
a viral strain of irregular warfare appeared. It was a nettlesome
doctrinal response to the orthodoxy of conventional mass-and-
drill military methods, and it took the form of a modern refinement of guerrilla warfare. This was a kind of hit-and-run
concept first used to great effect in the early nineteenth century
by the Spanish insurgents who resisted Napoleonic occupation.* At the close of that century, Boer and Filipino resistance
forces had used similar methods, fighting in small, dispersed,
yet networked groups.[†] But it was Mao Zedong who refined
guerrilla warfare during the decades before he finally gained
power in 1949, at the end of the Chinese civil war. His methods
were quickly emulated by others who saw they had little chance

---

*"Guerrilla" is the Spanish word for "small war."
[†]See Chapter 7's exposition of "Netwar 101" for a discussion of the similarities and
differences between classical guerrillas and modern networked insurgents.

of confronting their colonizers by conventional means; soon insurgencies erupted around the world, beginning in the 1950s in Algeria and Vietnam, and continuing ever since. Most of them have been successful, and have vexed the great powers, including the United States, whose military seems to have lost touch with its own colonial and revolutionary roots in irregular warfare.

Resistance to reforming our armed forces so that they may better confront the challenges of irregular warfare is just one more problem whose roots can be traced to staunch military traditionalism. Throughout all the changes described above—from huge enhancements in the accuracy and destructiveness of weapons to the rise of odd new concepts of operations—defenders of mass and drill have generally remained steadfast. They have repeatedly regrouped, seeing advanced new weapons as simply enabling new ways to "mass fire" or even to engage in "maneuver by fire." More to the point, they have stubbornly viewed the diffusion of improved new weapons and innovative operational concepts as impelling a reassertion of the primacy of sheer mass and dedicated drill.

Against this formidable resistance, those who have pushed for change have generally sought to find it in new practices rather than in new tools, trusting that innovative techniques would reenergize even old weapons systems. This has certainly been the main thrust of the Pentagon's office of "net assessment," where its longtime head, Andrew Marshall, first advanced this approach in the early 1990s, suggesting a deemphasis on tools by changing the notion of a "military-technological revolution" to one of a "revolution in military affairs." The T-word was deleted. Donald Rumsfeld, who believed that generals hated the word "revolution," replaced it with a new T-word: transformation. Still, ever since Marshall successfully deemphasized technology, American strategic thought—if it has shown any tolerance for change—has been focused for the most part on practice.

*

One of the best examples of an approach to the reform of processes, which might generally be described in terms of "old tools, new practices," was provided by the life and work of the late Arthur Cebrowski, an admiral and, in retirement, head of the Pentagon's Office of Force Transformation, an internal think tank that rose to prominence while Rumsfeld was defense secretary. Admiral Cebrowski championed the cause of networking the U.S. Navy in the hope that this new practice of vastly increasing the flows of lateral information would, among other things, reenergize and extend the life of aircraft carriers. He was both a naval aviator—with combat experience in Vietnam and elsewhere—and a computer specialist, so this perspective seems a logical one for him. And he was not alone among senior naval officers who thought along these lines: William Owens, who rose to become vice chairman of the Joint Chiefs of Staff, had similar ideas about creating a "system of systems" replete with interconnected sensors, communications, and very smart weapons-guidance packages.

To the extent that Cebrowski and Owens championed new technologies, they did so in the realm of information systems, as opposed to calling for radical changes in weapons or "platforms" like aircraft carriers. But after Owens's retirement, Cebrowski's death, and finally Rumsfeld's dismissal, the intellectual stirrings in the Pentagon seemed to wane. Cebrowski's concept of "network-centric" warfare continues to be debated but has gained little purchase outside the navy. Meanwhile the most visible sign of the return of traditional times—and ways of thinking—is that the Office of Force Transformation has been, as they say in Pentagonese, "disestablished."

But if the debate inside the Defense Department has been dampened, other sparks are still flying in the community of strategic thinkers and defense analysts who insist on the need for changes in both the tools and practices of war. Among the most exhaustive and articulate expositions of this point of view is that of George and Meredith Friedman, who seem to have successfully channeled the spirit of Ivan Bloch. From their perspective, every era of technological change is likely to imply the rise of new practices and to cast doubt upon the efficacy of older weapons systems. For the Friedmans, this means that the main battle tank and the aircraft carrier battle group must be closely examined to see how much of their costs is allocated to attacking the enemy and how much to defending themselves. A weapons system whose major costs are directed toward self-defense should be seen as increasingly suspect, suggesting the need to cast about for new tools that feature more offensive punch.

For example, if most of the expenditures of a carrier battle group are needed to keep the flattop safe—and estimates consistently reflect that well over three-fourths of the cost of a battle group *is* allocated for defensive purposes—one should consider alternative means for achieving the same amount of strike capability. Or for increasing strike capability while lowering the need for expenditures on vessel defense. One way to do this would be to put more missiles on more ships, relying less on attack aircraft for shore bombardment or even in battles at sea. The U.S. Navy actually did some of this sort of thinking several years ago, but then came up with the terrible idea of massing—here's "mass" again—huge numbers of missiles, perhaps as many as five hundred, on a handful of lightly crewed "arsenal ships." (It seems that the mentality of massing as much as possible in one place is alive and well.) In this case congressional and other critics were quick to point out the flaws of putting all our eggs in one seagoing basket, and the arsenal ship died a quiet, budget-deprived death.

The history of this ill-fated idea illustrates the continued pull of traditional thought, still (over-)asserting itself at the same time a range of increasingly sophisticated technological advances are being contemplated. In many respects, the current "war over war" within the U.S. military about its future course often seems to center on the "best practices" that were first introduced by the Swedes and the Dutch some four centuries ago. In the years ahead, the traditions they helped forge, if faithfully adhered to, are likely to lead us to failure.

If the impulse to hang on to well-established military practices is just as important as a willingness to innovate in the areas of organization, doctrine, and technology, why do I say traditionalist thinking is leading us toward disaster? The simplest answer to this question is that success in war, as in so many other competitive fields of endeavor, requires an equilibrium between the enduring and the innovative. Establishing just where such a stable equilibrium lies is sometimes difficult. And in the face of uncertainties that inevitably arise, military organizations throughout history have tended to rally round the known.

Averting risk is an understandable behavior, especially in the life-and-death business of war. Still, those who flock together to follow their instincts also tend to dismiss or devalue the risks of failing to change when it is appropriate to do so— even when keeping to the old course would engender much greater risks. For the military, the key question may be when and whether to change in order to *reduce* risks. Not eliminate them, but take a superior course that mitigates risks while exploiting new opportunities.

Today senior U.S. military leaders have grown more deeply risk-averse than ever, believing that radical change may undermine our existing advantages in conventional warmaking. They seem far less willing to contemplate the prospect that failure to initiate transformational change will doom us to go to war in traditional ways in an era when conventional practices have become ever less effective. Allowable changes are generally of a very incremental nature. For example, the U.S. Army is slowly shifting from its reliance on heavy armored vehicles with tracks—the Abrams "main battle tank" being emblematic—to the somewhat lighter Stryker armored fighting vehicle that has tires. So it goes throughout the services, the watchword being that evolutionary change is far safer than suffering the risks that might accompany a "military revolution."

How does one break from the pattern of modest change? One factor that can surely help overcome military professionals' inherent resistance to major change is defeat. Sometimes a single, terrible reverse leaves no other choice but to pursue a radical shift, as was the case when the U.S. Navy embraced the aircraft carrier as its primary weapon of war at sea in the wake of the loss of so many battleships in the surprise attack at Pearl Harbor. In other instances the effects that impel change are cumulative, as when both sides in World War I finally grew tired of the sheer slaughter that came with massed frontal assaults. Although it took more than three years to make really significant shifts, the Allies and the Germans finally responded to unacceptably high attrition. Of course, individual battles and campaigns aside, there is also the matter of the overall outcomes of wars, where defeat is seen as a catalyst for reform. The best-known example of this is the German development of blitzkrieg doctrine in the wake of defeat in World War I.

But one has to be careful about cultivating faith in the salutary effects of defeat on attitudes toward change. While it seems logical to try something new when something old has turned out badly, the historical record is replete with instances in which disaster has *not* spurred change. For all the fascination with German blitzkrieg, beside it is the troubling evidence that German naval leaders seemed to learn nothing from their experience of defeat in World War I. They kept right at the business of building battleships, neglecting submarines long after Hitler repudiated the limitations imposed on Germany by the Versailles Treaty. So the Germans failed to make the kind of quantum change in their navy that was necessary to give them an early opportunity to win the war.

The U.S. experience of defeat in Vietnam seemed to do little more than convince senior American military leaders to redouble their efforts to concentrate on conventional warfare—with the doctrine of "AirLand Battle," a blitzkrieg clone, emerging "seven lean years" after the fall of Saigon in 1975. A thoroughly new American counterinsurgency manual would not appear for another twenty-five years after AirLand Battle, its sometimes confusing new doctrine being an attempt to assimilate some of the lessons of Iraq. No, defeat does not necessarily lead to innovation.

How, then, does one proceed? Most important, with an understanding that, because of their habits of mind and institutional interests, our military leaders will consistently favor stasis over change. Hope may lie in emphasizing that change is not a simple, unitary concept; it has many facets and can take on many forms. For example, the U.S. Army faces a fundamental challenge to its organizational structure. Are divisions and brigades still the right formations to put in the field? The navy, on the other hand, confronts a set of hurdles that are principally technological. How should the aircraft carrier be viewed in an era of swift, smart guided weapons? The air force's doctrine of strategic bombing—which has survived virtually intact since the 1930s despite a spotty record of achievement—demands scrutiny. The Marines have essential questions to ask and answer at both the organizational and doctrinal levels—the future of divisions and brigades, like the army, and the whole approach to amphibious operations.

While organization, technology, and doctrine all matter, one or the other often comes to the fore. In land battles, for example, the ancient Roman manipular formation was an organizational innovation that breathed life into the legions. Yes, the short sword *(gladius)* was a well-suited "technology," but the real advance here was organizational. Conversely, at sea the Romans relied heavily on an innovative technology, the *corvus,* to give them a winning edge over the Carthaginians.

My survey of the American military today, service by service and issue by issue, forms the core of this book and comes at an opportune moment. Despite the quickening pace of technological advances, which have hugely empowered small field units through networking, U.S. ground forces still look much as they did at the end of World War II more than sixty years ago: heavy and mechanized. At sea the navy still relies on aircraft carriers, each of which deploys roughly one wing (between seventy and ninety combat planes), about the same as in 1945. For its part, the air force still adheres to a near-religious belief in the efficacy of strategic bombing, despite nearly a century of evidence suggesting that the intended "shock and awe" effects of aerial bombardment are largely illusory.

In an era when small, smart weapons are proliferating and opponents are unlikely to confront our incomparable conventional military forces in traditional ways, sustaining our spending on older weapons systems will prove both wasteful and increasingly risky. Just as troubling, the huge investment required to maintain heavy armored divisions, carrier battle groups, and super-expensive attack aircraft will also be held at risk by "high-end" opponents capable of developing and/or acquiring ever more widely available precision-guided anti-tank weapons and supersonic anti-ship and air-to-air missiles. We could find ourselves in the ironic position of outspending everyone else but still going into the next major war with outmoded weapons. Beyond the threats posed by other advanced militaries, our old-style forces will find few opportunities to fight the kinds of battles they would prefer: open confrontations between massed formations. The fundamental dynamic in future wars will more likely be that of "hiders and finders," with opposing forces surfacing only long enough to strike, then disappear.

This trend was foreshadowed by the anti-colonial insurgencies after World War II and has only deepened in the years since 1991, the year of the last traditional conflict, Operation Desert Storm. Since then the world has averaged more than thirty ongoing wars at any given time; and all of them have been waged in largely irregular fashion, save perhaps for the

American air war over Kosovo in 1999. Considering the course of military affairs since 1945, it seems that the Israeli military historian Martin van Creveld was right when he noted that the emergence of nuclear weapons—also in 1945—and other social and political factors have prompted a "transformation of war" which tradition-minded militaries have failed to appreciate. As will be seen in the following chapters, van Creveld's corollary point about the inability of militaries in general to perceive fundamental change applies in a particularly telling, and troubling, way to the senior leadership of the U.S. armed forces today.

CHAPTER TWO

The Once and Future Army

SINCE ITS INCEPTION, the U.S. Army has been torn between its attraction to new tools and practices and its loyalty to older, more established ways of war. This tension played out early and dramatically during the American Revolution, when George Washington championed the cause of building a European-style army and used it, with mixed results, in a conventional manner. At the same time a free-form, frontier-style of fighting manifested itself again and again, most notably in the decisive campaign in the South. A generation later, in the climactic Battle of New Orleans in the War of 1812, Andrew Jackson employed a skillful blend of frontier night-fighting and raiding tactics along with the most advanced weapons technology of the time. His was the first field army in history in which almost all its men carried rifles, and with them they defeated a British force comprised of veterans of campaigns against Napoleon's troops. Most of the Redcoats were still fighting with smooth-bore muskets that were far less accurate. By the time of the Civil War, however, both Northern and Southern armies seem to have forgotten the Jacksonian lesson. Instead they demonstrated their considerable devotion to Napoleonic methods of massed frontal assault—with horrific results in the form of needless casualties. But both sides also showed an aptitude for irregular warfare, with brilliant cavalry leaders emerging on each side. And both also strove to master the potential of the "high-tech" inventions of the time—railroad and telegraph—for moving and managing the operations of large forces across a vast theater of operations.

Even so, as the United States became more broadly industrialized, its way of war seemed to become ever less evocative of the "frontier" that the historian Frederick Jackson Turner believed exerted a mythic, powerful, and unique shaping influence upon all American social institutions. Yes, there was still some call for innovative tactics in the struggles against Native Americans and in colonial interventions like the counterinsurgent campaign in the Philippines (1899–1902). But for the most part the U.S. Army was increasingly driven by a conventional military orthodoxy, as demonstrated by its fundamentally unimaginative performance in World War I—relieved only by some brief thrusts with primitive tanks. Yet this basic stodginess was also accompanied by an appetite for acquiring new technology, so much so that the army would become, by the latter part of World War II, the most mobile ground force since the days of the all-mounted Mongol hordes of the thirteenth century. By 1944 the vast majority of American soldiers were moving around in tanks, trucks, or half-tracked vehicles; while, even at the height of their blitzkrieg successes, the German army was never more than 10 to 15 percent mechanized. And later in the war the Wehrmacht became far less so. Despite hard fighting at times, the U.S. Army was able to roll past the Germans again and again during the last phase of the war. The remarkable successes of the greatest American field general of World War II, George S. Patton—and his colleagues—inspired a new and highly appealing orthodoxy. It was based both on the traditional American affinity for accurate, powerful weaponry and on a newfound attraction to speed of movement. In the face of this love match between firepower and mobility, American skills at irregular warfare began to erode.

Here the pattern was set for what has followed ever since: a deep devotion to and hunger for the most advanced weapons and transport systems. While it was hard to adhere to the maneuverability dimension of this new orthodoxy in the indecisive Korean War (1950–1953), succeeding generations of senior military leaders have continued to embrace emerging technologies with a will, always keeping in mind the goal of sustaining their favored model of mobile warfare that was pioneered during World War II. Whatever else may have changed over the past half-century, homage to great tank generals continues to be paid, and a kind of "Patton paradigm" has persisted. As a succession of technological advances in weapons, transport, and information systems have been adopted, the army's organization and doctrine have seen precious little enduring change during this period.

Indeed, today's army would look quite familiar to George Patton or Omar Bradley, and either of these World War II field generals could easily have stepped out of the past and into command of our ground forces during Operation Desert Storm in 1991. Both could still command the army in battle today, and would likely have done at least as well as—if not better than—their descendants in uniform have during the United States' second war with Iraq. The army still possesses a few thousand tanks, several dozen motorized infantry battalions, even some brigades of parachutists—all redolent of earlier times and every last one of them neatly organized within the army's ten division-sized structures. All this continues despite the fact that quantum advances in the technology of war have come steadily on since the 1950s. That so little enduring organizational change has occurred is something of a puzzle, especially when one considers the army's initial belief that new inventions would make it incomparably stronger than ever before.

The first apparent change in land warfare after 1945 was sparked by the rise of so-called tactical nuclear weapons in the 1950s, which most military leaders initially thought of as simply adding another option to their existing arsenals. Atomic warheads were far more destructive than conventional artillery shells and so were seen as much more efficient. One atomic bomb could now do what had previously required massive, sustained barrages. This, of course, made nuclear weapons all the more desirable, and soon a whole body of military thought arose whose main line of argument was that acquiring all sorts of them would make it possible to do more with less against a wide range of targets. The "nuclear solution" seemed heaven sent, for this was an era when Soviet forces were thought vastly to outnumber those of the NATO alliance—even taking into consideration the large garrison of U.S. troops in Germany. It was thought that losses would run very high in the opening weeks of any war with the Russians, putting a premium on "follow-on forces" and reserves. Here NATO was at a grave disadvantage because the Soviets could move dozens of second-wave divisions simply by road and rail while American reinforcements were always an ocean away, taking far longer to reach the battle than their foes—and having to brave submarine attack during their transit. (Then, as now, sea transport was the primary means of reinforcement because heavy weapons could not be airlifted in sufficient numbers.)

For these reasons, tactical nuclear weapons were welcomed as *the* solution to a hitherto insoluble strategic dilemma. The key was to make sure they were big enough to defeat the enemy, but not so big that they would destroy Europe in the process of defending it. The guiding idea was that even very small warheads fired from artillery tubes—much less powerful than the bombs that destroyed Hiroshima and Nagasaki— could still decimate the enemy's massed forces or even take out small targets like bridges. NATO's tanks and armored personnel carriers, it was hoped, would learn to "button up," so as to be able to operate on the nuclear battlefield without soldiers becoming irradiated. With this vision of making what we already had even better, thanks to nuclear weapons, the "New Look" was born. With a bit of atomic assistance, armor would retain its pride of place in future land battles.

The eager embrace of nuclear weapons by the U.S. Army quickly had organizational effects. Soon there was talk of the "reorganization of the army division" (ROAD) and the even more ambitious concept of creating a "pentomic division" that would, many hoped, become the master of the irradiated battlefield. In short, the army was inclined to accept nukes rather than avoid escalation to the level of nuclear war. This attitude also came to apply to chemical and biological weapons, with U.S. forces preparing to fight in protective suits on ever more toxic fields of fire. All forms of weapons of mass destruction, it seemed, were viewed as usable options during the first decade of the cold war.

But this grim heyday didn't last long. The Soviets quickly acquired nuclear weapons of their own, and in sufficient numbers to guarantee that they could inflict unacceptable levels of damage on their foes. The prospect of such horrific levels of destruction, which all would suffer, led President Dwight D. Eisenhower to begin backing away from a general acceptance of and reliance upon nuclear warfare. He had come into office making veiled nuclear threats against North Korea to end a bloody, stalemated war, then went on to make similar threats against Communist China during the Taiwan Straits crises of the 1950s. Eisenhower even accepted the idea of declaring a national strategy of "massive retaliation"—that is, threatening to use nuclear attack in response to any aggressive acts by others, including very limited ones. In the event, though, he never backed up this standing threat with action, and massive retaliation was, as Thomas Schelling once put it, a doctrine "in decline from the moment it was enunciated."

This shift in the perceived usefulness of nuclear weapons soon affected the army. Gone were visions of motoring about desolate battlescapes in airtight tanks and armored personnel carriers in a kind of post-apocalyptic blitzkrieg. The idea of a pentomic division disappeared as if in a puff of smoke. Now it was imperative to think once more about having to fight a more familiar kind of defensive, attritional warfare for as long as possible, against a more numerous, very well-armed foe. In practice this meant the return of highly traditional military thought, which persisted for another thirty years, from the late 1950s to 1989, when the Berlin Wall finally fell.

The only nuclear vestige that remained during these years was the doctrine of "flexible response," by which the United States reserved the right to use atomic weapons in the event that its conventional forces were losing a new war in Central Europe. But the numbers of U.S. troops stationed there on a standing basis, which rose to about half a million at one point, suggested that Washington intended to do all it could to defend its allies by strictly conventional means. It seemed that the first great post–World War II development responsible for driving military change—the spread of tactical nuclear weapons—had come almost completely undone in less than a decade. To use the subtle, suggestive phrasing of a principal critic, General Maxwell Taylor, the New Look had simply sounded an "uncertain trumpet." But if the army's "brass section" was weak, other new instruments were being introduced that would soon be heard from.

*

By the mid-1960s a second major catalyst for change in the army had emerged. This time innovation was made possible by the rise of a new means of transporting large numbers of troops (albeit in small "packets") around the battlefield: the helicopter. Rotary aircraft had seen only the slightest use during World War II and were largely limited to the evacuation of the wounded during the Korean War, though they were also sometimes used for rescuing downed pilots. But by the time the

United States decided to become totally embroiled in Vietnam in 1965, improvements in helicopters—including giving them a modicum of firepower—had made possible what some senior military leaders saw as a wholly new kind of warfare, which they soon labeled "air assault."

In theory, helicopters were intended to restore a capacity for swift, decisive maneuver; and they would be even more flexible and far-reaching than Patton's World War II armored columns could ever have hoped to be. Variously known as "sky cavalry" and "air cav," the units' names conjure up the vision that was dancing in the generals' heads. Even the armored warfare concept of pincer attacks was contemplated in the heli-borne assault idea of "vertical envelopment." The fact that the overwhelming majority of helicopters used in Vietnam ("Hueys") were capable of moving only light infantry to distant points in the field—so that the soldiers would generally not be closely accompanied by armor or artillery—caused little concern. This deficiency was to be offset by precision airpower—including attack helicopters like the "Sky Cobra"—and a network of artillery firebases that could be called upon for support in a fight.

In practice, "vertical envelopment" did not work well. One big reason was that the helicopter, the heart and soul of this innovative new way of war, was slow, loud, and vulnerable. So the Vietcong (South Vietnamese insurgents) and regular North Vietnamese army forces generally knew when U.S. forces were on the move, and where their landing zones might be, simply by listening to the choppers and by being aware of the few locations where there were openings in the dense jungle large enough for them to alight. The Vietcong and North Vietnamese also knew of American reliance on artillery firebases, and recognized that heli-borne "leaps" would almost always be tethered to a range that would allow these bases to continue to provide fire support. This gave the enemy an edge in selecting battle sites as well as taking as much or as little of the fight as they wished. They could break contact by moving out of artillery range and generally not worry about being trailed by the Americans, because fire support from attack aircraft was often hindered by the dense cover of the jungle terrain.

After an initial reverse or two—most notably at Ia Drang, where North Vietnamese troops were too closely massed and their commander chose to slug it out at a spot inside American artillery range—the enemy figured out the best response. That was to initiate engagements at locations of their own choosing, usually by ambushing a ground patrol at a desirable point. Countless numbers of U.S. platoon-sized detachments deliberately "dangled the bait" right at the edge of firebase coverage, attempting to coax the enemy into a fight in which they could be "vertically enveloped." But this thinking opponent, having the initiative, was able to make excellent preparations for such battles, could throw more force into firefights early on, and would be able to shoot down more helicopters. And, unlike at Ia Drang, if American fire support became too hot to handle, insurgent forces were soon following a modified doctrine that called for breaking off rather than continuing an action under such circumstances.

Over the course of almost seven years of these types of engagements, American military leaders, including Gen. William Westmoreland and his successor as field commander in Vietnam, Creighton Abrams—not to mention the brain trust in the Pentagon—never found a way to cope with the strategic response to their air-assault doctrine that had been crafted by the leading enemy general, Vo Nguyen Giap. Sometimes Giap erred and undertook conventional offensives like Tet in 1968 and the Easter 1972 attack, both of which were defeated by sheer grit and massive firepower. But these military reverses seemed to generate political gains anyway; and Giap always reverted to his more successful ambush style of small-scale offensives. For its part, the U.S. military kept mostly to the air assault paradigm, losing thousands of helicopters along the way. And the war. Yet the air assault concept did not die. It was somehow able to survive this disaster and find an enduring place for itself in American combat doctrine.

For a while, however, in the immediate wake of defeat in Vietnam, the U.S. military happily put aside the problems posed by irregular warfare and focused once again on the difficulties associated with defending Europe against an armored Soviet horde. Because the attempt to solve this riddle with nuclear weapons had failed, due in part to the emergence of a competing nuclear arsenal on the other side, it seemed that a way would have to be found to overcome the Russians' numerical advantages by conventional means. Soon, less than a decade after the fall of Saigon in 1975, another major technological innovation began to take hold: precision-guided munitions (PGMs).

*

The simplest way to describe PGMs is to point out, first, that throughout history war has always been the business of hurling mass and energy at one's adversary. But in a new age replete with miniature on-board computers—a period that began in the early 1980s—it was now possible to provide many types of weapons with an "information package" to accompany their mass and energy. Thus, for the first time ever, the prospect appeared of decoupling range from accuracy. That is, all previous weapons, even ballistic missiles, were less likely to hit their targets dead-on the farther they were fired. Now it was possible to think in terms of shooting one's weapons over great distances with extremely high degrees of accuracy.

This new capacity for making deep, precise strikes gave NATO a way to cope with Soviet numerical superiority, the principal idea being to use cruise missiles to attack Red Army reinforcements while they were still a hundred miles or more from the "forward edge of the battle area" (FEBA). As to close-in fighting against an enemy possessing thousands more tanks than

NATO, strategists hoped that short-range PGMs would now prove effective enough to blunt a Soviet offensive—to do sufficient damage to delay the enemy advance until major reinforcements could cross the Atlantic in about a month's time.

Whether such a defense with PGMs was actually realistic was the subject of heated doctrinal debates. In the event, the matter was rendered moot, as the war NATO planned for never happened. But all the smart weapons that had been developed and fielded to fight the Russians were soon put to use against Saddam Hussein's forces in the brief 1991 war for Kuwait. The results were impressive, as both U.S. armored and anti-tank forces fired at will and with great accuracy upon a half-million-man Iraqi army, whose losses ran in the several tens of thousands of troops killed. American forces and their allies lost just a few hundred, winning one of history's more lopsided victories.

For some in defense circles, Operation Desert Storm was an absolutely perfect storm. It signaled a "revolution in military affairs" (RMA) based on smart new weapons, and at the same time appeared to reaffirm the enduring nature of modern armored maneuver warfare. Gen. Norman Schwarzkopf's famous "left hook" in the desert, outflanking most of the Iraqi army, looked very much like the right hooks in the desert that Erwin Rommel's Afrika Korps had repeatedly launched around British forces fifty years earlier. So the widespread use of PGMs—the army used far more of these in Desert Storm than the air force, over 90 percent of whose dropped ordnance still consisted of "dumb iron bombs"—seemed only to shore up traditional notions of armored battle.

As a piece of military "performance art," Desert Storm was compelling. As a basis for exerting powerful bureaucratic leverage on sustaining the level of U.S. investment in heavy, mechanized forces—even during a time when army manpower was being reduced by about one-third—it proved decisive. The ghost of failure in Vietnam had been "exorcised," as President George H. W. Bush put it. In practical terms, this meant that the army would continue to concentrate its energies on preparing for the next conventional war. The "scaling" problem—the balkiness of a big expeditionary force, especially its slowness in reaching distant theaters of war—was largely dismissed during Bill Clinton's two terms as president.

The inconvenient fact that it had taken more than five months of preparations to launch a ground offensive against the Iraqis was never given sufficient attention during these years. This despite President Clinton's 1999 Kosovo War, in which we were reminded of the central problem of having forces so large: that it would take several months even to bring nearby NATO ground forces into a position from which they could threaten the Serbs. In this instance we didn't have the luxury of that kind of time, given the urgent situation of the Kosovars. So an air-only war was waged and somehow won.* And in its wake the army kept doggedly to its traditional mind-set.

But even during the complacent 1990s a range of dissenting voices could be heard in the defense community. Their basic position was that the wrong lesson was being drawn from Desert Storm, and that a true revolution in military affairs must overturn, not reaffirm, classical notions of maneuver warfare. Their general insights included the belief that rapidly improving information systems—especially in the realms of sensors and communications—were driving developments far wider than just the rise of smart weapons. This view was best articulated in the soldier-scholar Ken Allard's incisive study *Command, Control and the Common Defense.*

The common stance of the dissenters also included an insistence that the changes under way in warfare—especially the shift toward irregular warfare that Martin van Creveld observed in *The Transformation of War*—were empowering new forms of military organization. Indeed, the scaling problem

*For a more detailed discussion of the Kosovo War, see Chapter 4.

itself soon came under direct scrutiny in the work of another soldier-scholar, Douglas Macgregor, whose *Breaking the Phalanx* began the process of thinking through how to move from an army comprised of a few large units of maneuver to one of the "many and the small."

My RAND Corporation colleague David Ronfeldt and I were deeply involved in the defense debates of the 1990s, trying to give voice to this emerging community of dissenters. We thought of them, and ourselves, as being "in Athena's camp"— our metaphor for an information age in which Mars, the old brute-force god of war, would inevitably give way to Athena, who welded together both knowledge and force. For us the future was one in which armies would grow smaller, smarter, and much more highly networked.

But none of us gained much sustained traction, and the army continued to do what it had been doing for decades: prepare for the next replay of World War II–style armored battles. So it continued to look much as it always had. When the urgent need arose after 9/11 to topple the Taliban, who were providing the al Qaeda terror network with a haven in remote Afghanistan, once again, as in Kosovo, the army's size and structure—and much of the Afghan terrain—ruled out the sort of conventional armored campaign for which it was prepared. Initially this led to another attempt to win with an air-only campaign; but after four weeks of bombing, to little apparent effect, Donald Rumsfeld told Gen. Tommy Franks and the uniformed Pentagon leadership to set loose the eleven special forces "A teams"—just a few hundred commandos in all—that had infiltrated into Afghanistan. Rumsfeld faced resistance, but he prevailed. As Bob Woodward put it, to get his generals to agree to unleash the commandos, Rumsfeld "increased the pressure on everyone involved in the chain of command. He was relentless as he laid down his own withering carpet of fire. Senior generals put their heads down on their desks in despair." Once they were authorized to proceed, the special operators teamed effectively with friendly locals, the function that had been envisioned for them from their formation in the 1950s, but which they had employed with mixed results in Vietnam. In Afghanistan, things went better. Much better.

Thanks to good networking and timely close air support, the Taliban were almost immediately put on the run, along with their al Qaeda allies. Although they escaped to the wilds of Waziristan, an untamed tribal zone only nominally under Pakistani government control, the fact is that they were driven out by a relative handful of American soldiers on the ground. Since then the Taliban have waged a protracted insurgency from this new haven, where U.S. military action is constrained out of fear of undermining the friendly authoritarian government in Islamabad. While nettlesome, Taliban raids are handled roughly by the relatively small garrison of allied forces that remains, and which routinely inflicts serious losses on the attackers.

In some respects the Afghan campaign, Operation Enduring Freedom, was a "war to change all wars." A very small force, closely linked with airpower, had swiftly deployed halfway around the world and, once set loose, won a signal victory while suffering casualties that were but a fraction of even those few losses incurred in Desert Storm ten years earlier. Despite all this, traditional strategists made a determined effort to insist that virtually nothing new had happened in Afghanistan. Rather, they argued, the campaign there was an anomaly. It worked as well as it did only because of the poor quality of the Taliban fighters.

Opposing views soon opened a fresh front in the war of ideas about war, with a sharp debate emerging that would be played out in the run-up to the invasion of Iraq in 2003, and throughout the protracted counterinsurgent campaign that ensued. On the one side were those of us who argued that there were indeed lessons to be drawn from Afghanistan, the principal one being that Iraq could be dealt with by a field force as small as a few tens of thousands of troops. These, we contended, could be broken into many small units of maneuver and linked to indigenous forces opposed to Saddam Hussein—the Kurds in the north, for example, and the Shi'a in the south—and closely supported by airpower. The traditionalists, noting that we had the five months' time needed for a buildup, plus access via the Persian Gulf, called for an army of 500,000 to be sent. In the end, a compromise was reached on a force almost exactly midway between the two camps' preferences. Neither side came away pleased.

Even so, for army traditionalists the Patton paradigm was strongly reaffirmed by the march up Mesopotamia in the spring of 2003. The U.S. mechanized field army of about 200,000 swept all before it—hardly a surprising outcome given that the 400,000-man Iraqi army basically melted away. Indeed, the military historian John Keegan considered the whole matter of the missing Iraqis something of a "mystery." To many others, however, there was nothing puzzling about the Iraqis' reluctance to confront U.S. forces in open battle, where they would be swiftly decimated. Instead it made more sense for them to rely on irregular *fedayeen* raiders and, later on, insurgent resistance cells. This they did, and soon U.S. forces were embroiled in a confounding, mostly urban guerrilla war. This war has highlighted the "scaling problem" that still bedevils the U.S. Army and has finally prompted its leaders to begin thinking seriously about organizational redesign.

*

American forces would have to stay in Iraq for half a century to suffer the same level of losses that were incurred during their half dozen years of heavy fighting in Vietnam. But in Iraq it took almost no time at all for the organizational vulnerability of the army to be made manifest. Very soon after the insurgency began in earnest during the waning months of 2003, just over half of the army's thirty-three brigades* were committed to Iraq. Given the goal of having troops serve one-year tours in-country, this meant that the rest of the army became tightly constrained by the need to be in a state of preparation for deployment to Iraq. There was no slack in the system; and if a second war were to erupt somewhere else—say, on the Korean peninsula—it would be virtually impossible to fight on both fronts simultaneously. It would also be impossible to look to the Marine Corps to retrieve such a situation, as its forces were nearly as heavily committed in Iraq as the army's and faced "rotation base" and sustainment problems that were equally alarming.†

At this point it became imperative for the army to create more units of maneuver, both to sustain the flow of forces into and out of Iraq and to reconstitute a strategic reserve that could respond to new contingencies. While there was agreement about the need for more units, once again there was spirited debate about just what size and shape they should be. And once again the traditionalists triumphed, and the lessons of Enduring Freedom were neglected. Instead of a radical redesign centered on small units, closely interconnected with friendly indigenous forces, the choice was made to create more brigades—albeit slightly different-looking ones, in the form of "brigade combat teams" (BCTs).

Without changing its fundamental organizational structure—divisions, brigades, and battalions, in descending level of strength—the army began the process of moving from the thirty-three traditional brigades it had at the outset of the Iraq war to forty-eight BCTs.‡ The hope was to achieve this almost 50 percent increase in what were now being called

---

*Three per division, across the army's ten divisions, and three more from reserves and Guardsmen.
†For more on the Marines' role in Iraq, see the discussion in Chapter 3.
‡By late 2007 the number had risen to thirty-eight.

"units of action" over the next several years. It is important to note, however, that this increase in numbers came at something of a price in terms of combat battalions. Where the old brigades had three battalions each, the BCTs had just two, with the third formed up mainly to provide intelligence, surveillance, and other key information flow and influence functions.* So while there was no change in manpower, conventional "combat power" was reduced.

On the positive side, the development of BCTs would indeed provide marginally more organizational capacity for the army. This focus on the brigade level was also accompanied by a further easing of the requirement that divisions be made up of like units. That is, an armored division had always been made up mostly of tank brigades, an infantry division of infantry brigades. Under the BCT system—in which divisions were likely to exceed the "rule of three" brigades—it would be theoretically possible to mix and match the new teams in creative ways, depending on the theater of operations and the type of mission. Thus in some campaigns an armored division might have only one tank BCT—and even this might be a lighter armored vehicle, with tires rather than treads (the "Stryker")—with the remaining BCTs made up of infantry or even "information operations" functions such as psychological warfare.

While this appeared to be a considerable degree of change, it wasn't. For decades the army has been mixing and matching brigades, to such an extent that an infantry division today often has nearly as many tanks as a designated armored division. And the new plan did little to change the almost equal apportionment of army brigades between heavy (armored) and light (mostly infantry) forces. For a long time we have had a "bifur-

*Historically, nearly everything that comprises a brigade has "come in three's" for the U.S. Army. At the most basic level, the squad of six to ten soldiers, three squads have made a platoon. Three platoons have constituted a company, three companies a battalion, and three of these a brigade. This ideal is often relaxed in practice, but the basic point is that even a fully fleshed out brigade is generally comprised of no more than two thousand to three thousand front-line soldiers.

cated army." Under the BCT initiative we will continue to have the same proportions, despite the fact that the far more likely need will be for lighter forces to move swiftly to distant theaters and engage in conflicts that look very little like World War II. Or even Desert Storm.

If traditional mechanized warfare has grown less likely, what about relegating tank brigades to the Reserves and National Guard units? This would seem a natural move, as it would hedge against the return of a "good old-fashioned war" yet maximize the standing army's ability to deal with smaller-scale contingencies. A decade ago former Senator Gary Hart, in a thoughtful meditation on military reform, *The Minuteman*, made a similar recommendation to put old-style capabilities into Reserve and Guard units. Unfortunately the BCT initiative was pursued with exactly the opposite goal in mind: under plans as of late 2007, the vast majority of Guard and Reserve units would be light rather than heavy.

The principal rationale for the reluctance to reduce the emphasis on heavy forces in the standing army is the fear of being unprepared for a classical-style mechanized war. Over the years this line of reasoning has dominated the resistance to change. It presupposes that an old-style enemy must be fought in the old way: mass on mass. But if the emergence of precision-guided weapons and networked sensors and communications has taught us anything at all, the lesson should be that the bigger the old-style force, the harder it will fall to the new way of war. Many senior military leaders will acknowledge this, but entrenched habits of mind and institutional interests are highly resistant to change, even though the need for radical reform of the army is now urgent.

*

What ought the army to look like? Very simply, it should become a force of the "many and the small," not the "few and the

large." Today the army has far too few units of maneuver because of its reluctance to depart from reliance on the brigade.
Not only will there still be too few of them, even when the forty-
eighth BCT is at last fielded, perhaps a decade from now, but
it will take too long to get them where they need to go if significant distances are involved. We cannot bet on the luxury of
having more than five months to deploy our forces gradually
and ready them for battle, as we did during the run-up to both
our wars against Iraq. Instead it is imperative to plan for having to commence combat operations at the earliest possible
moment—perhaps in just a few weeks, a response time much
more like that of the eleven special forces A-teams that toppled
the Taliban in the waning months of 2001.

This doesn't mean that the entire army must become
"special," but it does suggest that our elite forces have been
functioning as something of an organizational redesign "laboratory" over the past several years. While special forces are few
in number—only five small groups of them exist, a few thousand soldiers all told, and they generally operate with friendly
indigenous forces—the army is blessed with several hundred
thousand troops. These could be organized into units that look
a lot like the A-team/indigenous force combination, with the
benefit that those taking the role of the friendly local units
would be well-trained U.S. troops. Add to this the high likelihood that American airpower would achieve control of the
skies over the theater of conflict, and would be tightly interconnected with our forces on the ground, and something very
appealing begins to emerge. This scheme is very different from
what we have been doing. It could easily take us from the
planned incremental increase of forty-eight BCTs to a much
larger shift—the fielding of several hundred smaller but no less
deadly units of action.

If this vision of main combat forces operating with as few as
100 to 200 troops per unit is simply too unsettling, think of a
less ambitious organizational innovation: moving from the

brigade down to the battalion as the army's basic building block. If the B in BCT stood for battalion instead of brigade, a decade from now we would have 144 units of action rather than just 48—that is, nearly a hundred more. Were this to become the case, it would be much more difficult for a ragtag group of insurgents, numbering in the few tens of thousands at most, to hamstring a great, modern military, as they managed to do for so long in Iraq. Consider also the strategic flexibility that would come with organizational redesign along these lines. Suddenly the specter of a simultaneous second serious conflict becomes less dire. And the ability to move swiftly to avert an impending genocide in an ethnic conflict or other type of small war would also be greatly enhanced. Even this slight change in preferred organizational size, down from brigade to battalion, could produce important advantages.

If one believes in the combat power of networking, it is possible to see the real strength of even smaller units. Here the greatest gains could be made, conveying to the U.S. Army a hitherto undreamed of operational capacity. In the war against widely distributed small terror cells, this new organizational structure would give us much more ability to seize and hold the initiative, mounting raid after raid against their training camps and their units in the field.

Whether army change is incremental or transformational, the idea of moving in the direction of smaller, nimbler, and more networked forces should also prompt us to rethink our devotion to some long favored combat formations. The armored division itself heads this list, given that its heavy "force package" requires months for overseas deployment, and the fighting vehicles themselves—tracked or with tires—are increasingly vulnerable to smart anti-tank weapons, especially in urban environments, where tanks' great strengths are limited and their weaknesses magnified.

The weakness of armor was first exploited by small Chechen irregular forces during the Battle of Grozny in 1996. Armed with nothing heavier than rocket-propelled grenades, and organized in bands of just twelve to twenty fighters, the insurgents drove Russian armored forces from the city, then out of their country. When the Russians fought their way back into Chechnya nearly five years later, recapturing Grozny, they came with far fewer tanks and many more small detachments of infantry that had trained to fight in urban terrain. While the insurgents in Iraq have never come close to demonstrating the kind of tank-killing skills of the Chechens, U.S. forces have been careful to make sure that their armor has been well accompanied by infantry. After the opening week or two of the invasion in 2003, armor had little impact on the course of the Iraq War. Even without armor, the "thunder run" from the Kuwait border to Baghdad could have been successful, given American air supremacy and the general unwillingness of the Iraqi forces to fight in the open.

Whether to retain the army's heavy armored divisions should clearly be the subject of an unflinching debate, as should be the case with at least one more major combat formation: the Eighty-second Airborne Division. Why do we still have a whole division's worth of parachutists? The last division-sized jump by American forces was in late 1944, during the World War II battle at Arnhem, where American and British parachutists suffered a costly defeat. More than sixty years later, what are the prospects for this sort of operation ever happening again? There is simply no reason to keep a whole division's worth of skydivers.

Instead we should be thinking of many small detachments capable of striking from the sky—whether by parachute, glider, or even some of the more exotic modes of delivery under development, like personal "bat wings" and power packs. All these have in common a reliance on small numbers and stealth for success. Even those using traditional parachutes seek to minimize the amount of time during which they might be detected, particularly with such techniques as "low opening," in which soldiers drop like stones until very close to the earth, deploying their chutes at the absolute last moment. The iconic image of a sky filled with gently floating mushroom caps is gone. So too should be the division designed for such drops, replaced by far fewer airborne specialists organized in much smaller assault teams.

The historical record of parachute deployment in battle suggests that such an organizational move should have been made many decades ago. The Germans, who pioneered airborne attack, succeeded in their one major assault by parachutists on the island of Crete in 1941. But their casualties were so great that Hitler was forever reluctant to use them again. By way of contrast, a few small German airborne detachments, fewer than two hundred troops in all, played a key role in enabling the Nazi victory against Anglo-French forces in the 1940 Battle of France by taking the well-defended Belgian fortress of Eben Emael.

On the Allied side, parachutists performed ably during the D-day invasion of Normandy in June 1944, but their success was due in part to the fact that the three divisions dropped (two American, one British) were widely scattered in the wind and dark, and began engaging the German defenders from many directions simultaneously. These little groups of paratroopers (to this day reverentially called LGOPs, pronounced ell-gops) had a profoundly dislocating effect on their adversaries. The other great success came in 1945 against a Japanese force defending the fortress of Corregidor in the occupied Philippines. Here, as at Eben Emael, a small airborne assault detachment was able to employ stealth successfully and overcome a large garrison— yet more evidence that, when it comes to airborne operations, "small is beautiful." It's time to deactivate the Eighty-second Airborne and replace it with a set of small detachments capable of striking from the sky in a variety of ways, using some of the cutting-edge technologies that combine speed and stealth in new delivery systems. The rest of the old division, which has basically been employed in a regular infantry role for the past half-century, should become part of the new, networked ground forces. This is one of the most obvious reforms waiting to be pursued. Other reforms are subtler, more complex, and more debatable.

*

Since the Vietnam War the helicopter has retained a powerful hold on the military imagination. Even though that war ended in defeat for the army and its pet doctrine of air assault by helicopter, the 101st Air Assault Division—formerly a division of parachutists—remains an essential element of the overall force. Partly this is due to improvements in the doctrine for the use of the 101st, which specifies that a lot of flying be done close to ground, so low as to reduce vulnerability to anti-aircraft fire. Another reason for holding on to helicopters is that, as a principal beneficiary of the rise of precision weaponry, they now pack more punch than ever before. A third reason for the army's reluctance to give them up is that rotary aircraft are the only kind the army controls. From an institutional perspective, jettisoning them would make ground forces totally dependent on another service for air mobility and close-in fire support.

Beyond these conceptual points there is the practical matter that continuing experience also seems to point to the need for helicopters. In the army's effort to counter the Iraqi insurgency, the threat from snipers, suicide bombers, and improvised explosive devices was sufficient to encourage continued reliance on helicopters for tactical mobility. Save for a brief flurry of shootdowns of helicopters in early 2007, the U.S. military has indeed been able to rely on them to provide both speed of movement and reasonable levels of security—for all the infantry in the army, not just elements of the 101st Division. And there has been nothing like the very high attrition rate suffered by helicopters during the Vietnam War.

In addition to their ability to transport troops and provide fire support, helicopters may also have a key role to play in supplying small detachments located at outposts deep in "Indian territory," or on a discontinuous postmodern battlefield where dispersed small units might be fighting a war without identifiable "fronts." Indeed, it is hard to think about the future of logistics without a role for helicopters. Perhaps supplies can be dropped to far-flung detachments by parafoils (think of a remotely piloted hang glider) or even by missiles that release packets of food instead of cluster bombs (think "ballistic logistics"). But even on a generally desolate battlefield, with few troops spread out over great distances, the helicopter will be needed to help provide necessities—and, of course, to evacuate the wounded.

Still, the helicopter's fundamental problems remain: it is slow, loud, and highly vulnerable to ground fire. And these are weaknesses that will prove ever more exploitable by our adversaries in the years to come. Alternatives should be considered now. The Marine Corps, whose forces also depend on helicopters for tactical mobility, has tried to forge a high-tech solution with the Osprey, a tilt-rotor aircraft that can fly like a plane *and* a helicopter. The theory is that it can speed to a desired location, thus reducing its vulnerability, but still be able to land in rough settings like a rotary aircraft. The Osprey's sheer complexity, however, has made it a delicate machine, prone to crashing; and it has taken many years to bring even one squadron of these hybrid aircraft into service.

If a high-tech approach to providing army forces with good mobility and solid fire and logistical support presents serious problems, some low-tech solutions can be explored. Some might even draw upon tools and practices of our potential adversaries. For example, the North Korean army, particularly its large special-forces component—which amounts to nearly 100,000 troops, or 10 percent of the total force—has figured out how to make considerable use of the Antonov 2 "Colt" biplane. This is a canvas-covered aircraft that can hold a few dozen soldiers or be jammed full of supplies, and is fast, flexible, and able to evade radar detection, anti-aircraft missiles, and much ground fire, because of its ability to fly low along the terrain. What's more, the Colt is very easy to fly and can land in almost any grassy field. It's a whiff of World War I aviation.

Why couldn't the U.S. Army make wonderful use of the Colt or a large biplane of our own manufacture? It would serve a force comprised of countless small detachments very well, giving these units the mobility and logistical support they need. And many more soldiers could become pilots, as the process of flying a biplane is much simpler than handling a modern helicopter. The point here is that innovation need not always demand wholly new technology. On some occasions, older tools can be put to creative new uses. Sometimes, when trying to look ahead, it helps to look back.

But bringing back biplanes, even large ones, won't solve the fire support problem that distributed small detachments will confront. And it would not be prudent to rely completely upon the air force as the sole provider in this important area. So here I suggest a shift in doctrine: moving from the notion of massing artillery to distributing it widely, in "one-gun batteries." Every outpost and detachment would have its own piece of field artillery.

In almost every setting, but especially in irregular warfare scenarios, one howitzer can dominate an area of operations— much like the lone long cannon in *The Gun,* C. S. Forester's classic novel of insurgent Spain during the Napoleonic occupation. Supported by mortars and supplemented with airpower, even the smallest army outpost would have a huge firepower edge over its opponents. And the fact that every single gun could have such an effect would mean that a network of mini-firebases could be created, one without the gaps in coverage that bedeviled this concept in Vietnam. The guns could be driven to the outposts or, if the site were too remote, brought in by helicopter (yes, there would still be occasional uses for them) or disassembled and flown in parts on a Colt biplane. The biplane could also handle ammunition resupply issues.

Could one-gun batteries work against a traditional foe advancing with massed forces? Absolutely, given that these mini-batteries would be networked together, enjoying a common operating picture—that is, though physically dispersed, their fire could be unified. Of course airpower would play a significant role in defeating such a conventional attack, as would the precision-guided anti-tank munitions of defending (or attacking, as this scheme could work on the offensive too) infantry detachments. Artillery is ripe for reform.

*

For all the areas touched upon in this chapter, I have argued that the army's most urgent need for reform is organizational. We have too few units of maneuver, a point depressingly proven by the ability of a relative handful of insurgents in Iraq to wear down U.S. forces and stretch them to the breaking point. The answer to this is a simple one: shift from an army of a few large units to one of the "many and the small." The division and the brigade need not be sacrosanct military formations. They appeared a few centuries ago, coincident with the rise of massed firepower and, later, industrialization. Now we live in a post-industrial age with smart weapons that can empower even very small units. It is time to become nimbler.

Doing so would echo developments throughout the history of warfare, which has seen alternating periods in which mass was first sought then avoided. The Greek phalanx, the first great massed formation, dominated warfare from the Persian Wars of the fifth century B.C.E. to the Battle of Zama, where the distributed, checkerboard formations of Roman maniples (Latin for "handfuls") defeated Hannibal's Punic phalanx.

Looser formations dominated until the gunpowder revolution, which began just as the Eastern Roman Empire was dying in the mid-fifteenth century, at which point the need to mass fire swung the pendulum back toward larger formations. But in the seventeenth century the great Swedish soldier Gustavus Adolphus rediscovered the value of smaller, more maneuverable units, as did Prussia's Frederick the Great a century later. The tendency toward massing reasserted itself under Napoleon and quickened with the Industrial Revolution. Even so, the need for smaller formations on an increasingly deadly battlefield drove the rise of German storm troopers in World War I and an emphasis on loose formations of infantry platoons in World War II. Later, in Vietnam the U.S. Army slid back toward "big-unit warfare," and even in the wake of defeat retained a bias toward bigness. That preference has been sorely tested in recent years and cries out for reexamination and reform.

Unfortunately the army has been using the information revolution to try to sustain its big units, hoping to revitalize them with digitization and its emerging "future combat system," an amalgam of more than twenty new sensors, communications devices, and high-accuracy weapons. Many in the Pentagon hope these developments will keep big units strong, even though every technological advance along these lines is actually empowering smaller formations. Using one of the most promising features of advanced military information technology, tele-operations, some of these small formations might actually be remotely controlled. Just as the air force has the Predator and other flying drones, the army has the potential to move into this arena aggressively—not simply in de-mining operations but for a whole range of missions, including maneuver warfare and urban fighting. Currently there is polite interest in pursuing tele-operated ground combat systems—for example, field experimentation with an "Urbie," which might one day engage in street fighting. But there is not yet a commitment that will make a real difference on the battlefield. To the extent to which "Big Army" prevails in this particular aspect of strategy, we may see an innovative new tool supporting old practices. Such a development, if coincident with other successful efforts to shore up and sustain our traditional way of war, will light the way to a future of conflict where, despite massive expenditures and amazing technological advances, we will be organizationally and operationally crippled.

CHAPTER THREE

War at Sea . . . and from the Sea

IF THE ARMY'S principal challenge is to improve its organization, the navy's need is to embrace technologies that will sustain American sea power in the twenty-first century. Since
ancient times, seagoing vessels have always represented the
cutting edge of technology in their day. And at least since the
first stirrings of industrialization two centuries ago, navies
have been subjected to regular, clearly observable episodes of
radical change. At the dawn of the nineteenth century, for example, sea power was epitomized by Lord Nelson's *HMS Victory*, a classic ship of the line of the age of sail, and a key to
Britain's victory over Napoleon. But by the close of the American Civil War in 1865, half a century after Waterloo, the capital
ship of the day was now armored instead of wooden, steam-
driven rather than moved by the wind, and it fired high-
explosive shells in place of the old solid-shot cannonballs. Just
one or two of these ironclads would have been more than
enough to blow all of Nelson's fleet at Trafalgar to matchsticks.

Fifty years later, by 1915, navies were contending in World
War I. The ships were still ironclads, but their size had grown
immensely, as had the range and accuracy of their weapons—

particularly on the "all big gun" dreadnoughts, which wreaked bloody havoc in their one great encounter, at Jutland in 1916. More than seven thousand sailors died in the Great War's lone major fleet-on-fleet engagement. Just one of the dreadnoughts engaged at Jutland—either German or British—would have sunk the whole Union "monitor" fleet of 1865. And the aircraft carriers that next came to dominance could do the same to a whole squadron of dreadnoughts. Taking another fifty-year-interval snapshot, one would see the navy of 1965, the first year of deepened U.S. involvement in Vietnam, exercising its command of the sea almost wholly through aircraft carrier strike groups, which had come into their own during World War II. Today, more than forty years after the Gulf of Tonkin naval incidents, aircraft carriers are still the dominant naval vessels of our time. Why?

Given the regular pattern of radical change in capital ships over the past two centuries, and the astonishing pace of high-tech innovation, how can it be that the aircraft carrier retains its pride of place as the queen of naval battle? After all, its predecessors' dominance came and went swiftly. Sailing ships of the line were in serious decline from nearly the moment steam was introduced; and the need for "castles of steel" was immediately realized by navies around the world in the wake of the 1862 battle between the *Monitor* and the *Merrimac*. Refinements to ironclads were almost constant, with some classes of vessel facing technological obsolescence from the time of their launch.

The same has not been true at all of aircraft carriers, whose fundamental principles have changed very little in the roughly seventy years they have been around in their recognizably current form. Many of them now patrol the seas using nuclear propulsion, but the size of an aircraft carrier's strike force is still almost identical to what it was during World War II—roughly one wing, between eighty and ninety attack aircraft. Why the carrier has not become outdated is puzzling, but thinking through the sources of its resilience will reveal much

about the personal characteristics and bureaucratic preferences of those who defend the flattops with such zeal. Indeed,
it is clear that if senior leaders in and out of uniform are allowed their preferences, the aircraft carrier will continue to be
the centerpiece of American naval power for the indeterminate
future.

It is tempting to draw an analogy with the ships of the line
of Nelson's day, which had undergone little fundamental
change in more than two hundred years—only incremental differences in length, area of sail, and weight of armament. For
the most part, from Drake to Nelson, the great sailing warship
type had remained constant: it was completely wind-driven (as
opposed to being equipped with both sails and oars), and almost all its gunfire shot out at an angle roughly perpendicular
to its direction of movement. Could the aircraft carrier, which
has also seen only incremental changes over the past seven
decades, be enjoying a similarly long lifetime? Might the carrier be another of these enduring, archetypal naval vessels?

Perhaps, but likely not. The ship of the line's longevity
stemmed from a lack of major advances in naval architecture,
propulsion, and armament. The carrier exists in an era of near-
constant technological change in each of these areas, a time
when there is a profusion of new types of vessels, missiles,
mines, torpedoes, and aircraft. It simply beggars the imagination to believe that carriers can survive such a broad scope and
rapid pace of change when all preceding capital ships in the industrial era have been superseded with such regularity. But it
seems that, at the highest levels of navy leadership, sufficient
imagination can envision a future in which the flattop remains
the hallmark of U.S. maritime strength.

And so the U.S. Navy's eleven aircraft carriers remain the
heart of American sea power in the twenty-first century. Thinking through the reasons for their longevity—and the possible
threats and alternatives to them—will be central to the introduction of naval innovation, reform, or transformation.

*

The starting point for any such analysis along these lines is a set of dual observations: first, how sheer budgetary inertia has helped keep the carriers afloat (they represent the largest single line items in the defense budget), and, second, how little competition is being posed by foreign naval powers. The U.S. Navy's share of the defense budget is well over $100 billion annually, and aircraft carriers and the groups of ships needed to protect them account for the lion's share of this allotment. So there is no doubt a powerful institutional impetus to continue to rely on these vessels.

But the absence of a clear rival on the seas also makes it easier to maintain the carriers indefinitely. The situation today, when there is no serious challenge to American sea power, is vastly different from that of a century ago, when the Anglo-German naval antagonism fueled an arms race in dreadnoughts. It differs sharply, too, from the situation in the 1930s, when both Japan and the United States realized they might soon be propelled into a wide-ranging sea war in which aircraft carriers could strike at battleships—or even enemy carriers—in engagements that would be fought at such long ranges that opposing ships might never make visual contact with each other. No international situation today conveys a similar sense of urgency for naval power; and this lack of an apparent threat serves to shore up the carrier's status as the only capital ship that apparently will not give way when faced with major technological change.

Still, some disturbing signs have foreshadowed trouble for the carrier, and thus for American naval policy. The most unsettling development occurred during the cold war, when the Soviet navy rejected an emphasis on carriers in favor of submarines. For one of the few times in history, a rival navy did not try to imitate the superior force it faced. Soviet strategy instead relied upon the belief that the stealth of submarines, greatly enhanced by technical advances that allowed them to remain submerged for long periods, would vastly increase their potency. Combined with the improved range and accuracy of their torpedoes and missiles, some of which might even be nuclear tipped, it was thought that submarines would now be able to defeat or disable a carrier-centered navy and the hundreds of surface vessels that complemented the flattops. Beyond combatting the opposing warship fleet, the Soviets knew that their submarine flotillas would also be useful in striking at transatlantic convoys that might bring reinforcements to beleaguered NATO troops trying to defend against a Soviet ground offensive. For all these reasons, Russian naval strategy, best articulated by Adm. Sergei Gorshkov, made good sense, and at the height of its powers the Red Navy ended up deploying several hundred submarines.

In the event, there was no Soviet-American sea war that might have proved whose approach was correct. Instead we have been left for the most part to ponder the matter at a conceptual level. But one real sea war during this period, waged between roughly evenly matched foes, yielded some tantalizing insights. This was the three-month South Atlantic War in 1982, a struggle between Britain and Argentina over control of the Falklands/Malvinas Islands. In the conflict, both sides suffered heavily at sea, and submarines demonstrated their ability to engage a much larger force, even one with an aircraft carrier. With just two attack submarines on station, the Royal Navy was able to drive the entire Argentine surface fleet back into port—after sinking the cruiser *General Belgrano*, which went down with severe loss of life. The Argentines had a few submarines of their own but had trouble locating the British carriers that were supporting landing operations on East Falkland, as British Adm. Sandy Woodward wisely kept them far from the islands. This skillful deployment also insulated the British carriers from Argentine attack aircraft that were based on the mainland, barely able to reach the islands and with no chance to strike a task force steaming far to the east. Of course, the need to safeguard the British carriers by keeping them at such a remove came at the price of reduced air coverage for the transports and combat vessels supporting the landings on the islands. Six of these ships were sunk and a dozen others suffered varying degrees of damage.

In all, naval operations during the South Atlantic War suggested that aircraft carriers could still function in the face of threats from submarines and aircraft, but at the price of deploying far from the fight, imposing the primary costs and risks of battle on other vessels and units. The submarine, on the other hand, showed that it could indeed engage a superior force and imperil an aircraft carrier—presuming the surface forces could be located. The South Atlantic experience speaks to a point made by the military historian John Keegan in his magisterial study of modern sea power, *The Price of Admiralty:* that the great debate about whether the submarine or the carrier was the true capital ship of the late twentieth century was never resolved, but that all the evidence suggests the edge went—and will increasingly go—to the submarine. Keegan bases his judgment in part on the course and outcome of the South Atlantic War, concluding emphatically: "The era of the submarine as the predominant weapon of power at sea must therefore be recognized as having begun."

Today, while the U.S. Navy continues to double down on its big bet on aircraft carriers, it seems that the rest of the world agrees with John Keegan's view. Instead of investing in flattops, other nations are building navies of small, swift vessels and are acquiring very quiet submarines—stealthier and far less costly than our nuclear boats—that move by means of an ever-improving form of "air-independent propulsion" (AIP). Today the Iranian navy is following this alternative approach to sea power with perhaps the greatest fidelity, fielding swarms of small but heavily armed speedboats and other light forces, along with quiet submarines. But Iran hardly stands alone.

Many other nations are moving along this path, not least the North Korean navy, which has a few dozen submarines and hundreds of light combatant vessels. Indeed, only a handful of countries have even a single aircraft carrier. Only a few have more than one. The Indian navy may now be one of the latter—assuming that purchase negotiations late in 2007 have concluded favorably—when it acquires Russia's ironically named *Gorshkov*. India was the last naval power to mount a major, World War II–style carrier strike—in 1971, in a spectacular raid on Karachi during one of the Indo-Pakistani wars.* But India is the exception among rising naval powers, most of whom have chosen to follow Russian Admiral Gorshkov's model of predominantly submarine- and small-vessel-based sea power that has come to the fore in naval affairs.

*

The "Gorshkov approach" has clearly been adopted—and built upon—by the navy of the People's Republic of China, where there is a deep appreciation of the need for potent sea power and a determination to avoid building the kinds of naval forces for which the United States is well prepared. China's navy relies on submarines and swift, light vessels instead of aircraft carriers. But the Chinese are going a step further than the Russians did, further than any other country today, by trying to develop what I would describe as "sea power without a navy." In short, the Chinese are trying to utilize technological advances in the range and accuracy of weapons, emphasizing these armaments rather than the types of vessels from which they would be deployed.

In this undertaking they are true trailblazers in the annals of naval affairs, pursuing what some of their strategists call "remote warfare." The World War II Battle of the Coral Sea, in

*This ended with East Pakistan becoming Bangladesh.

which neither battle fleet ever came in sight of the other, was an early example of remote warfare, and ever since the U.S. Navy has relied on attack aircraft and, later on, missiles to achieve this stand-off capability. But we have retained our reliance on heavy vessels. What the Chinese admirals have in mind today seems light-years ahead: they are not only looking to engage us "remotely"—in every sense, including perhaps remote control—but foresee doing so without coupling such a concept to a big fleet of expensive ships.

What, then, will Chinese "sea power without a navy" look like? There are basically three types of weapons on which Chinese capabilities at sea will be concentrated. First is the "supercavitation" torpedo, a weapon distinguished by the creation of a bubble of air in front of it as it runs through the water, sharply reducing resistance. The exact speed gain achieved by this innovation is highly classified, but it can be said that reducing drag in this fashion allows the torpedo to achieve speeds reaching hundreds of knots—much faster than American torpedoes, and much too fast for large U.S. naval vessels to evade. Currently the Chinese are world leaders in developing supercavitation torpedoes, though teething problems with guidance systems have slightly impeded their progress. Nevertheless the time is not far off when these weapons will be deployed, and not just on Chinese submarines. These torpedoes might also be fired from surface vessels, or one day even from aircraft.

The second great new weapon of sea power in which the Chinese are specializing is the supersonic anti-ship cruise missile. To date, cruise missiles, whether intended for use in land or naval warfare, have moved at about the speed of a commercial airliner (that is, about six hundred miles per hour). This makes it somewhat easier for them to be shot down, though their ability to fly low and maneuver gives them a good chance of reaching their targets. This chance would increase significantly if the missile could move some hundreds of miles per hour faster without loss of accuracy, and this sort of improvement in speed is being addressed by the Chinese navy today.

The third new initiative in Chinese naval tactics is the development of "brilliant" seagoing mines. We are familiar with the notion of naval mines blocking harbors or landing zones, and needing to be cleared by the brave crews of small, usually wooden vessels.* During World War II the English Channel became a maze of minefields, as both the British and Germans planted these small, deadly weapons in large numbers on both sides of these narrow waters for both offensive and defensive purposes. Think of these kinds of mines, but now with the ability to rest stealthily on the ocean floor, rising up when the enemy's approach is sensed, and maneuverable enough so as to be able to detonate right under a big ship's keel, breaking its back. China is a leading developer of this weapon, applying to a nineteenth-century device a real information-age twist.

The strategic approach of the Chinese navy today in fact suggests more than a little flavor of the nineteenth-century French *Jeune Ecole* ("Young School"), which tried to revolutionize naval warfare in its time. Instead of imitating the British emphasis on battleships, as the Germans fatefully chose to do before World War I, the French sought to offset the Royal Navy's relatively few, large vessels with hundreds of swift, small boats armed with torpedoes and able to lay mines. The French idea was that this naval force of the "small and the many" would overwhelm a fleet of the "few and the large." Of course, all this was happening while a fierce Anglo-German naval antagonism was unfolding, and when European power political fortunes were driving Britain and France into closer alliance. Thus a clash between these two differing approaches to sea power never materialized. Instead the Royal Navy's principal challenge at sea during World War I came from an opponent whose forces looked very much like its own.

*Wooden because metal vessels would be more likely to trigger magnetic mines.

Clearly the Chinese navy is channeling the spirit of the French *Jeune Ecole.* I am in no way arguing the likelihood of a sea war erupting between the United States and the People's Republic of China; but I am suggesting that, should one occur—say, over the future of Taiwan—stubborn American insistence on keeping with bigger, older ship types will put the U.S. Navy at great risk to the smart weapons being developed on the other side. So we return to the question of why, in the face of such a clear challenge to our conception of modern sea power, does the navy cling to its carrier-centered fleets and battle groups?

*

The navy does offer answers to this question. The first is that it feels the need to hedge against the return of a classic sea war, like the great struggle against Japan from 1941 to 1945. But this line of reasoning falls afoul of the fact that almost no other country is producing carriers, much less in numbers that could challenge our naval mastery. If this were the only concern, our carriers could be mothballed today, to be taken out again with years of comfortable advance notice if we spotted anyone building a capacity for this kind of naval warfare. And this would presuppose that one would have to fight a carrier force in the old way—with aircraft carriers—a big assumption in its own right, much like the army's concern about having to keep its armored forces in order to fight the hordes of tank divisions of some unnamed foe at some indeterminate future date. But at least in the naval instance, an enemy with one or even several carriers could be bottled up by our attack submarines, as the British did to the Argentine fleet during the South Atlantic War. And couldn't our airpower, or even missile-firing surface naval vessels, destroy enemy carriers before they ever went into action? Why should we assume that we would have to fight an old-style naval threat with operational concepts drawn from the 1940s?

The navy also argues that its aircraft carriers can provide vital support to military operations ashore, whether related or not to an amphibious landing. A variant of this "land attack" mission would consist of using the navy to engage a shore-based enemy strictly from the sea. Each of these activities falls within the contemporary category of "littoral warfare," an updated version of the classic naval notion of shore bombardment, one of the archetypal elements of sea power. Carrier attack aircraft have been used to support major land campaigns in this manner since the Korean War (as portrayed in James Michener's classic *The Bridges at Toko-Ri*). Today this capability has been enhanced by the profusion of sensors and communications systems that ever more closely connect the needs of the ground forces with the capabilities of carrier strike aircraft armed with smart weapons. The idea of revitalizing naval strike forces with interconnected "sensor and shooter grids" was the brainchild of the late Vice Adm. Arthur Cebrowski, something he called "network-centric warfare." In many respects it was a direct outgrowth of an innovative earlier concept, Adm. William Owens's notion of creating an information-based "system of systems" designed to employ advanced sensing, communications, and weapons guidance capabilities to empower naval strike forces in fundamentally new ways.

While Cebrowski acknowledged that any types of naval strike vessels—not just carriers—could support networked operations, he made it clear that the flattops would become far more efficient if employed in this way. And it is true that in one "fleet battle experiment" after another over the past decade, ever higher levels of performance by the carriers have been reported. It seems as if Cebrowski found a way to employ new practices to revitalize an old tool. If any man could do it, he seemed the logical candidate, as he was both a naval aviator—with Vietnam-era combat experience—and a qualified computer scientist. He also had a reputation as one of the navy's most innovative spirits; but this just makes it ironic that his legacy would be to provide a basis for retaining the aging, hugely expensive, and increasingly vulnerable aircraft carrier as the hallmark of American sea power.

The cooptation of Cebrowski's network-centric concept by carrier advocates has allowed the navy to keep what it has (and prefers to have) while appearing to be on the cutting edge of strategic affairs. But it is a costly finesse, for it stifles more creative, and far less expensive, approaches. For example, the entire aerial bombardment function of the carrier can be shifted to a combination of land-based aircraft and missile-firing naval vessels. In fact, carriers routinely practice sending their planes off in small groups to a variety of airstrips ashore, from which they then operate. This routine has the effect of turning the aircraft carrier into the world's most expensive limousine service. If one takes seriously the notion of "substitutability," a continued reliance on the carrier for shore bombardment can no longer be justified.

An egregious example of the costliness and limited utility of the carrier in this role was provided by the deployment of the *USS Carl Vinson* to the Persian Gulf between January and June 2005. For six months this carrier supported counterinsurgent operations in Iraq. During that whole time its planes dropped just *four* bombs on the enemy, one of which was dropped at too low an altitude for it to arm, and had to be dismantled by an explosive ordnance disposal team. As shocking a waste as this was—considering the billions it cost to keep the *Vinson* there in the Gulf—it was not particularly out of the ordinary. None of the carriers that have deployed in support of operations in Iraq have ever come anywhere near the level of bombardment activity that was routinely reached during the Korean and Vietnam wars.

While our aircraft carriers' strike capabilities could easily be replaced by air force attack aircraft, or by missiles or even artillery, the navy would be quick to point out that the pace of flight operations in the Persian Gulf has often reached an extremely high tempo. Why? Because it soon became routine to use carrier jets to serve as "eyes in the sky" for our ground forces. That is, an attack aircraft would spend almost all its time aloft providing tactical information to patrols on the ground. This is a key part of the "sensing" function envisioned by the network-centric warfare concept, and the real-time interconnection between the carrier pilot and the company commander on the ground is a wonderful thing. But, again, it is a far too costly way to employ carrier personnel, and there are myriad alternative ways to provide the same information, including the use of land-based jets, Predator drones, dirigibles, aerostats, and tethered balloons. Ground troops themselves increasingly have access to hand-launched tactical unmanned aerial vehicles (TUAVs). In short, there is a wide range of ways to keep an eye on the battlefield from above. The aircraft carrier is by far the least cost-effective way to do so.

The navy's leadership has not been in complete denial about the diminishing value of the aircraft carrier, especially the huge costs associated with maintaining its relatively modest strike capabilities. Beginning three decades ago, debates focused on the idea of getting rid of our relatively few, large carriers in favor of constructing more small ones. The "super carrier" lobby prevailed in this fight, partly by making an economy-of-scale counterargument that turned the cost-effectiveness issue back against the "small carrier" advocates. This line of reasoning proved less effective, however, when the idea of creating "arsenal ships"—huge vessels filled with hundreds of cruise missiles but with tiny crews—was advanced. Arsenal ships, though not offered as part of a direct critique of carriers, would have created tremendous cost savings. But this concept had two problems: it centralized vulnerability, and the same kind of strike capability could be achieved by relying on a network of smaller missile-firing ships in a battle group, instead of on just one golden goose. The arsenal ship, despite enjoying a considerable rooting section among naval officers, died a quiet death.

But the aircraft carrier, which suffers from the same problem of being a big, single "point of failure" if sunk, seems to be immune to this and other arguments against its continued primacy. A recent study by Benjamin Lambeth, a leading scholar of twenty-first-century aerial warfare, admits that "the well-worn criticism of the aircraft carrier by some as a 'self-licking ice cream cone' with respect to its continuing need to protect itself as a first priority remains valid enough as far as it goes." Lambeth's conclusion, however, greatly favors a continuing investment in and incremental improvement of our flattops, in the hope that, as he puts it, "this process of evolutionary change in naval strike aviation will continue to develop in a way that portends a revolutionary improvement . . ." Lambeth believes in the widespread preference, among the navy and elsewhere, for small steps in an improvement process that will ultimately result in a great leap forward.

So the aircraft carrier retains its pride of place, despite a long list of compelling reasons why it should not. Further, if navy leaders have their way, the carrier will be joined in the coming decades by exotic new radar-evading surface vessels armed with "rail guns" able to propel their shells possibly hundreds of miles by relying on electronic rather than chemical explosives as triggers. Curiously, at the same time the navy is trying once again to improve the reach of its surface ships' gunfire, it has adopted a doctrine aimed at fighting close to shore, often at "eyeball range." This concept is the genesis of the new wave of "littoral combat ships" (LCS) that are on the way. The irony of such ideas about naval operations, that have been given rough-sounding names like "Streetfighter," is that close-in fighting is being cultivated at the same time that potential opponents will be better armed with smart weapons that can be fired from swift small boats, or even from ashore.

This sense of irony only deepens when one acknowledges that the vast majority of U.S. naval vessels are so constructed as to suffer serious damage from even single hits by torpedoes or missiles. For example, the *USS Stark* was very nearly lost when accidentally struck by two Iraqi missiles in the Persian Gulf twenty years ago. Similarly grave damage was done to the *USS Cole* in 2000, off the coast of Yemen, by a suicide boat bomber. If the intention now is to send our ships further into harm's way in narrow seas or coastal waters, where they can expect to be struck, a whole new generation of better-armored vessels would seem to be needed—but current designs give the LCS all-aluminum superstructures. A simple alternative would be for the navy to operate their existing ships from a safer distance offshore—removing the need for carriers to protect them from land-based enemy attack aircraft*—where the increased range and accuracy of their smart new weapons systems would enable them to be used with telling effect.

*

As already noted, shore bombardment is one of the basic functions of waging war from the sea. Another way to achieve effects on land is by means of amphibious operations, ranging from small raids to large-scale invasions. Smaller operations have usually been undertaken by naval commandos, known as SEALs (for sea-air-land), while the Marines have taken on the primary responsibility for larger incursions. There is some overlap: SEALs have often helped provide hydrographic reconnaissance before major landings, and Marine amphibious raiding forces were used very successfully in World War II, Korea, and Vietnam.

But today SEALs and Marines have wandered far from their founding responsibilities in waging war from the sea. Naval commandos have increasingly concentrated on counterterror

---

*At this point, if the only need for naval aircraft was to protect surface ships, an argument could conceivably be made for small carriers—like the World War II "jeep carriers"—using vertical- or short-takeoff-and-landing jets. No super carriers would be needed for fleet protection.

operations, much as they had shifted to a focus on counterinsurgency tactics during the Vietnam era. The Marines, for their part, have virtually lost sight of their statutory purpose of assisting in the prosecution of naval campaigns; instead they have become something of a "second army." Or, from their perspective, the first. This doctrinal drift on the part of the service elements most responsible for thinking through the future of amphibious warfare runs the risk of leaving us without a capacity for mounting effective "land-sea operations," as the great strategist and RAND analyst Bernard Brodie called the range of activities from raids to invasions.

To some extent this relative neglect of amphibious operations grows out of a belief that invasions from the sea are becoming ever less possible, precisely because of the rise of attack aircraft, missiles, mines, and other smart weapons. This was certainly the feeling even during Desert Storm in 1991, when many thought that threatening a landing in Kuwait had value only as a deception.* U.S. leaders believed that even low-quality Iraqi forces would be able to inflict sharp losses on Marine landing forces. In the event, Gen. Norman Schwarzkopf's "left hook" in the desert got the job done against Saddam Hussein's forces, so the Marines weren't put to the test. Nearly forty years earlier, during the Korean War, there was similar skepticism about being able to mount amphibious invasions, despite the string of successful landings during World War II. Yet at Inchon the Marines and the army together showed once again the profound potential of striking from the sea at an enemy's vulnerabilities, completely turning the tables on North Korean forces and setting them to flight.

Even before these events, the Marines had performed the signal service, during the 1920s and 1930s, of resurrecting the concept of amphibious warfare from the grave that had been

---

*And the possibility of a Marine landing in Kuwait did indeed divert a substantial number of Iraqi troops, perhaps as many as ten divisions.

dug for it at Gallipoli. In that World War I campaign, the brain-child of Winston Churchill, an Allied landing aimed at seizing the Dardanelles from Turkish control turned into an absolute disaster, seemingly discrediting the whole notion of invading from the sea. But the U.S. Marine Corps, instead of giving up on amphibious operations, studied Gallipoli closely and de-cided on solutions that would ensure the swift movement of masses of landing forces from ship to shore, as well as provide them steady and sufficient supporting fire. The Marines' ge-nius, as John Keegan has observed, was in sweating the details that attend all opposed landings—details that the British had neglected at Gallipoli, and paid for dearly. As Keegan wrote, the "Marine Corps put forward the idea that transit between ship and shore must be essentially a tactical movement. The idea, so arrestingly simple, had been grasped by none of the oceanic powers before."

By the time the United States entered World War II, the Marines—with conceptual and material help from the navy— were ready for the island-hopping campaign against Japanese forces, a counteroffensive that would commence just eight months after the attack on Pearl Harbor. These successful Ma-rine examples of amphibious warfare in the Pacific were ob-served carefully and later replicated in the European theater of operations, where Allied forces mounted one well-crafted land-ing after another, from North Africa to Sicily, Italy, and France. Indeed, the Axis powers lost the war, in large part, because they were never able to defeat a major landing force. Despite tech-nological advances in landward defense—from motorized movement of reinforcements to land-based attack aircraft and better artillery—amphibious operations succeeded.

Today, however, we must ask some crucial questions about the World War II model of land-sea operations. Can a Normandy-style massed invasion from the sea succeed against an opponent armed with smart, guided weapons? In an age of global access to satellite imagery, how can any measure of tactical surprise be achieved by the assault fleet and its landing forces? D day was a success in June 1944 because the Germans had only a very limited ability to strike at an invasion fleet, and were uncertain as to where the landings would occur. Basically they had only a small number of U-boats, some light coastal forces, whatever artillery was already in the landing zone, and a handful of aircraft with which to oppose an immediately available invasion force of about 100,000 troops backed by thousands of aircraft and naval guns. On top of this, beleaguered German troops in Normandy were never fully reinforced because of their high command's continued belief that the invasion was a feint aimed at drawing forces away from the "real" assault that would come in the Pas de Calais.

In the future, the landward enemy will more likely be armed with a multitude of guided weapons, and will be able to detect and monitor the movements of any large expeditionary force. So the situation may come to be somewhat analogous to the period between the world wars, when the apparent lessons of Gallipoli indicated that aircraft, artillery, and well-armed defensive forces had made amphibious warfare too risky an undertaking. But this time the Marines' solution, apotheosized on D day, will no longer obtain. Any future amphibious attack by a large force will have neither stealth nor the usual expected benefits of coming in a steady, streaming mass of humanity. The well-informed foe—if well armed too—will be able to decimate such a force.

Does this signal the end of major seaborne invasions? Perhaps. But there may be another way to bring ground forces from sea to land that can, once again, extend the life of amphibious warfare in the modern era. Instead of thinking in terms of large-scale landings involving concentrated masses of tens of thousands of troops, what if invasions were undertaken by smaller, dispersed expeditionary forces that would come ashore at several points? They might be brought in on hovercraft, meaning that their landing zones would be far less restricted by the terrain requirement of landing-craft-friendly beaches. Or invading troops might be delivered from the sea by gliders, helicopters, or on tilt-rotor aircraft, once again greatly increasing the possible number of landing points. For added stealth, landing forces might even come off of submarines, given that a reconfigured ballistic missile submarine (a "boomer") can be retrofitted to accommodate—albeit in less than cruise-ship style—a battalion of seven hundred–plus Marines.

Why can this work? Because of the great and growing power of even very small units, especially when they are net-worked together and connected to attack aircraft and support-ing missile and naval gunfire. This small-scale approach to amphibious warfare also cultivates a renewed capacity for sur-prise, given that the range of landing zones would be far greater than it ever was in traditional amphibious warfare. Thus defenders would have great difficulty trying to prevent an initial lodgement, and they would then be outmaneuvered again and again by the swift and inherently surprising move-ments of these small expeditionary units. If greater numbers were deemed necessary, their landing would be eased by the disruptions caused by a first wave of these small, swarming units.

But if history is any guide, following up an amphibious at-tack by a nimble, networked force with a large, traditional ex-peditionary group might not be necessary at all. I have in mind another example of doctrinal innovation that comes from the same period as the Marine Corps' advances—the 1920s and 1930s—but this time from the other side: the Japanese. For they too spent the interwar period thinking about the possibil-ity of having to wage a protracted campaign in the Pacific, one that would hinge on the seizure of key islands and strategic coastal points. And they devised a concept of operations that was diametrically opposed to the Marines' solution. Instead of large landing forces backed by massive firepower and an endless stream of logistical support structures, the Japanese saw the possibility of waging war from the sea in small, dispersed units, operating without much direct control. Such forces, they thought, would continually gain the advantage of tactical surprise, and would to some extent be able to provide their own supplies—beyond ammunition, of course. Their fundamental approach has been neatly summed up by Allan Millett, a leading scholar of amphibious warfare (and Marine officer), as being based on "infiltration and exploitation."

The great proof of this concept of operations was offered during the several months after Pearl Harbor, a period in which small Japanese landing forces mounted a far-flung, amphibious blitzkrieg that ranged from the Philippines and Micronesia through the Dutch East Indies (basically today's Indonesia) and on to a campaign in Malaya that culminated in the capture of the mighty British fortress of Singapore. This last conquest was the toughest test of the concept of small-unit amphibious operations using powered barges. In this campaign, about 100,000 British and Empire troops were thoroughly outmaneuvered and outfought by a significantly smaller Japanese force. Of Gen. Arthur Percival's surrender of Singapore, along with some seventy thousand troops, Winston Churchill said it was "the worst disaster and largest capitulation of British history."

Given the current state of technological play in modern weapons systems, the future of amphibious operations is likely to look much more like the Japanese than the American model from the interwar period. But this future is unlikely to be realized if the Marines continue to shift away from amphibious warfare and toward variants of land warfare. Their current path may allow them to command greater budgetary resources and to continue to raise the overall statutory troop limit on the size of the Marine Corps, but it will take them too far from their core competency: war from the sea. When amphibious operations are needed once again—as they surely will be at some point—the Marines will be saddled with old doctrine at a time when the ability to effect landings in strikingly new ways will be urgently needed.

If the Marines are to continue to be masters of their historic mission of amphibious warfare, they must stop thinking of themselves as a slightly smaller version of the army. Perhaps the best way to achieve this change of mind-set is to *draw down* Marine manpower from its current level in excess of 180,000 (as of late 2007), to make the point clearly that by statute the Corps exists to support naval campaigns. Such assistance to the fleet could very well include some aspects of irregular warfare, as many counterinsurgency campaigns have featured the navy and Marines playing key roles in blockading coasts being used by insurgents, and mounting raids from the sea on their coastal hideouts. Until the shift to a "big unit" war in Vietnam, the navy and Marines were doing this with great success, interdicting supplies to the Vietcong and driving them away from coastal communities throughout South Vietnam.

The navy's SEALs should make a similar return to the fleet. They are likely to prove crucial to any future effort to rekindle the amphibious doctrine of infiltration and exploitation by small units that led to so many early Japanese successes in the Pacific war. Indeed, the SEALs are already well habituated to operating in this fashion. There is little purpose in using them on land in day-to-day counterinsurgent operations. Like the Marines, they can and should participate in raids from the sea in the ongoing terror war and in future wars; but they should not routinely form part of the task forces that spend all their time manhunting for al Qaeda cadres in Afghanistan and Iraq. While SEALs take great pride in the fact that some of their officers have commanded these task forces, this is not their reason for being. Like the Marines, the SEALs should come home to the sea. There they will rediscover their fundamental purpose and may also find a world of new possibilities in the realm of "naval special warfare," particularly as the latest technologies for tele-operations become more widely available.

*

While remotely piloted aerial drones have found a place in the military consciousness—even to the point of their sometimes being used as strike weapons rather than just reconnaissance platforms—the air force has so far resisted remote control of fighter aircraft, and the army has only slowly begun to contemplate "tele-operated ground combat systems." Sadly, the navy has shown even less interest in this emerging possibility of an almost wholly new element in naval special operations, and perhaps in sea warfare more generally. It is not entirely new because others have previously experimented with such techniques.

The best historical example of employing tele-operations in naval special warfare was provided by the Germans in World War II, especially in their efforts to attack the Allied fleet that was supporting the Normandy invasion. By this point in the war Germany had lost almost all its major surface combatant ships, and so had to rely on light coastal forces to strike at the Allies. These consisted primarily of swift, well-armed, but unarmored E-boats, the Reich's counterpart to the British motor torpedo boats and American PT boats. These light German forces were sometimes able to hit quite hard, as they did at a landing exercise off Slapton Sands before D day, where they killed some four hundred Allied troops in a single raid. But the Germans also deployed manned torpedoes and remotely operated speedboats jammed full of TNT. All these irregular means were used in the fight against the Allied landing fleet and, though they ultimately met with defeat, they often inflicted stinging losses. The official American naval historian of World War II, Samuel Eliot Morison, noted particularly that "remote-controlled explosive motor boats were employed with some effect."

Today there is an opportunity to replicate these "effects," sixty-odd years later. The long hiatus in the development and use of tele-operated naval systems seems puzzling and unnecessary. Far from being just an exotic element in naval special warfare, remote-controlled vessels should instead be finding their way into more general naval operations. Perhaps a twenty-first-century incarnation of the Battle of Jutland will be fought by tele-operated fleets, waging what the Chinese strategists call "remote warfare" by remote control.

The basic vision of this new kind of naval warfare consists of a swarm of small drone craft—something even smaller than a boat, perhaps the size of a Jet Ski, but one chock-full of high explosives. Imagine a number of these remote-controlled craft coming at a traditional warship—a destroyer, cruiser, or even an aircraft carrier. The larger the number of drones, the greater the chance some will get through, sinking or seriously damaging expensive naval vessels at little cost, and virtually without risk to one's remote pilots. Of course such a concept is not limited to armed Jet Skis. A larger speedboat could be employed, one big enough to launch anti-ship missiles. This capability is within the reach of the American naval special warfare community today, and scarcely any other traditional navy in the world could cope with it. Even navies that might operate their own swarms of light coastal forces, such as those of Iran and China, could be engaged effectively in this fashion by our own, similarly configured forces.

To date this approach has not been adopted. Instead, the American naval special warfare community has invested heavily (more than $1 billion so far) in the "midget submarine" concept of "advanced SEAL delivery," which has proven highly problematic. Even if the midget submarine—which worked poorly for the Japanese during World War II but slightly better for the Russians during the cold war—ever comes to fruition, its value will be far less than that of even a modest-sized tele-operated naval special warfare flotilla. So the opportunity is there, waiting for someone to seize it.

The Iranians, who have clearly concentrated on building a substantial body of light coastal forces, appear to have rejected tele-operated vessels in favor of creating a swarm of manned craft, whose one- or two-person crews would simply sacrifice themselves in kamikaze attacks. A senior U.S. naval officer, who went on to serve on the Joint Chiefs of Staff, once told me that his greatest concern was how to defend a carrier deployed in the relatively narrow waters of the Persian Gulf from such attack. And this form of assault is hardly unprecedented: the "Sea Tigers," the naval arm of the Sri Lankan Tamil rebels, have for many years employed suicide-boat tactics of this sort against government ships. Against such a threat, wouldn't it be handy to have a drone Jet Ski that could be sent to collide with and blow up a manned enemy speedboat bent on a kamikaze attack? Even if the U.S. Navy holds to its fleet posture of having a relatively small number of large capital ships—aircraft carriers in this instance—and a fleet's worth of supporting vessels, tele-operated systems could play a crucial role in defending them.

I almost hesitate to suggest this tactic, for fear of even slightly encouraging those devoted to super-carriers in an era of their rising costs and diminishing benefits. But any line of argument that promotes our serious investment in small, swift, remote-controlled craft should probably be employed without reservation. This is an area that we simply must explore. Other nations will surely do so in the coming years. If the history of developments in naval technology since the onset of the Industrial Revolution is any guide, the systems we cherish will soon be outmoded. Why wait until we find ourselves on the short end of a high-tech Trafalgar?

*

In his classic study of the effects of the Industrial Revolution on maritime affairs, *Sea Power in the Machine Age,* Bernard Brodie concluded that industrial advances had had the somewhat perverse effect of reducing the "reach" of navies. Instead of being able to circumnavigate the world with the only demands being fair winds and enough citrus, capital ships were now tethered to supply bases and a host of other complex support systems. This state of play undermined the nineteenth century's leading naval power, Great Britain, and allowed the rise of new challengers at sea such as Germany, Japan, and the United States. Industrialization also ushered in a century of near-constant technological refinements to ships and their propulsion, weapons, and communications systems. So great was this effect that the life span of the best-designed capital ship of its time was probably not much more than a decade or so before it demanded radical retooling. Thus, both strategically and technologically, sea power was swiftly, fundamentally, and continually transformed.

Now we are in the midst of the Information Revolution, some of whose effects are already being felt, others of which may be inferred with a bit of creative thinking. What seems apparent is that the Information Revolution's effects on sea power are likely to be similar to those of the Industrial Revolution. That is, the ease with which other nations are gaining access to fast, far-ranging, and highly accurate weapons suggests an emerging constraint on the ways in which a "modern navy" might hope to operate against serious opposition.

Coupled with the pressure imposed by the growing "reach" of hostile navies is a second factor: the effect on the form and function of capital ships and other vessels. Here too the pattern will be repeated, to some extent, in that the nature of the capital ship will be subject to rapid and radical change. But instead of driving navies toward ever larger—and fewer—capital ships, the information age will impel development toward fleets comprised of far more numerous but much smaller vessels, replete with swift, smart, long-range weaponry.

The U.S. Navy today seems scarcely cognizant of these trends; it appears intent upon retaining a first-rate twentieth-century fleet well into the twenty-first century. The navy may have to sail this staggeringly expensive form of sea power into harm's way against opponents who will, most curiously, await our ships with much more modern weapons and even more advanced concepts of naval operations. For us to maintain this course is to bear a growing risk of suffering future defeats that would make Pearl Harbor look like a mild reverse. But to make the right adjustments now calls for questioning virtually all the conventional wisdom about sea power that has been accumulated and nurtured for nearly seventy years—a task about as daunting as the one the army faces as it considers organizational redesign. In some ways, however, the navy's challenge to understand the implications of technological change is less demanding than the air force's fundamental need to accept the possibility that its cherished doctrine of strategic bombardment—which comes under scrutiny in the next chapter—may have to be jettisoned. In this comparative respect, at least, the navy enjoys the small luxury of being able to concentrate primarily on retooling, though in the long run it cannot hope to escape the need for rethinking.

CHAPTER FOUR

Airpower in the Information Age

FROM THE DAWN of powered flight a century ago to the present, the impulse to drop bombs on one's enemies has proven irresistible. The basic notion behind this desire has been that attack aircraft (and, since 1944, guided missiles) make it possible to strike an enemy homeland without a prior need to defeat opposing land or naval forces. And so, in the hundred years since H. G. Wells first conjured up a vision of this kind of conflict in his prescient *The War in the Air* (1908), an expanding body of theory and practice has aimed at proving that wars can be won primarily from the air. Both theorists and practitioners have remained remarkably consistent in their approach to airpower: strategists have maintained a near-religious belief that bombing can break the will of the enemy people; and practitioners have kept trying—largely unsuccessfully, despite huge increases in the accuracy and destructiveness of air-delivered munitions—to prove this notion true.

Everything the theorists have said about the ability of airpower to triumph over physical constraints of time and space and to deliver lethal force anywhere is true; but little of what they have believed about the effects of bombing on the human spirit is. In World War II, when aerial bombardment came into its own, the British people bore up amazingly well in the face of the German Luftwaffe's intense blitz. When their time came to suffer, the German people remained resilient too, though Allied bombers killed more than 600,000 civilians—with many of these casualties caused quite intentionally, as in the deliberately planned firebombings of Hamburg and Dresden. In both the British and German cases, industrial production actually rose, rather than fell, in the face of sustained bombardment.

As to the deliberate bombing of civilians with nuclear weapons, at Hiroshima and Nagasaki in 1945, Japan was already defeated militarily, blockaded by sea, and tottering on the verge of surrender. Some historians believe that no costly invasion of Japan was necessary to bring an end to the fighting. So these nuclear attacks hardly provide a basis for justifying one's belief in strategic bombing—though latter-day proponents of "shock and awe" still point to weapons of mass destruction (WMD) as illustrating the amount of force needed to make aerial bombardment work.

This notion of winning wars by deliberately striking with WMD first appeared in the thinking of the Italian soldier and strategist Giulio Douhet, who, in his 1921 treatise *Il dominio dell'aeria* ("Command of the Air"), called for the use of chemical weapons on civilian populations. But both sides in World War II initially found this unthinkable. Still, by war's end, the one country that did develop an ultimate weapon—the United States—was very quick to use it at Hiroshima and Nagasaki. Even so, in all the strategic bombing campaigns waged ever since by those with access to chemical, biological, or nuclear weapons, they have almost never been used.* It would appear that ethical inhibitions are simply too powerful to allow such

---

*There seems to have been a period in the 1980s when these inhibitions were relaxed. The late Saddam Hussein bombed both insurrectionist Kurds and Shi'a with chemicals during the Iran-Iraq War, and it is widely thought that the Soviets used chemical toxins in their bombing campaign against the *mujahideen* resisting their occupation of Afghanistan. Both wars ran mostly from 1980 to 1988.

weapons to be employed other than in retaliation for an enemy's first use. This is the basis of nuclear deterrence, which has played such a powerful role over the past sixty years in helping prevent the onset of another great war between leading states.

The same degree of restraint, what the great theorist of world politics Kenneth Waltz once described as "the mutual fear of big weapons," has not characterized the use of conventional munitions, for which a great enthusiasm has remained. A few years after World War II, the conflict in Korea (1950–1953) featured massive aerial bombing, to the extent that Pyongyang, the North Korean capital, was so heavily damaged by American-led air attacks that hardly a single building remained standing. Still, the people endured, North Korean and Chinese forces fought on, and a bitter stalemate ensued. Bombing certainly did not work in Korea. As the journalist and historian Max Hastings summed it up: "In Korea, the USAF belief in 'victory through air power' was put to the test and found wanting." Nor did strategic bombing prevail in Vietnam, where the massive "Rolling Thunder" and "Linebacker" bombardment operations did little to break the enemy's will, to disrupt their dispersed manufacturing sector or supply lines, or to restore faltering American fortunes on the battlefields of that terrible war.

The next major test for strategic bombardment came during the conflict between Iran and Iraq (1980–1988). This war featured an extended test of guided missiles, employed by both sides, as the principal means of strategic attack designed to weaken the will of the enemy. This too failed, just like the pioneering use of early cruise and ballistic missiles (so-called V weapons) by the Germans against Britain in World War II. Even so, the 1980s were years in which long-range missiles, fired from underground silos on land or submarines at sea, almost fully supplanted manned bombers as the preferred means of waging strategic nuclear warfare. Again, the sheer destructiveness of such weapons made their use highly unlikely; but the specter of being attacked by unstoppable missiles catalyzed a major movement to try to defend against them. Known as "Star Wars" twenty years ago (or, more properly, the "strategic defense initiative") and "national missile defense" now, the idea of thwarting missile bombardment in this manner still captures the imaginations of many air strategists.

Despite decades of poor results in conventional aerial bombing campaigns, normative inhibitions against the use of weapons of mass destruction, and the sheer, daunting power of mutual nuclear deterrence, airpower theorists were not at all disheartened. They soldiered on near the cold war's end, their spirits boosted by advances in sensing, guidance, and information-gathering systems. They restated the ideas of Douhet and other early airpower advocates like Gen. Billy Mitchell and Alexander de Seversky in clever new ways. And their continued devotion was seemingly rewarded in the first U.S. war against Saddam Hussein, when six weeks of bombing in January and February 1991 decimated many of the Iraqi field units that had been placed in static positions in the open desert, with no defensive air cover. Still, the lessons of the air campaign during Desert Storm were viewed as mixed, according to the Pentagon's official *Gulf War Air Power Survey*. Iraqi forces had not retreated from Kuwait under bombardment, nor had Saddam Hussein or the Iraqi people wilted under an unrelenting air assault against the length and breadth of their country. Instead an offensive by half a million coalition ground troops had been needed to expel the occupiers. Even then, Saddam Hussein remained in power at war's end, further clouding the results. No, Desert Storm could not be seen as validating aerial bombing as a primary instrument of war.

Beyond the sheer destruction visited upon Saddam Hussein's forces in this conflict, there remains the question of whether the outnumbered and outgunned Iraqis represented a real test of the potency of aerial bombardment. Can one make a definitive judgment about airpower when it has been applied against a completely overmatched opponent? Probably not. The converse is more likely true, given that this weak opponent resisted in the face of a fierce, sustained aerial assault.

The next great test of strategic bombing came in the Balkans. While a short, sharp series of air strikes in 1995 does seem to have encouraged the Serbs to sign the Dayton peace accords, allowing Bosnia to break away fully from Belgrade, the real test for airpower came in Kosovo in the spring of 1999. In this conflict, apparently sparked by concerns over the mistreatment of Muslim Kosovars by Orthodox Christian Serbs, American-led NATO forces waged an air-only campaign that continued for seventy-eight days. The bombing was intensive, both in Kosovo and throughout Serbia proper. But little actual damage was done to the armed forces of the Federal Republic of Yugoslavia during the campaign. Even so, in the view of some analysts the bombing worked, persuading the Serbs to withdraw their military forces from Kosovo after eleven weeks of air attacks.

Perhaps. If so, the Kosovo conflict, however much it demonstrates a problematic process of "winning ugly," is one of the few instances on record in which airpower has succeeded on its own in achieving one side's war aims. But this case presents some problems. The first is that the Serb surrender of Kosovo was not quite that, as the peace was conditioned on emplacement of a multinational stabilization force, one that initially included Russian forces, not only NATO troops; and Russia was the Serbs' strongest ally. The second issue also involves the Russians, since they had threatened to pull their support for Serb leader Slobodan Milosevic if he refused to deal with NATO. This looming loss of a major supporter may have had as much effect as the bombing, if not more, in encouraging the Serbs to sue for peace. Finally, the renewed political controversy that erupted in 2007 over Kosovo's future—that is, about whether it would remain a part of Serbia—suggests that the outcome of the fighting in 1999 was, in the largest sense, indecisive.

Two years after the Kosovo War, U.S. airpower was unleashed on Taliban and al Qaeda forces in Afghanistan, in a wide-ranging strategic bombing campaign whose goal was to topple the regime that had provided terrorists a haven for planning and mounting the 9/11 attacks on America. For about a month, the aerial bombardment had little effect on the enemy, even in the northeastern part of the country where friendly insurgent forces were engaging Taliban and al Qaeda forces on the ground. As one Pentagon spokesman, Adm. John Stufflebeam, put it at a press briefing, "It seems they're tougher than we thought." But then everything changed in a flash, in the wake of a decision taken by Defense Secretary Rumsfeld—over the resistance of many uniformed leaders in the Pentagon and at the Central Command—to set loose eleven special forces "A teams." These contained fewer than three hundred troops combined, and were embedded with small bands of insurgent forces. Soon they were using laser devices to "paint" targets for attack aircraft dropping smart bombs that would home in on the "tag," greatly enhancing the efficacy of the bombing. In a few weeks the Taliban had been toppled, and in many ways this campaign, Operation Enduring Freedom, could be seen as a major innovation in warfare. Strategic bombing alone had not worked; but airpower used in conjunction with a small, initially horseback-mounted force, had shown tremendous potency. Nothing quite like this had ever been seen before.

Although some experts saw this campaign as analogous to World War II battles in which allied air superiority helped overcome German resistance, there was a big difference. The Germans were almost always fighting huge ground forces that outnumbered them, in addition to having to cope with the crippling effects of aerial attacks. In Afghanistan, it was U.S. forces and their local allies who were outnumbered by the Taliban and al Qaeda, by about three to one. The key point of this campaign was that the accuracy of aerial bombardment had been greatly enhanced when airpower was used in conjunction with ground forces capable of providing key targeting information. In this respect it was not strategic bombing that succeeded in Afghanistan but an information-age version of classic "close air support." This high-quality tactical air support has enabled a modest-sized U.S. force (one much smaller than the expeditionary forces used in Iraq) to wage an effective counterinsurgency campaign in Afghanistan in the years since the Taliban's fall.

Less than two years after Enduring Freedom there would be yet another major application of U.S. airpower, this time against Iraq. While intermittent aerial sniping had occurred since the end of the Gulf War in 1991, growing out of U.S. Air Force patrols of "no fly zones" that covered about two-thirds of Iraqi airspace, these operations were nothing like the scale of air attacks planned and launched in support of the 2003 invasion of Iraq. The intensity of the operation was so great that the favored catchphrase used by policymakers to describe it was drawn from the mantra of the bombing enthusiasts: "shock and awe."

In the event, terrible destruction was wrought upon Iraq from the air. (Once again a major ground invasion was also necessary, even though the 400,000-man regular Iraqi army simply melted away.) The tonnage dropped on Iraq in the second U.S. war against Saddam Hussein was more than five times the amount used in the first Gulf War, tremendously complicating reconstruction efforts that got under way after the start of the American-led occupation. Beyond the sheer material destructiveness of the bombing, which was not necessary to topple Saddam, the psychological effect on those who were bombed was to kindle a great and growing hatred of Americans, due in part to the deaths of thousands of innocent Iraqis who became part of the air campaign's "collateral damage."

This resentment would help fuel the grassroots insurgency that soon rose against the U.S. occupiers, making a mockery of the noble intent of "Operation Iraqi Freedom."

Some voices in American defense circles—a significant minority—were raised in opposition to the continued devotion to a strategic bombing mind-set. For those of us in the dissenting camp, operations in Afghanistan, particularly in the period after U.S. special operations forces had been inserted, suggested a far more effective way to use airpower in close support of small ground-combat formations. Our view was that in an invasion of Iraq, air elements could be used much as they had been employed from November 2001 on in Afghanistan. This perspective was dubbed "Afghanistan-plus," because it called for the method employed in Enduring Freedom but with a somewhat larger force (between 25,000 and 50,000 troops overall) on the ground than had been used in Afghanistan. The retired head of the U.S. Special Operations Command, army Gen. Wayne Downing, was one of the principal proponents of this approach. But even his advocacy proved insufficient to create the momentum needed for a shift in strategy, particularly since the chairman of the Joint Chiefs of Staff at the time, Richard Myers, was an air force general who greatly favored strategic bombardment. His predecessor, Gen. Hugh Shelton, a Special Forces officer, had retired three weeks after 9/11.*

Recently the bombing enthusiasts have had their confidence shaken by two other events: the frustrating Israeli experience in the Lebanon War of 2006, and the equally nettlesome results of the intensive planning done to conceptualize an air campaign against Iran. In the Lebanon War the Israelis mounted a countrywide aerial blitz, destroying communications, power, and transportation infrastructure in an attempt to cripple the Hezbollah network in Lebanon. While there were

---

*When I urged a high-level defense official to suggest keeping Shelton on, he dismissed the very thought of doing so, telling me curtly, "He's a Clinton general."

limited ground operations, this was primarily an air war—on both sides, for Hezbollah relied principally on missile bombardment of northern Israel.

After more than a month of intense bombing, the Israelis gave up their effort to destroy Hezbollah from the air, and Hezbollah ceased its materially ineffectual missile bombardment as well. Most Israelis believed that their nation had somehow lost the war. Ironically, about 90 percent of Israelis had strongly supported an air-only campaign against Hezbollah in the first place, perhaps in the belief that this approach would reduce ground fighting and its resulting casualties—another reason why strategic bombing retains its attractiveness. But six months after the war ended, its chief architect, the Israeli chief of staff, air force Lt. Gen. Dan Halutz, resigned. Soon after, Israel's official inquiry into the conflict produced a harshly critical assessment of the conduct of the war, shaking the stability of the governing coalition.

Given that military ties between the United States and Israel are extensive, the Pentagon watched this war *very* closely. The results of the fighting in Lebanon during the summer of 2006 have had palpable effects on American strategic debates. One could see this almost immediately in discussions about the effectiveness of airpower in confronting the perceived threat of Iranian nuclear proliferation. Given that U.S. policy clearly opposes Iran's development of nuclear weapons, and that the Iranians probably believe they cannot be truly secure from American attack without them, a considerable chance of conflict exists. This seemingly intractable confrontation has sparked a great deal of strategic analysis of potential military operations, with special emphasis on the likely effects of a massive strategic bombing campaign, one loosely labeled "a thousand points of light" (a reference to the fires that would break out all over Iran). Before the Lebanon War—and despite contrary evidence from the Iraq campaign—the estimates as to what could be achieved by such aerial bombing were rosy. Afterward, the message sent by even the most enthusiastic air-power advocates was that bombardment alone would be un-likely to halt an Iranian proliferation program or destabilize the regime in Tehran.

This scaling down of strategic assessments was a healthy development: it helped reenliven the American debate over the uses and limits of strategic airpower. This debate is long over-due for a revisit, given the extensive, uniformly unsuccessful history of U.S. attempts to win wars by trying to bomb oppo-nents into submission. But the U.S. Air Force is a supple insti-tution, and it has already readied another response to these criticisms of its central strategic paradigm. As a number of air force generals have told me recently, "We're going to space!" The idea is that while the United States commands the air, space is increasingly up for grabs. And so a new arms race is being promoted, this time for control of what some believe will be the most commanding of heights, eminently suitable for new and advanced strategic bombing initiatives. While propo-nents of "space power" echo many of the sentiments that moti-vated cold warriors of the late 1970s and early 1980s, the difference today is that, because of a variety of technical ad-vances, what were once just far-fetched fantasies now appear tantalizingly close to becoming achievable.

*

In 1967, as the Vietnam War was nearing its greatest intensity, the United States and the Soviet Union, along with most other countries around the world, signed the Outer Space Treaty.* It affirmed the desire of all civilized peoples to encourage the ex-ploration of space, but without militarizing it. While the treaty

---

*So it is commonly known. But its legal name is the "Treaty on Principles Govern-ing the Activities of States in the Exploration and the Use of Outer Space, Includ-ing the Moon and Other Celestial Bodies."

explicitly outlaws the use of nuclear weapons in or from space, it is vague about deploying other kinds of weapons, from traditional explosives to more exotic lasers and other directed energy devices. Four decades after the treaty took effect, however, there are still no weapons of these kinds in space. Instead, the approach by nations in space has been, for the most part, to make increasing use of space to support military operations—particularly in the areas of intelligence gathering, surveillance, and advanced communications—but to refrain from establishing orbital weapons platforms.

The tracking and information-gathering functions of satellites matured fairly quickly, with the "Talent Keyhole" (TK) system providing important intelligence beginning in the 1970s. The value of these "national technical means" was rated so highly that Adm. Stansfield Turner, Jimmy Carter's director of central intelligence, felt comfortable enough to allow the CIA's networks of human spies to wither in the late 1970s. With the dissolution of the Soviet Union at the end of 1991, the principal duty of the satellite spies to locate and count Russian tanks, planes, and ships declined in importance. But even though there has been no comparable military threat to track, the TK system and other assets have remained on duty at a cost of about $1 billion per week. Unfortunately the rise of small, dispersed terror networks over the past decade cannot be tracked by satellites as easily as the movements of the Red Army during the cold war, and the decline of American human intelligence capabilities has thus been keenly felt.

Beyond the realm of espionage, though—for which satellites now seem somewhat less relevant—orbital assets have continued to prove their tremendous worth in battle. Ever since Desert Storm, the U.S. military has relied more and more heavily upon space assets to provide targeting data for terrestrial operations, and to enable the global command and control of our far-flung forces with lightning speed. This is especially true in more conventional battle settings, where an accurate picture of an adversary's dispositions can be quickly provided. But the value of satellite surveillance, tracking, and communications links has also been demonstrated in some irregular warfare settings, particularly in the rough-and-tumble counterinsurgent operations of U.S. and NATO forces along the Afghan-Pakistani border. In this sense, at least, space has become seriously militarized, edging up against—but not going beyond—the bounds intended by the framers of the Outer Space Treaty.

Today a troubling development threatens the integrity of the treaty and could ignite a war in space that would disrupt the vital stream of satellite support for our terrestrial military operations. In October 2006, President Bush quietly articulated a radical new policy calling for the United States to develop a military capability that could deny others the chance to make "hostile use of space." In the wake of this announcement, which comes close to contravening the spirit of the Outer Space Treaty, the Pentagon has begun thinking about how to move from militarization to full "weaponization" of space.

To senior leaders in the armed services, this means not only creating an ability to stalk and kill other satellites; it also extends to the notion of adding a new twist to the whole idea of strategic bombardment. The vision includes creating orbital battle stations that drop their deadly packages to earth at several times the speed of sound. The preferred munition in this instance would be poles made of the strong metal tungsten—no explosives needed, no "physics package," and thus no treaty violation—"rods from God." These, strategists believe, would be of particular use in knocking out deep underground bunkers (in Pentagon parlance, "hardened, deeply buried targets," or HDBTs) where the illicit development of weapons of mass destruction might be going on. Using a bundle of tungsten rods, whose velocity at impact would be about Mach 10 (more than seven thousand miles per hour), would be like hitting the target with a meteorite.

Another use of an orbital battle station would be to serve as a strike platform for knocking out missile launch sites on the ground, making it a key component of any future national missile defense. If beam weapons were to come on line, the missile-defense role of these "battle stars"—and the anti-missile beam-firing satellites working with them—would only grow in importance. Beyond this, the air force is contemplating development of a new generation of bombers that can fly into orbit, then swoop down anywhere in the world within an hour or so. Both the Marines and special operations forces have expressed interest in using such a space plane to move small combat teams to any target with similar speed, and without a need to negotiate overflight rights.

The obstacles associated with such paths of development are many. Perhaps the greatest is that the attempt to create space-based combat capabilities faces daunting technological dilemmas and gargantuan costs. Sustaining a fleet of satellites in space is difficult enough. Creating one or more "battle stars" would be many orders of magnitude more challenging. Not to mention the complexities and costs involved in developing an aircraft that could reach orbit, descend upon a target, then fly its way back to friendly territory.* Even if these hurdles were overcome, we might end up imperiling the existing combat-support functions now provided by space assets—because others will surely be impelled to learn how to fight in space, to shoot down or cripple our orbital "eyes and ears."

This has been the great paradox of war in space all along: the potential attractiveness of being able to destroy enemy satellites or bombard one's opponents from orbit is offset by the terrible vulnerability of one's own space-based weapons platforms to retaliation. It has been clear since the dawn of the space age that the fragility of satellites or orbital stations is

*The U.S. space shuttle fleet is composed of craft with no ability to do more than make a "dead-stick" (unpowered) landing when coming back to earth.

great. Just a few years after the Russians launched Sputnik in 1957, the U.S. military was attempting to build space vehicles that could get close enough to attack enemy satellites. While the euphemistically named Project SAINT ("satellite inspection technique") proved too difficult to pursue and was shut down in 1962, it was soon replaced by a simpler "sense-and-strike" system. Satellite tracking was done by legions of ground radars, whose function was to provide a target for earth-based ballistic missiles to strike at with nuclear warheads. Despite the Outer Space Treaty's clear ban on nukes in space, this strategy stayed in place until at least 1975—for nearly a decade after ratification—in the form of nuclear missile batteries deployed at the Kwajalein Atoll and on Johnston Island in the Pacific.

The Russians fared somewhat better in these earlier days, when blinding the enemy's eyes in space seemed so important. In 1978 their Cosmos 1009, an attack satellite about a hundred feet long and three feet in diameter, successfully maneuvered within about half a mile of another of their satellites, a position from which it could have attacked by firing steel pellets—effective, and probably allowable within the letter of the Outer Space Treaty. But the Russians too slipped over the line with their plans to disrupt satellite communications by using nuclear weapons in the upper atmosphere, perhaps even in orbit, to generate a crippling electromagnetic pulse (EMP). As their own economic pressures mounted, Soviet reliance on nuclear weapons to degrade the perceived American advantage in space systems only grew.

Around the time the Russians were working on the Cosmos 1009, President Jimmy Carter signed Presidential Decision Memorandum (PDM) 37, dated May 13, 1978, which has served ever since as a guide to American strategic space policy. The document reflected a deep concern about any weapons that could destroy or blind U.S. satellites. This was an especially worrisome issue in an era when even a few minutes' advance warning of an enemy's launch of intercontinental ballistic missiles might mean being able to retaliate against a first strike. Assured ability to retaliate was—and still is, in a mechanistic sense—the key to deterring a nuclear war. Carter, a nuclear engineer by training, sought to make sure that the United States would not be vulnerable in space; but PDM 37 went beyond defense to include the call for an "integrated attack capability." This reference to the offensive side of space operations—an early foreshadowing of the position that George W. Bush would expand upon in the fall of 2006—gave the document its real punch among soldiers, scientists, and defense bureaucrats.

Off and on for thirty years, the United States has quietly been thinking through the issues in developing a capacity to shoot down or cripple other nations' satellites. Where the Russians had Cosmos 1009 in the 1970s, we began developing a "miniature homing vehicle" (MHV) during the Carter years, a paint-can-sized device that could be deployed from a high-flying aircraft or a rocket. Once launched, the MHV's thrusters would be used to propel it into a collision with a satellite target. Less exotic approaches were also cultivated. As early as 1982 a missile was launched from an air force fighter aircraft that destroyed an aging U.S. satellite. Many other approaches to hitting targets in space were considered, and some were developed. All have remained highly classified, but no doubt they fall into categories that reflect the various modes of attack that have been discussed for decades, including "directed energy weapons" like lasers, and devices designed to transform the kinetic energy of electrons into lethal microwave fields.

In the nearly twenty years since the end of the cold war, the Russians seem to have fallen behind in the area of war in space; but the Chinese appear to have ramped up their capabilities considerably. A dramatic demonstration of Chinese ability to engage in anti-satellite warfare came in January 2007, when the People's Liberation Army fired a ground-based ballistic missile with a conventional warhead that destroyed one of their own old satellites, still in orbit about five hundred miles above the earth's surface. Coming as it did on the heels of George W. Bush's announcement that the United States intended to accelerate its efforts to engage in offensive action in space, this test seemed to presage a new kind of arms race.

The basic Chinese approach to space warfare—directly attacking satellites with earth-based missiles—differs from the earlier Russian emphasis on striking in space from maneuverable orbital vehicles. And even though much of Moscow's space warfare capability has fallen into disarray since the end of the cold war, American defensive efforts have continued to focus on thwarting just such "Moonraker"-type attacks on U.S. satellites. This mind-set is most evident in the ongoing program to develop orbital ANGELS, "autonomous nano-satellite guardians for exploring local space." These tiny spacecraft are intended to act as scouts, capable of providing warning of the approach of a hostile object to one of our satellites, allowing the latter time to fire thrusters and relocate to a safer place. Whether ANGELS may one day have swords to go with their shields is a matter beyond our ability to discuss openly now.

Beyond the daunting technological state of play, which currently finds it so much easier to knock things down from space than to put them there and keep them in orbit, several other factors bedevil the pursuit of waging war in and from space. The first is that dropping weapons from greater heights—even from as high up as an orbiting battle station—is no guarantee that target populations will be any more likely to crack psychologically than when they come under more traditional bombardment. As long as the munitions used are traditional explosives rather than nuclear weapons, why would it matter that an attack aircraft had come from outer space rather than from neighboring airspace?

Would the meteor-like impact of iron rods dropped from orbit terrify people into submission? Not if they were used as intended, to destroy deep underground bunkers in remote places far from population centers. Even in this example, their use would be problematic, as there would be no way to go in and prove illicit activity at the site that was hit. The victims could still react with unchallengeable, righteous outrage. Worse, if these "rods from God" were used against an urban population, the world outcry against the carnage would quickly surpass any benefit gained from the effects of the bombardment itself. No, space will not be the saving new means of strategic bombing.

The idea of empowering a generation of Robert Heinlein–like "starship troopers" by putting them on space planes that could drop them off anywhere in the world in about an hour's time also has serious flaws. Only a small degree of force can be applied in this fashion, and these new orbital commandos would quickly be put down if they could not link up with other forces once they reached their target. And if others could rendezvous with them at the site, why would the commandos have had to come from space in the first place? Even if this method of insertion were to succeed, the problem of exfiltrating the plane and the troops would remain. They might be able to move anywhere in the world without needing overflight rights—since they would drop in straight from space—but getting out would require flying through the atmosphere and crossing international boundaries, no doubt with enemies in hot pursuit. Unless the space plane could somehow find the fuel and external tanks to become a rocket capable of making its way back into orbit on its own—a practical impossibility—it would become a new, exceedingly costly kind of kamikaze.

The foregoing suggests that the U.S. Air Force, which has grown increasingly aware of the fundamental problems with its strategic bombing paradigm, is trying to revitalize this tattered concept by seeking to dominate space militarily. It is thought that once this ultimate high strategic position is secured—by an ability to attack others' satellites and space stations—strategic bombardment, and even national missile defense, can be reenergized, both with surveillance and strike capabilities.

Further, the notion of airdropping military forces might be greatly enhanced by a capacity for mounting "space drops."

At first blush, the air force move into the military use of space seems an inevitable development, to some even a welcome one. The United States has long been the world's dominant air power, and Americans are, as the great apostle of aerial bombing Gen. Billy Mitchell put it more than eighty years ago, a naturally "air-going people." Isn't it logical that we should now become a "space-going people"? And if we don't, other nations will surely try to forge their own mastery of space. Today China, Russia, and Japan all have the resources for such an undertaking. This stark prospect first confronted us with the Soviet launch of Sputnik, the first man-made satellite. It resonates today in China's advances, both in the manned space flights of their *taikonauts* and in their successful testing of anti-satellite weapons. The Russians too remain interested in space and have banked a great body of knowledge and expertise in the area of space warfare.

While it seems inevitable that space will grow ever more important to military affairs, seeking a capacity for combat in space, or for using orbiting weapons to strike at terrestrial targets—as senior U.S. military leaders would like—is a path to failure at ruinous cost. Space bombardment as a dominant tactic is unlikely to work where nearly a century of traditional aerial bombing has already failed. Orbital attack suffers from even more limitations, not least the great, growing vulnerability of satellites and manned or unmanned stations. Even if the United States develops better space-based anti-satellite weaponry to deal with hunter-killers in orbit, there will remain the fundamental risk that almost any earth-based ballistic missile can relatively easily be used to destroy objects in space.

A major war in space would likely harm the United States far more than other nations. As of 2007 there were about 850 satellites in orbit, more than half of them American, a significant portion of these dedicated to military use. Their orbits range from about 100 to 22,000 miles above the earth, with the higher number representing the altitude needed to sustain a geostationary orbit that keeps the satellite moving at the speed of the earth's rotation. More than 300 satellites—the vast majority of them American, many used for "military imaging"— are in "low earth orbit," below 550 miles.* The Chinese missile test in January 2007 shot down a satellite 540 miles above the earth, demonstrating that a large proportion of the world's satellites are already imperiled. If space warfare were to erupt one day, destroying many, if not most, satellites and filling the orbital circuits with debris fields that would linger for decades, U.S. commerce would suffer significantly, and American military forces would be denied the vital imaging intelligence, targeting, and other communications capacities that now so greatly empower them. The likely losses in space warfare far outweigh almost any possible gains.

Before such a misadventure is allowed to unfold, military leaders should realize that the greatest advances they are likely to make in the years ahead will depend on retaining secure flows of information from space. The clear implication for American policy is to reaffirm the 1967 Outer Space Treaty, which allows all to use information gleaned by their space assets but prohibits more direct means of warfare in orbit. This treaty, which made such good sense forty years ago, makes even more sense now. The avenue toward transformation that the air force is most eager to take turns out to be the one that should be most carefully avoided.

*

If devotion to a doctrine of strategic bombing and a strategy to dominate space are wrongheaded notions, what, then, *ought*

---

*This tally is based on the number of satellites that come within 550 miles when they are nearest to the earth. Many of them spend at least a portion of their time above this level, as orbits are elliptical rather than circular.

the air force to be thinking about? The answer is, refocusing air doctrine on the support of ground operations, and pursuing a technology strategy that skillfully blends old and new aerial platforms, weaponry, and information systems. In both areas the opportunities are almost self-evident and require only a change in habits of mind in order to begin a reform process that can revitalize airpower and restore its relevance to twenty-first-century military affairs.

The choice is starkly illuminated when it comes to doctrine. While strategic bombardment has a poor track record, the opposite is true of close air support (CAS). Where it is hard to identify more than one or two instances in which the bombing of infrastructure and the deliberate targeting of civilians may have been decisive, it is overwhelmingly clear that when commanders have been able to call upon airpower in support of their ground combat operations—on offense or defense—the effects have often been profound.

Airpower used in a close-support role has produced remarkable results across a wide range of wars over the past seventy years, beginning during the Spanish Civil War (1936–1939), which saw German pilots of the Condor Legion helping ensure a fascist victory. Many of these same German airmen would take the lessons of the Spanish conflict and apply them at the outset of World War II, when the close cooperation of armored and air forces formed the heart of the blitzkrieg doctrine that won so many striking victories during the period 1939–1942. But the Allied forces that opposed them were learning as well and, between 1943 and 1945 first-rate German ground forces were defeated again and again because they lacked air cover. Even many of the irregular conflicts that erupted during the late colonial period and the cold war saw close air support playing a major role, with the British exhibiting particular skill in their counterinsurgency operations in Malaya and Kenya in the 1950s. The American experience with close air support after World War II was less successful, the Korean War ending in a stalemate and Vietnam in defeat. But Desert Storm in 1991 and the campaign in Afghanistan ten years later both saw a return to timely and highly effective close coordination between air and ground forces.

Clearly the U.S. Air Force *can* excel at close air support. In the years ahead it should emphasize this doctrine over and against strategic bombing or space warfare. It will be especially important to focus on tight coordination with ground combat forces engaged in unconventional warfare, which will remain far more prevalent than good old-fashioned conventional wars. In irregular wars our opponents are unlikely to have attack aircraft, and will probably possess only a very limited ability to threaten U.S. planes with shoulder-mounted or other types of anti-aircraft missiles. So it will be possible to concentrate on *exercising* air mastery rather than on having to expend a great deal of effort to *achieve* such a level of control.

The key to using airpower in close support against irregular adversaries is threefold, demanding the ability to: provide timely, targeted information on enemy dispositions; have strike forces always at the ready; and limit the damage to noncombatants. There are a number of simple ways to become very, very good at each of these functions—but each challenges the air force to move away from existing orthodoxy. For example, it now tends to associate tactical intelligence with space assets or, more often, unmanned aerial vehicles like the Predator. But there is a faster, cheaper, better way: networks linking patrol aircraft and ground forces. The great need is for persistent aircraft rather than just fast-moving, fuel-guzzling jets that linger only briefly over the battle area. This means thinking in new ways, like using dirigibles for intelligence, surveillance, and reconnaissance. A blimp can fly above the reach of ground fire, stay on station for many days, and be replaced by another with no lapse in coverage when it leaves. Weather need not be much more of an issue for a blimp than it is for other aircraft. Even small, unmanned aerostats and balloons can easily be interconnected with ground units, sharing voice, text, and video in real time. The practical experience with aerostats used to monitor drug-smuggling "go-fast" boats in the Caribbean, along with advanced experiments conducted by research teams at the Naval Postgraduate School, have showed the feasibility and utility of this approach again and again.

A blast-from-the-past technology like the dirigible can do more than relay information: it can also serve as a strike platform. Why require a costly cap of attack aircraft to be flying constantly overhead, or call on them to make their way to a distant target, perhaps taking hours to scramble and get there, when blimps can be on station and armed to the teeth with bombs? The payload-carrying capacity of a Goodyear-sized blimp is quite substantial, allowing for hundreds of heavy bombs. Or much more light ordnance. Think of the navy's now-discarded concept of the arsenal ship, but a much safer and more sensible aerial version of it, with an air crew optional but probably desirable in the early going. Since airships can fly at high enough altitudes to be virtually invulnerable to enemy ground fire—unlike attack helicopters, which were shot down by the thousands in Vietnam—the only essential condition for their employment would be air force control of the skies. Given the overwhelming U.S. superiority in jet fighters, this requirement can easily be met.

Because weapons dropped from the dirigible can be "smart" (for example, guided by troops who have laser-tagged the ground target), the likelihood of collateral damage is sharply reduced. It's important to realize that, when it comes to bombs, small is beautiful. The standard two-thousand- and five-hundred-pound bombs that the air force uses to support counterinsurgent ground operations will be too heavy for the job much of the time. These bombs may make sense in the context of a major land campaign with large field armies. But in a pitched battle waged by small teams of fighters on both sides, in settings where the killing of innocents causes resentments that will dry up intelligence flows and serve as a recruitment tool for the enemy, what is needed is something far more precise. The downsizing of ordnance is another important change.

Dirigibles can also contribute to a "hearts and minds" campaign by bringing relief in the wake of disasters. Instead of carrying bombs, on appropriate occasions they could be loaded with food, medicine, and other supplies. The payload-carrying capacity of several airships—again, using a Goodyear-sized blimp as a model—would roughly equal that of a whole squadron of air force Hercules transports. And the dirigible has the added advantage of being able to land in almost any open space, with no runway required, so that relief could be delivered exactly where it was needed, without having to build or repair airfields in disaster areas. In recent years the U.S. Air Force has found itself repeatedly involved in relief missions, as in Indonesia after a tsunami hit in December 2004, and in Pakistan in the wake of a killer earthquake in 2005. Both times this led to what Carroll Doherty of the Pew Research Center called an "uptick" in favorable opinions toward the United States. In Pakistan, for example, the favorable rating among the general public toward the United States was 23 percent before the relief effort, 50 percent after. By enhancing this relief capability with airships, the favorable effect on public opinion will be still greater. The air force's eight "contingency response groups" (CRGs), designed to fight but usable in relief, should acquire blimps, which can support combat operations or humanitarian responses to natural disasters.

This idea of seeking a "return of the Zeppelins"—the slowest powered military aircraft ever built—comes at a time when almost all the emphasis in the U.S. military is still to develop "fast-burner," high-performance jets. This preference goes beyond the air force; the navy and Marine Corps seek the same properties in their attack aircraft, which explains the genesis of the "joint strike fighter" concept: one plane, good for all the services, with the exception that the Marines would also like their

version of this aircraft to have a short takeoff and landing capability. It would be foolish to neglect our fighter aircraft component; but too much emphasis on squeezing the last ounce of
high performance out of this type of aircraft stifles interest in
other important concepts, like airships, and starves them of research and development resources. And the air force is still fixated on fighter aircraft.

*

Why the obsession with the fastest and most maneuverable
jets? Is it for the same reason that men are endlessly fascinated
with sports cars? Perhaps there is an element of this passion.
But such performance characteristics have always been crucial
to fighter aircraft, where an overall advantage in speed, maneuverability, and firepower has generally proved decisive in
aerial combat. This has been so from the dawn of the air age,
from the Sopwith Camel of World War I to the Spitfire of World
War II and on to the Tomcats, Hornets, and Eagles of more recent times. It has remained so because all fighter aircraft, until
now, have had to be pointed directly at the enemy aircraft in order that the pilot could fire with any hope of hitting the target.
This is why the dogfight tactics of the Red Baron in World War
I remained relevant in the "Top Gun" era, and why, to the extent that guns are still used by fighter pilots, "pointing" still
matters. It is why there remains such a strong emphasis on ek-
ing out every last bit of performance from each new generation
of fighter aircraft. And there is usually a great sense of urgency
about doing so, as other militaries always seem to be leaping
ahead with their own fighter models—the Russian MiG series
being our principal competitor for almost sixty years now.

But there are at least two ways to tamp down the ardor of
the "fighter jock" community without damaging national security. The first would be a greater concentration on air-to-air
weapons, taking advantage of improvements in the movement

and guidance of munitions that now make it possible to fire one's weapons without also having to point one's plane directly at the enemy long enough to lock on the target. This is a sensitive area of military research and development, but it can be said openly that this capability is real. Putting more emphasis on developing such weapons would soon transform air combat as we have known it. Both the Israelis and the Russians have been emphasizing such weapons for years; but our late entry into this field is somewhat offset by the greater sharp-angled "backward reach" of our missiles. Specifics remain classified, but, for example, Russian "reach-back" missiles cannot be aimed at anywhere near the angles that American air-to-air missiles already use. All the more reason for us to pursue this development, and to work out such kinks as the problem that these missiles lose much of their speed as they turn backward to chase enemy fighters.

Another breakthrough approach to the future of fighter aircraft would continue to emphasize high-performance characteristics but would deliberately take them so high as to make it impossible for pilots to remain in their cockpits. It is already feasible to build attack aircraft that zoom and turn in ways that the human body could never tolerate, despite being encased in the best-tailored "G-suit" possible. How, then, would the plane be guided? Today it would be possible to pilot such an aircraft remotely, the same way that the Predator and Global Hawk unmanned aerial vehicles are flown. In the future the piloting function could be fully programmed, much as the space shuttles are already almost entirely flown by means of artificial intelligence, and many commercial flights are conducted with a near-complete hands-off being the norm among their flight crews.

While pilots might embrace the idea of having weapons that could be fired at the enemy even when running away, they are sure to oppose any notion that takes them out of the cockpit.

Beyond the general devotion of most airmen to strategic bombing, there is an absolutely unshakable, John Henry–like faith, shared by virtually all, in the superiority of the human pilot in the cockpit. Even if the physical limits of the human body are recognized, the community of pilots would assert the continued need to exercise human judgment in air combat or ground-attack missions. Indeed, the specter of a wrongful shootdown by a thoughtless, computer-driven aircraft is scary. Even a remote pilot's field of vision can never be as broad or as flexibly refocused as a human pilot's.*

These are powerful concerns, but they should not deter innovators from continuing to develop remote and fully automated piloting, sure to be a large element in the future of aerial warfare.

*

The air force's greatest challenge is to move away from its beloved but ineffective doctrine of strategic bombing, and to replace it with a much sharper emphasis on the close support of ground operations. The allure of space should also be seen as illusory. Taking warfare to this ultimate high frontier is more likely to result in degrading our own ability to support terrestrial operations than in depriving our potential adversaries of orbital assets. Finally, in terms of technology strategy, the obvious choice of developing ever faster, more maneuverable manned aircraft should be reconsidered. The change in weapons' capabilities now matters more than airframe performance. If air-to-air weapons can be fired in any direction, speed and turning ratios matter less. Just as smart bombs have

---

*Remote piloting refers to an aircraft being guided from a ground station by a human operator. Fully autonomous aerial vehicles—and there are some—are entirely controlled by computer programs.

extended the life of the aged B-52 bomber as a tool of close air support—and could even prompt a renaissance for dirigibles—air-to-air weapons could make fighter aircraft design issues almost moot. For those who insist on continuing to improve fighters, the call should be to look unflinchingly at the future of remote-controlled and robotic aircraft. The point is not to take all the pilots out of all the cockpits, but skillfully to blend men, women, and intelligent machines so as to forge a fundamentally different kind of airpower.

CHAPTER FIVE

Thinking About Nonlethal Weapons

THROUGHOUT HISTORY the central goal of weapons makers has been to increase the striking and killing power of the tools of war. Sometimes they have focused on improving range and accuracy, as was the case with infantry weapons from the long-bow to the rifle. In other instances they have emphasized ever-larger explosives, a clear pattern that can be perceived in the development of modern artillery, aerial bombs, and even atomic weapons. Today the rise of exceptionally sophisticated guidance systems has reduced the demand for greater destructiveness of weapons, precisely because they can often be delivered right on target, often over great ranges. The mission can be accomplished with "less bang," a point well illustrated by the overall reduction in the megatonnage of nuclear weapons arsenals that occurred—well before the end of the cold war—as guidance systems made it possible to deliver these deadly payloads virtually on top of enemy silos. But even these sometimes important reductions in the need for kinetic power pale next to the emergence today of a whole new stream of advanced research and development that aims at fielding "nonlethal weapons" (NLW). In other words, a major new goal of arms producers is to figure out how force can be used without killing.

This may be the greatest paradox in the long course of military affairs. Even more puzzling, a significant number of those whose profession calls upon them to use force in the field against their nation's enemies are among the strongest advocates of NLW. How can this be? Almost surely the reason is that more and more military interventions must deal with conflicts that feature subtle cultural intricacies and ambiguous strategic characteristics. Sensitivities to death are often higher on both sides. The combatants may be guerrillas or terrorists who blend in with a relatively innocent general population that must be protected, or at the very least not alienated. Perhaps even those who were saved or "liberated" resent and resist the presence of the intervening force, as happened in Iraq in the wake of the 2003 American invasion. In such situations, both the age-old ethical principles of "noncombatant immunity" and "proportionality" impel soldiers and statesmen alike to strive to use force in the least lethal ways possible. And beyond these rationales is the growing problem that, in an age of global media and real-time streaming webcasts, the perceived excessive use of force by one's troops is likely to be shared with a world audience immediately, causing a grave defeat in the "battle of the story" that now matters so much to the outcome of these perplexing conflicts.

So, for the last several decades, while traditional wars have been on the wane and irregular conflicts, insurgencies, and other kinds of mass uprisings have been on the rise, advanced militaries have been trying to figure out how to use force less lethally. The idea behind the NLW concept is to be able to deter or defeat such enemies by using coercion, without applying so much force that the killing of innocents will cause serious blowback in the court of public opinion. This tacit admission of the importance of public opinion has increasingly driven the development of NLW.

Constabularies in many countries around the world are carefully constrained in the degree of legal violence they can employ, so they often resort to NLW—water cannons to disperse mobs being an iconic image. This is true even in authoritarian states, where instances of the police massacring large numbers of demonstrators are exceptionally rare. Whenever the levels of violence are ratcheted up, matters tend to move quickly beyond the police, with the military entering the picture, as the Chinese People's Liberation Army did at Tiananmen Square in 1989. Given the increasingly blurring line between civil unrest and outright insurrection—and the fact that almost all the thirty-odd major conflicts in the world today are civil wars—militaries have found themselves, like the Chinese PLA and many other armies, more often involved in restoring order. This is so not only at home but sometimes in interventions abroad, where the restoration of "security and stability" has become a major military mission for United Nations peacekeepers and for those working under the auspices of regional security groups.

One of the longest-running cases of violent civil unrest can be found in the struggle of the Palestinian people for statehood. Because Israel has resisted the presence of international peacekeeping forces on its own soil, or even in the "occupied territories" of Gaza and the West Bank, the Israeli Defense Forces (IDF) have had to move seriously into the nonlethal realm. The IDF is among the first militaries to thoroughly explore this area. Its first sustained engagement of this kind came in response to the initial Palestinian *intifada* (1987–1993), when activists and militants fought the Israelis mostly with slings, stones, and jeers. A lethal response would have appeared (and, in truth, would have been) disproportionate, so the Israelis adopted some traditional police methods, introduced some new tactics, and made particular use of "rubber bullets" that were designed to injure or incapacitate but not to kill. In these ways, they thought, the protesters' will could be worn down without world opinion shifting decisively against Israel's position on Palestinian rights and statehood.

In the event, the militants—many of them women and children—continued their street actions for years, and it was the Israelis who eventually acceded to the call for a negotiated solution (which came in the form of the 1993 Oslo Accord). Still, little real progress toward mutually agreed-upon goals was made, and seven years later a second *intifada* erupted, comprised of both the familiar stone-throwing and a new wrinkle: small-scale suicide bombings. Over time low-level street violence gave way to ever more numerous acts of terrorism, an escalation that seemed to make a mockery of Israel's reliance on nonlethal solutions to its security problems in Gaza and the West Bank. Indeed, the Israeli experience with NLW seems to be a sobering, cautionary tale about the risks of not being forceful enough when faced with a smart, determined adversary. In this case, reliance on NLW may actually have toughened the will of the insurgents, given their foreknowledge of the Israelis' self-imposed constraints on the level of violence that might be used in response to their actions.

The U.S. military has also been developing its nonlethal capabilities in recent years, spurred no doubt by humanitarian interventions in the 1990s in Somalia, Haiti, and Bosnia. In each of these cases, providing "stability and security" was the primary objective, not the decisive engagement of a clearly known enemy on the battlefield. While the situation in Somalia did end up escalating into more general fighting—a debacle that led to the unraveling of U.S. policy there at the time—Haiti and Bosnia both turned out to be qualified successes, with peace and order being restored. The possibility of more missions like these in the future suggested to American civilian and military policymakers the need to develop a whole range of nonlethal capabilities. The primary goal was to give U.S. troops the flexible options they might need in order to keep the peace and ensure that aid flowed to those who were suffering—without necessarily having to kill those who opposed and intended to thwart the intervening force.

Over the past decade a great number of nonlethal devices have been designed and built, many of which have been tested, some of which are now being fielded. Most of these programs have been pursued under the auspices of the Defense Advanced Research Projects Agency (DARPA) and are highly classified. But this does not preclude a general discussion of the many types of NLW under development and their various properties, which range from incrementally improved versions of older devices to exotic high-tech systems.

*

Among the more traditional NLW that can be fired by riflemen are rubber bullets and "beanbags." Rubber bullets hurt a great deal and occasionally kill people, particularly the very young or those who are struck in the head. Each incident of this kind undermines the credibility of NLW and the policies supporting their use. This proved to be a nettlesome problem for the Israeli Defense Forces during the *intifadas,* as the handful of Palestinian women and children killed in this fashion caused resentment of Israel to rise sharply, both in the conflict zone and worldwide.

Shotgun-fired canvas bags filled with small lead pellets are unlikely to kill inadvertently, as they spread out and dissipate their impact over a larger area; they have been rising in relative value. But these "beanbags" can be defended against simply by holding up mattresses, a practice that has driven a counter-move—the creation of grenades filled with as many as one hundred small, hard rubber pellets, with enough explosive to propel them in all directions with great force. The perceived value of these grenades is that they can be tossed among those huddling behind mattress walls or other types of protective cover.

A further refinement has been to fill the grenades with dye, so that insurgents and rioters may be identified and sorted out among crowds of mostly innocent people. But the illogic of this line of reasoning should be obvious: anyone hit by the hard rubber balls in these grenades is assumed guilty, when in fact the innocent may be crouching and hiding alongside the guilty. They may in fact be deliberately used as human shields, much as Somali "technicals" fired at American troops from behind women and children during Operation Restore Hope, especially during the infamous "Blackhawk Down" firefight in October 1993. People have the right to be out on the street, whether to demonstrate or simply to go about their business. This is one of the reasons for constraining the use of lethal force in such settings, as most of the masses are innocent. That insurgents will take advantage of this, and even attempt to provoke the killing of innocents by "stabilization forces," seems a given. The problem is a difficult one, and has done much to spur the development of a variety of other kinds of nonlethals.

Moving beyond the NLW that are intended to be wielded by the average infantryman/peacekeeper, there are also systems designed to inhibit movement, from nets that can be fired over groups of people to sticky foams that freeze them in place. These can be effective in the right settings but are of limited use in large crowds and also suffer from the problem of not being sufficiently discriminating. This limitation is also a concern for the nylon netting intended to stop automobiles, and with the synthetic fiber filaments that can be dropped in waterways to stop vessels by entangling in their propellers. These filaments may be swept along by currents and do damage far from the site of their initial deployment. Still, the idea of encumbering the movement of insurgents and violent protesters is a logical one, and will remain a central element in continuing NLW research and development.

The problem of discriminate targeting bedevils other kinds of NLW, in particular devices designed to "dazzle," or temporarily blind, and those that would use acoustic means to incapacitate people. Both of these are "area weapons" that can affect all those in the target zone, not just the malefactors. Further, these weapons run the risk of occasionally causing permanent damage. Like rubber bullets that sometimes kill, dazzle can seriously impair vision, and acoustic weapons may cause a permanent loss of hearing or the onset of a variety of hearing-related maladies.

It seems ironic that, when NLW *are* actually useful, their chief benefit lies in helping to "get the drop" on terrorists in hostage situations—so that they may be killed. A famous example of this was the rescue of hostages being held on a Lufthansa jet in Mogadishu, Somalia, in 1977. German Grenzschutzgruppe GSG-9 commandos used "flash-bang" grenades to temporarily blind the terrorists, making it easier to take them down before they could kill their hostages. So it may be that one of the very best uses of NLW is to enable more deadly actions, particularly in rescue operations.

Grave risks, however, come with the effort to use nonlethals in hostage situations. Perhaps the most spectacular failure to date for NLW in such settings occurred in October 2002 when Russian security forces pumped a kind of sleeping gas into the ventilation system of a Moscow opera house where Chechen terrorists were holding hundreds of patrons hostage. Instead of simply incapacitating everyone, the gas killed 129 of the hostages. In such situations, more traditional special rescue operations may still be superior, as was demonstrated in 1997 when Peruvian military forces rescued hundreds of hostages being held at the Japanese embassy in Lima by the Tupac Amaru terrorist group. In this case Peruvian commandos dug a tunnel that brought them in amidst the terrorists. At the right moment they swarmed out and freed everyone, in a raid as spectacularly successful as the 1976 Israeli rescue mission at Entebbe in Uganda.

Perhaps the most innovative—and most highly classified—effort to develop NLW today lies in the realm of what the Pentagon confusingly calls "active denial." What can be said about this system is that it generates millimeter-length electrical waves that heat human skin, giving the target a sense of being

burned.* More familiar microwaves are much longer and penetrate deeper than an inch, which is why they're good for heat-
ing up food but would do severe harm to humans. So the very
short wavelength employed by active denial is designed to have
a powerful, shocking effect; but, since it scarcely penetrates the
skin, the hope is to avoid causing serious injury to internal or-
gans. This system is still under development and must grapple
with issues of power generation, discriminate deployment, and
susceptibility to countermeasures, such as a terrorist using a
human shield, or a suicide driver with his hands strapped to the
steering wheel and his foot to the accelerator, who may dearly
wish to turn away when his skin is superheated but cannot.

Taking this concept further, the idea of harnessing the kinetic energy of electrons and transforming it into a powerful
field—in this case what is called a high-powered microwave
(HPM)—poses the prospect of using NLW against objects
rather than people. This is also a highly proprietary area of advanced military research, conjuring up visions of sophisticated
new defenses against cruise or even intercontinental ballistic
missile attacks. Another possibility for this technique is a new
kind of strategic bombardment, which could be undertaken
without doing much destruction. Think of developing an ability to knock out an opposing nation's power infrastructure
without having to blow it up. The range of applications of HPM
could be quite broad, and might even serve to send a strong signal to one or both disputants in a crisis, letting them know that
the consequences of going to war would include much hard-
ship at home, right from the outset.

The best notional example of this form of attack came more
than fifty years ago in the classic science fiction tale *The Day*

---

*In the early 1990s there was also a proposal to develop chemical agents that could
make enemy troops' skin hypersensitive to light. Other exotic proposals, which apparently went unfunded, included tools designed to give enemy undercover operatives persistent halitosis so that they could not blend in among the innocent; and
there was even talk of building a "hormone bomb" that would turn enemy soldiers
gay.

the Earth Stood Still. In this story the alien, Klaatu, seeks to prevent earthlings from one day taking their warlike ways into space. To underline human vulnerability to whatever punishment might be meted out by the aliens, he uses the non-lethal approach of briefly knocking out power all over the world. In the story the problem of collateral damage is finessed. No one is killed, because Klaatu keeps the power on in hospital intensive-care units and such. In real life an ability to discriminate in order to rule out adverse effects will be virtually impossible—still, the prospect of influencing an adversary by primarily disruptive rather than destructive means seems inherently attractive. If strategic attack ever hopes to achieve its intended psychological effect, it will likely be due to an increased ability to disrupt other societies in this way. That said, we are a long way from having the kind of capacity that Klaatu commanded. Perhaps it's time we got moving in this direction.

*

The foregoing discussion suggests an interesting dynamic: nonlethal weapons may have more practical uses in warfighting than in the peacekeeping, humanitarian assistance, and rescue operations for which they were originally envisioned. For it seems that using NLW in these smaller-scale contingencies—beyond the problems associated with discriminating between innocent civilians and insurgents or terrorists—is that the very fact of choosing a nonlethal approach may embolden one's adversaries. If enemies and the mass publics sympathetic to their causes are aware that only NLW will be used against their riots and demonstrations, they are more likely to riot and demonstrate. Their downside risk is controlled as long as they avoid threatening escalations in their use of force.

This was the principal reason for the success of the first Palestinian *intifada,* which resulted in Israel's signing on to the Oslo Peace Accord in 1993. The Palestinians were willing to continue going into the streets to demonstrate and throw rocks, because they knew that the Israelis were constraining their own response largely to NLW. As long as the insurgents did not give the IDF an excuse to escalate, they were bound to win what had become a kind of psychological war of attrition. This is a model for insurrection that others are sure to emulate if the United States or other powers interested in humanitarian operations rely more heavily on NLW in such settings.

It may be that a new kind of "lose-lose situation" will emerge for those who would intervene, even when guided by high-minded motivations. Those in possession of nonlethal weapons will be induced to intervene more often, while at the same time those who are confronted by these humanitarian forces that are constrained from using their lethal weapons will be far more likely to oppose them. The deadly interplay of this new dynamic, fueled by NLW, would generate pressures on both sides to escalate to lethal levels of violence. This is precisely what happened in the second *intifada*. It will happen elsewhere too when the limits and curious side effects of nonlethal weapons become apparent in new crises and interventions. Putting NLW in the hands of troops trained primarily in the use of lethal force imposes a special strain on them that will be hard to mitigate, even with excellent preparation and thoughtfully crafted rules of engagement. It will always be hard to know precisely when to keep one's phasers on stun.

*

Is a computer virus a nonlethal weapon? It may not be able to disperse an unruly mob in the streets, and would probably be useless in freeing a hostage held at gunpoint by a terrorist. But in a world of complex, interconnected information systems that control communications and power infrastructures, as well as oil and natural gas flows, malicious computer code may have enormously disruptive effects. This looming mode of strategic attack—"strategic" in the sense of being able to strike at an adversary's homeland without prior need to engage defending military forces—might one day achieve the elusive psychological effects that have driven theorists of airpower to distraction for the better part of a century. Perhaps this is why today's air force strategists are as interested in cyberspace as they are in outer space.

Computer-based attacks—if they ever do achieve strategic impact—would do so principally by disruptive means, rather than by wreaking the destructive havoc that always comes with war from the air. True, some destruction might occur if, say, an automated oil pipeline flow were stopped, causing a rupture or even an explosion in the area of the leak. Similarly, a power outage might cause deaths on operating tables and in intensive-care units, or even in automobile accidents caused by cyber attacks having knocked out traffic lights. But these possible losses pale in comparison to the damage routinely caused by even modest amounts of aerial bombardment.

So it is fair to describe cyberspace-based means of attack as employing an important kind of nonlethal weaponry, a point of view held by most experts on the subject. Serious efforts are under way in many countries to identify and study the various means by which computer viruses, logic bombs, and the like can be set loose, and what effects they might have. Most of these concoctions of malicious computer code have the common purpose of inducing the targeted information systems to damage themselves, often by freezing up so they can't operate at all, or sometimes even by getting them to erase their own hard drives. The primary means of deploying the viruses is in attachments to email messages; but sometimes they are included in innocent-looking software that is installed—the "Trojan Horse" approach. Other means of insertion cannot be openly discussed, but many around the world have been energetically exploring them for years.

Another kind of cyber attack aims at achieving control over immense numbers of computers, creating so-called zombie farms, some known to have as many as 250,000 "slave botnets" (a word derived from ro*bot net*works), some even more. Estimates of the number of computers that come under remote control from time to time now exceeds 50 million. In a world where many more millions of computers are connected to the internet as soon as they are turned on, it makes for a happy time for hackers, who can quickly figure out user identifications and passwords, then take command of a particular machine much as its legitimate owner would. These botnets, clusters of which are often widely separated in the physical world, can be united in time and cyberspace for purposes of striking at, overwhelming, and thus crippling particular commercial, charitable, governmental, or military websites. Few of these sites can continue operating for long when they are on the receiving end of hundreds of thousands of hits per second in what are called "distributed denial of service" (DDOS) attacks.

To date, both forms of attack described above—viruses and DDOS—have been routinely used throughout the world to mount costly but nonphysically destructive attacks, with damage estimates from single viruses often mounting into the billions of dollars. My own experience with this phenomenon extends to close study of, and sometimes involvement in dealing with, a number of cyber campaigns that have been mounted by hackers, operating on their own or in service to some network or nation. These include the "cyber jihad" against Israel, Chechen efforts to launch destructive computer viruses against Russian targets, and a number of al Qaeda–related efforts aimed at our and our allies' information systems. Beyond the realm of Islamic extremists there have been more instances of what Martin Libicki has termed "Gibson warfare"—fights waged entirely in cyberspace, so named in recognition of William Gibson, the great writer of speculative fiction who first envisioned this new arena of conflict. Among them are the ongoing forays between

Chinese and Taiwanese hackers, similar struggles between North and South Koreans, and even an apparent Serb hacker effort to slow electronic commerce in Kosovo in the wake of the 1999 war there. More recently, concerted attacks were mounted on several of the main servers—at a dozen locations around the world—upon which the internet relies. And in the spring of 2007, pro-Russian hackers appeared to be behind a protracted series of cyber attacks on Estonia, in seeming retaliation for the removal from a prominent display setting of a statue of a Soviet soldier from World War II. In all these cases the defenders have been able to cope with and swiftly recover from cyber attacks. Even so, much more sophisticated offensive actions are possible and will likely emerge in the coming years.

For all our advanced technology, Americans will likely prove to be most vulnerable to Gibson warfare. Warning flags are already snapping in the virtual breeze, as the insured damage being done by all sorts of cyber mischief—reckoned mostly in terms of the financial cost of business interruption or reduced productivity—now amounts to more than $40 billion per year. This is roughly the amount of insured property damage claims paid in the wake of the 9/11 attacks on the World Trade Center. The big difference is that the costs of cyber attacks are widely dispersed throughout a $14 trillion–plus economy rather than concentrated in damage to a few big buildings, making the "virtual hurt" harder to feel and visualize, and suggesting that there is not yet a single controlling mind, unified purpose, or strategy behind the attacks. This may change.

For the U.S. military, the prospect of defending against cyber attack is proving to be daunting. First, there is a clear and undoubtedly growing need to help protect American infrastructure, commerce, and society from such disruptions, a technically and bureaucratically complex problem, and a duty to be shared with civil government, law enforcement, and the private sector. Given that the United States is one of the world's most heavily "wired" countries, there is much to protect—too much, it seems, in the face of skillful, determined assaults in which the attackers will almost always have the advantage of surprise. The looming possibility of having to cope with simultaneous (or sequential) attacks on natural gas flows, power transmission lines, air traffic control, and more must be carefully considered. So does the need to identify those who might be capable of mounting such strikes, and to deter or preempt them. These are stern challenges.

Beyond the general need to protect civilian infrastructure—which is analogous to the air defenses that seek to protect the homeland from bombardment—there is also the task of ensuring that the military's own needs for secure information flows in the field can be met and maintained. For example, deployments of U.S. forces, coordinated with the transport of their equipment and weapons, is a logistical feat of staggering intricacy. It is configured largely by highly automated systems, such as the "time-phased force deployment list" (TPFDL, or "tip fiddle"). Air tasking orders (ATO), which are often essential to area bombing or interdiction campaigns, represent another key area where computers are almost completely in control. If they are compromised, the American military response to a crisis or conflict will be delayed—some studies have suggested by as much as several days or a few weeks. In a relatively confined theater of operations like the Korean peninsula, where Seoul is within artillery range of the North Korean border and susceptible to bombardment or ground attack, a delay of a week or so would be a difference that really made a difference. Certainly this would be true in terms of casualties and costs, but in such a theater of operations, cyber-induced delays might prove to be the margin between victory and defeat.

An important "existence proof" of the military's vulnerability to cyber attack on its sensitive systems was provided in an exercise, held just over a decade ago, called "Eligible Receiver." Details remain classified, but officials have never disputed public reports that a controlled hacker team was able to invade sensitive military information systems and gravely undermine the ability of the Pacific Fleet to perform in the war game at hand. More recently, exercises called "Silent Horizon" and "Cyber Storm" have pointed out the continuing vulnerability of both civilian and military information systems. Testing the defenses of both is important, not only to gauge the threat to the general populace but because the overwhelming percentage of military message traffic is still transmitted via the commercial, civilian information infrastructure.

In addition to the world of Pentagon war games, there have been disturbing real-life reminders of the insecurity of even highly protected information systems. Shortly after the Eligible Receiver exercise, it became apparent that a series of extensive, hostile intrusions into our defense databases and communications systems was under way. The purpose of these hacks was not, it seems, to destroy anything, but rather to gain access to specific information and engage in extensive mapping of American defense information systems. The investigation into these hacks was called "Moonlight Maze," a process that went on for several years and eventually determined that a site in Moscow was being used by the intruders as a jumping-off point.* This does not mean that the Russian government was behind the operation, or even that Russians were the perpetrators. All that can be said is that a location in Moscow was the terminus of the "back hacking" operation. Indeed, this case proved that the veil of anonymity is extremely hard to pierce in cyberspace. An awareness of this problem has only grown in recent years, because of our inability to identify those who have released "Code Red," "Nimda," and a number of other highly disruptive viruses. It is not hard to see that a chief attraction of operating via cyberspace is that it can exploit or attack one's enemies in clandestine ways.

---

*The aspect of the "Moonlight Maze" story pertaining to the type of information sought remains classified, as do other facets of this vexing case.

Yet another sensitive, real-life experience with cyber-intruders has appeared within the past few years. Much less can be said about this situation, except that it is called "Titan Rain" and involves attempts to extract classified data—about nuclear matters, among other things—and again includes extensive mapping of defense information systems. "Back hacks" in this case seem to point to the use of sites in the People's Republic of China. Again, this does not necessarily mean that Beijing is behind Titan Rain, as clever hackers may simply be trying to shift blame to the Chinese. But this latest series of protracted hostile actions demonstrates our continuing vulnerability to such attacks, more than a decade after Moonlight Maze first set off the alarm bells.

Why does there seem to be so little sense of urgency about dealing with such threats? And so little progress in precluding them? The main reason, probably, is that so little damage has been done. Yes, some sensitive information may have been compromised. But the attackers have never taken the trouble to commit costly, highly focused acts of disruption, such as those undertaken by the hacker team in the Eligible Receiver exercise, or by the various "red cells" (friendlies who act as the enemy would) in other, more highly classified tests of our systems.* Many in the Pentagon see this absence of evident malice as a sign that there may be "less than meets the eye" to the whole idea of cyber attack; so they are reluctant to link this kind of nonlethal weapon with the lethal effects it could have on far-off battlefields, where U.S. troops might one day find their crucial communications lines cut at a vitally important moment.

Our vulnerability requires thinking differently about cyber defenses. The prevailing view, both in the United States and around the world, is that cyberspace can be defended with vir-

---

*In these cases, not even the operations' names may be given. They too are classified, and in these cases there have been no public reports of them.

tual fortifications—basically the "firewalls" that everyone knows about. These consist of software designed to identify potential threats. But as one of the world's best hackers once told me, "There are no firewalls. They can only recognize what they already know. Almost anything new or different goes right through them." This reality is alternately resisted and dismissed by decision-makers. For the most part, a kind of Maginot Line mentality prevails, driven by misguided faith in firewalls. Our military services—and the commercial, civil, and governmental users of the internet and the web—have taken this traditional perspective with them from the real world into cyberspace, fully confident in their security even as skillful hackers easily penetrate or outflank such defenses, much as German tanks went around the real Maginot Line in 1940. As a result, we live in a world where cyberspace, and all the realms of activity that depend upon it, are seriously, increasingly vulnerable to disruption by any smart, hostile power, or even by small groups of determined individuals.

In conceptual terms, the strategic state of play in cyberspace-based NLW can be described as offense dominated. Despite the thwarting of some invasions already noted, it is far easier to intrude or attack with a reasonable expectation of success than it is to defend effectively. In practical terms, the balance between offense and defense is harder to perceive, because the ease that has characterized exploitations like Moonlight Maze and Titan Rain has not been matched by any direct attack. There has been no "digital Pearl Harbor" or "virtual 9/11." But the clock is ticking toward such events, because our fundamental defensive paradigm—based on a faith in firewalls and other linear notions of cyber conflict—is flawed.

What is the remedy? In a word, encryption. We would all be far better off if virtually all civil, commercial, governmental, and military internet and web traffic were strongly encrypted. This means basically that all data flows would be encoded, and the keys to these codes would be unbreakable because of their

length and complexity. Beyond passwords, computers can encode all of one's data in unbreakable ways, and in just fractions
of seconds, ensuring security while at the same time maintaining speed and efficiency. In this age of high-performance computers, code makers have a huge advantage over code breakers,
and will for the foreseeable future.

The ubiquitous use of strong encryption would make it
much more difficult for intruders to invade others' systems.
Even if they did make their way inside, as happened with the
Moonlight Maze and Titan Rain incidents, they would have a
hard time making sense of any of the data they tried to access.
In this way, e-commerce—routine corporate, governmental,
and even private communications—would grow far more secure, and the military would be able to embrace highly automated, interconnected combat and combat-support systems
with less fear that forces in the field might be crippled by hack
attacks.

If this encryption-based solution is so simple, why has it
not been embraced? For the most part because people—from
average citizens to generals, admirals, and national security
officials—still believe that the absence of a major cyber offensive means that this form of attack is impossible or highly im-
probable, and certainly exaggerated. Other interests are also in
play. From the perspective of government, for example, law enforcement would be concerned about its inability to monitor
suspected criminals via the web and the internet if people routinely used strong encryption. Intelligence agencies would have
similar concerns when it came to tracking terrorists and their
sympathizers by cyberspace-based means. Even officials in
government who are involved in the regulation of commerce
and the collection of taxes would be worried that strong encryption might provide a new basis for energizing and enlarg-
ing the "subterranean economy"—that portion of commercial
activity that is "off the books," which some economists believe

is already about one-sixth the size of the known U.S. gross domestic product.

For all these reasons, government officials have been reluctant to spread the gospel of "security through strong encryption." The gradual relaxation of laws against purchasing and using strong "crypto"—which ensured government's ability to monitor cyberspace—has occurred only because cyber rebels, among them the Silicon Valley icon Whitfield Diffie, have pushed to make crypto available to the people. Until they came along, the only individuals who had unbreakable codes were terrorists and criminals whom the government was supposedly trying to keep from having secure communications. Today drug lords still enjoy secure internet and web communications, as do many in terror networks, while most Americans don't—seven years after 9/11.

The Pentagon has none of the government's excuses for failing to embrace strong crypto—and in some settings it does. But overall the military remains reluctant to shift to an "all encryption, all the time" approach to information security. Old habits die hard, including faith in firewalls. This is certainly what I have seen over the past fifteen years or so, as I have tried (largely unsuccessfully) to encourage widespread adoption of strong encryption routines. Rather than encode all its data with much longer keys, the Pentagon has chosen to build ever more firewalls, seeking a new, unassailable "defense in depth" scheme—like the layers of forts that the Duke of Wellington built nearly two hundred years ago to defend Portugal against Napoleon's forces. The difference is that Wellington's Lines of Torres Vedras worked against opponents who massed in columns and pushed against them, while we already have evidence that our cyber depth defenses have been deeply penetrated. The most striking example of this is the effect of the "MS Blast" virus on the $10 billion Navy/Marine Corps Intranet (NMCI). This costly system, touted to be totally secure from cyber attack, wasn't even targeted by the virus but saw many thousands of Navy and Marine Corps terminals affected for extended periods of time.

What would happen if determined bands of cyber attackers were to mount a sustained campaign against our military "infosphere"? Computer viruses may be nonlethal weapons, but their potency in degrading the performance of forces in the field could cost the United States many lives if such attacks occurred during a shooting war. If air support were slowed or otherwise compromised, or reinforcements failed to marry up with their equipment at the right time and in the right place, the consequences in battle could be dire. So there is much reason now to take this threat quite seriously, and to act before a "digital storm" is unleashed against us. Better firewalls cannot keep us secure. We must move to a strong encryption regime, and stick to it.

*

For the moment, though, offense dominates cyberspace, which raises the question of whether it might be wise to use selective cyber strikes as a tool of conflict prevention. If the American military's functions can be degraded by cyber attack, the systems of other advanced militaries are likely as vulnerable. This poses the prospect of disrupting forces massing on both sides of an impending conflict—or on only one side if there were a clear aggressor in the case at hand. The idea is that shutting down the disputants' command and control capabilities would give them serious pause, perhaps even dissuade them from the path to war. In this way, cyberspace-based attacks would function as a kind of strategic-level ultimate nonlethal weapon, keeping crises from mushrooming into conflicts.

As appealing as this vision may be, it presents problems at a practical level. Parties on the verge of conflict might suspect each other of mounting such attacks, spurring them to respond by going to war with whatever military means had not already been disrupted. In the case of potential disputants like India and Pakistan, both of whom possess nuclear weapons and substantial military capabilities of all sorts, a cyber attack during a crisis over, say, Kashmir, might have the most dire unintended consequences imaginable. To mitigate this risk, the party initiating the cyber intervention might come forward openly in the immediate wake of the virtual attack. There would be some reluctance to do this, as it would reveal the cyber capabilities of the intervening party, but the likelihood of escalation to general war between the disputants might be reduced.

At this point, however, legal issues would arise, for the cyber intervention would be an act of war in its own right, and would presumably have been undertaken without authorization from the United Nations—or from the legislature or general public of the intervening country either, for to be most effective the cyber attack would have to be mounted with the utmost secrecy. Cyber deterrence, in fact, is an area that runs ahead of the international laws of armed conflict. Yet the prospect of warding off a bloody fight by the nonlethal means of disrupting military command and control via cyberspace-based weapons is one that should not be passed over easily.

It behooves the UN to consider a kind of international "nonlethal war powers" convention that would require those engaging in such actions to come forth publicly and promptly to provide their rationale for having taken such actions in the interest of saving lives. A somewhat analogous area is intervention in the form of rescue operations intended to prevent genocide—something clearly allowable under the 1948 UN convention against genocide. Both types of preemptive action should be provided for, as there will be situations like Rwanda in 1994 and Darfur a decade later, where cyber preemption would do little to forestall the brutal slaughter of innocents, more than a million of whom perished in just these two instances. Much conflict might be prevented between relatively advanced nations by means of cyber deterrence; but much other violence, so concentrated in lesser-developed areas of the world, can only be dealt with by the rapid deployment of armed forces.

Because of the inability of one nation to maintain a monopoly on cyber intervention, it makes sense for the United States to embrace such a tactic in a systematic, transnational manner, under the rubric of existing notions of international "security and stability" operations. And there needn't be the usual attendant concerns about slipping into a "nation-building" mode.

What about the "human capital" that might make up a cyber corps? For the most part, the military, law enforcement, and intelligence communities have been growing their own, because of the persistently hostile relationship between hackers "in the wild" and institutional authority. In the United States, a hacker caught breaking the law while in the course of conducting his virtual activities can end up serving more time than an armed robber. For their part, terrorists are probably just as reluctant to recruit and employ cyber mercenaries, since the security risks of hiring hackers are prohibitive.

But this needn't be our mode of operation. Hackers could be hired, monitored 24/7, and given the chance to help defeat terrorism, or to preempt crises and conflicts in the world's trouble spots. I have come to know a number of master hackers (like Neo from *The Matrix*—and Trinity too, as some whom I've met are women) over the past decade, and have come to think of them as resembling the German rocket scientists after World War II. The rocketeers may have been helping bombard London while the fighting still raged, but both sides in the cold war courted them, and they ended up determining the contours of nuclear strategy. They also took both the United States and the Soviet Union into space long before either country would have gotten there without the help they offered. Hackers are much like this today, but their realm isn't outer space, it's cyberspace. The ones I know simply want an opportunity to contribute.

To a small extent, our military and intelligence communities already recruit hackers. It is yet another sensitive area, about which nothing specific can be said. I can only share openly my considered view that not enough is being done. The hackers I know are generally acknowledged as being in the top dozen or so in the world today—*and none of them is being used.* This is particularly frustrating given that the terror networks now operating rely almost completely on the internet and the web for their communications, money movement, and many other functions. So far, as one of the Joint Chiefs of Staff observed to me before his retirement, "We have given the terrorists a free ride in cyberspace." A damning admission, and an especially troubling one all these years after the onset of the terror war.

As conflict migrates into cyberspace, with the urgent need to better defend both our civilian and military systems, the situation also offers some opportunity. One is to prevent conflicts from breaking out; another is to use this form of nonlethal, virtual force to mount more humane types of strategic attacks when we do find ourselves at war. Finally, there is the chance to defeat terror decisively, as al Qaeda and other militant networks simply cannot survive without the web and the internet. How curiously appropriate it would be if terrorists were ultimately brought to justice not by field armies but by the best of a generation of hackers, who had finally been given an opportunity to click for their country.

CHAPTER SIX

The Rise of Influence Operations

ONGOING EFFORTS to create a new generation of nonlethal weapons reflect a deepening concern that the use of traditional deadly force often breeds resentment and resistance rather than submission. The same concern explains the U.S. military's current interest in the potential of "influence operations." Intoning the mantra of what are called "effects-based operations" (EBO), the services have been seeking ways to achieve their aims while using minimum force. While EBO are generally viewed as precisely targeted violent military actions that have maximum psychological impact, over the past fifteen years a school of thought has emerged within the services dedicated to the idea of achieving influence without having to blow things up at all.

The rationale behind this effort to aim directly for psychological effects, perhaps even eliminating the use of force, is that violent imagery, televised almost immediately to a global audience, can undermine even the noblest cause. See, for example, the unraveling of the humanitarian mission to Somalia some fifteen years ago, which initially saved hundreds of thousands from death by starvation. Broadcast images of a long, bloody firefight between tribal militiamen—the so-called

Somali technicals—and U.S. special operations forces in October 1993 appalled the world and soon after led to American withdrawal from that sad land. The media's worldwide dissemination of graphic images of violence from more ambiguous military interventions, like the controversial invasion and subsequent counterinsurgency campaign in Iraq, may pack even more of this kind of "punch."

The growing power of words and images to trump traditional military outcomes has for some time been fueling institutional interest in improving American influence operations. Ten years ago this issue area already concerned the U.S. military and was known as "perception management." This phrase, however, was soon deemed to have dark, propagandistic connotations, and fell under a cloud, reemerging only in the wake of 9/11 as, variously, "public diplomacy" and "strategic communications." Both of these notions carry a hint of being on higher moral ground; and the recently completed Pentagon "road map" for information operations clearly seeks to guide the military in an ethically untarnished way through the thickets of this domain. The same is true of the State Department's own contribution to the influence area, its official *U.S. National Strategy for Public Diplomacy and Strategic Communications.*

Lest influence operations are thought of as nothing more than propaganda—as too many in government and the military are wont to do—it is important to note that this concept includes other types of activities. The most familiar are classic deceptive and psychological techniques that have long been employed to trick or dishearten one's foes. Today's challenge is to integrate such activities with advanced military operational concepts. Where leaflet drops and loudspeakers were effective in an earlier era of massed forces and relatively fixed front lines, today's influence specialists must think about things like using the internet and the worldwide web to pass demoralizing messages to small cells of widely dispersed insurgents and terrorists.

In this way, hidden adversaries might be lured or flushed out of their lairs, providing our "hunter networks" with targets.

In addition to psychological operations and deceptions, military activities in the realms of civil affairs and reconstruction should be considered key tools of influence—friendly, grateful populations are more likely to provide information that helps ferret out enemy operatives. Another important aspect of influence operations has to do with the approach to interrogating—perhaps eventually co-opting—enemy combatants taken prisoner. And beyond the military realm, "influence" should also be thought of in terms of diplomatic strategies that involve negotiation, perhaps even to the point of making concessions. At a minimum, this last area implies that influence extends to listening as well as actively communicating our own views. All these aspects of influence operations are considered in this chapter.

Although there are many different dimensions to influence, there appear to be a few core principles that have been identified as guides to American strategy and policy. For the military, the most important one, a kind of prime directive, is that influence operations are not to be used on the American people. But since Americans are very likely to see broadcasts from overseas sources—either live or taped, or streamed out on the web—the range of freedom to engage in this form of influence is sharply constrained. The rules do allow for a little slack in situations where the primary target is demonstrably foreign; but most practitioners are encouraged to be extremely prudent about crossing this line. Which means that, in practice, very little is actually done.

This constraint on employing influence operations that might somehow affect the American public is clearly taken very seriously by the military. But such reserve is hardly mirrored by political leaders of both major parties, who spend much of their time actively trying to shape the public's views of foreign affairs and issues of war and peace. Occasionally this is done on the basis of flimsy evidence, or out of sheer rhetorical verve. And sometimes our armed forces are used by politicians in ways that imply support for their positions, the most egregious example of this being President George W. Bush's landing on an aircraft carrier soon after the fall of Saddam Hussein, followed by a speech given with an unfurled "Mission Accomplished" banner clearly visible in the background. Bush's frequent use of military audiences as backdrops for major policy speeches on national security issues over the years only reinforces the point that, though our soldiers may not engage in influence operations aimed at the American people, there seems to be little restraint on the part of others who would use them for this purpose.

The second basic principle of American influence operations is to avoid lying. This seems eminently sensible and recalls Thomas Jefferson's injunction to tell the world public "the naked truth always, whether favorable or unfavorable. For they will believe the good, if we tell them the bad also." One problem with this approach, of course, is that the truth may seriously undermine support for one's own cause, as happened when it became apparent that Saddam Hussein had neither weapons of mass destruction nor ties to al Qaeda, the twin pillars that supported the stated case for invading Iraq in 2003. But in this instance the real question should perhaps be whether sufficient care was given to asserting only known truths in the run-up to the invasion. Had Jefferson's injunction to hew to the "naked truth always" been adhered to in the first place, a congressional authorization to use force against Saddam Hussein in 2003 might have been much more difficult to obtain—perhaps too difficult, and the result would have been peace, accompanied by an intrusive inspection regime. Truth can have powerfully beneficial effects.

But the benefits of truthfulness in one aspect of statecraft may be offset in other areas. For example, hewing to an honest path would seem to rule out the use of deception—throughout history an important tool of military strategy, from Joshua's capture of Ai in biblical times to the Allied landing in Normandy during World War II. In the wake of the 9/11 attacks on America, the Pentagon sought to establish an Office of Strategic Influence that would aim to outfox the terrorists in just such fashion. But when it was publicly admitted that the new office might engage in deceptions—Donald Rumsfeld even went so far as to quote Winston Churchill's axiom that "in wartime, truth is so precious that she should always be attended by a bodyguard of lies"—it was quickly dismantled. Despite the undeniable power of trickery in conflict—it is, after all, a principal basis for achieving surprise in war—open societies appear to have developed a strong allergy to deception.

The third tenet of American influence operations can best be described as the belief that affecting the behavior of others requires only the careful crafting of content followed by its repeated use until the message takes hold. This approach is the governing doctrine for efforts ranging from psychological operations leaflets dropped on rural villages to high-level "strategic communications" broadcast worldwide. It is a notion rooted in theories of political propaganda, mass commercial marketing, and public relations. Thus the Pentagon, throughout the war on terror, has come to rely heavily on professionals in these fields for guidance. This was something of a trend during the Clinton years as well, and to some extent in earlier presidencies, but in the ongoing "long war," the hard-sell approach to influencing others has tightened its hold on American information strategy.

While it is entirely understandable to think about influence in these terms, there are two problems with adhering to this concept of information operations: it undervalues listening, and it rules out the idea of making concessions in order to induce others to change their behavior. In my experience, neither the Pentagon nor the State Department adequately consider the possibility that careful listening might allow us to craft better messages, or perhaps even encourage us to modify the policies that most greatly offend others. When I made this point at a meeting of high-level military and diplomatic officials in November 2005—a gathering convened specifically to consider the role of listening in the war on terror—a senior member of the State Department's strategic communications office dismissed the whole matter by noting that "listening is fine, but we cannot make policy concessions." American information strategists are generally loath to include concession-making as one of the tools of influence, though our nuclear diplomacy toward North Korea in recent years has shown at least some willingness to provide "side payments" as inducements to prompt behavioral changes. In the U.S. military a few voices have been raised from time to time in favor of give-and-take negotiations, even with regard to dealings with terrorists and insurgents. One retired army general with extensive experience in counterterrorism has made the argument that "it would be very beneficial to have a mechanism—most likely secret—that could enable an opportunity to dialogue with terrorists."

*

The three basic constraints I have noted—not to influence the American people, not to deceive them, and not to make concessions based on hoped-for changes in behavior by the target audience—have led some observers to give up on the prospect for our ever engaging in successful influence operations. Others, who see the clear value in methods that can help achieve our goals without always requiring military action, and who also believe that violence can often undermine our strategic aims, have attempted to work within these constraints. In practice, this effort has come to resemble something like trying to jog while immersed in water up to the shoulders. The chief obstructions come from legal, ethical, and other experts and levels of command that are part of an increasingly cumbersome approval process, one that sometimes demands sign-offs from the highest levels of the national command authority. Even the most basic psychological operations leaflet generally requires between a dozen and sixteen levels of review and prior approval before it may be distributed. While such careful scrutiny seems ethically admirable, the process often makes it impossible to use influence operations in a timely manner in the field.

This apparent urge to overcontrol our influence operations is not mirrored in traditional military operations. Raids by ground forces, as well as air strikes, are often quickly approved, sometimes on the basis of poor or mistaken intelligence, the result, all too often, being the killing of innocents. Yet military leaders are apparently inured to collateral damage of this sort, which they—and the broader public—expect and to some extent discount. When it comes to influence operations, where acting wrongly is more likely to cause a failure to achieve the objective, rather than lead to the deaths of noncombatants, there is a much greater perceived need to avoid mistakes. Perhaps the right way ahead here would be for soldiers to become more sensitive to the problem of bringing harm to the innocent. Combat errors can have a profound effect in the information domain. At the same time, cultivating more willingness to accept mistakes in the prosecution of influence operations is also a good idea, as blunders in this realm are far less likely to cost innocent lives.

Just as violent military action shapes attitudes and beliefs, nonviolent military operations in the field may also have profoundly influential effects. The army's civil affairs specialists are the most likely candidates for demonstrating this point. Their specialty is in an area known as "security, stabilization, transition, and reconstruction" (SSTR), and what they do often lies at the heart of our ability to forge ties with locals, building bonds of trust that can make the difference between success or failure in a counterinsurgent campaign. Indeed, their ability to improve sanitation and health, restore electricity, and bring about a general amelioration of suffering can prove crucial in developing sources of intelligence about adversaries as well as in denying our enemies fertile grounds for recruitment.

Yet it is important to note that the "reconstruction" part of SSTR can be one of the most problematic aspects of civil affairs, illuminating the divided nature of influence operations. That is, efforts to rebuild a country in the middle of an ongoing conflict may simply provide insurgents and terrorists with an inviting set of "soft targets." In Iraq, for example, the percentage of reconstruction funds dedicated to on-site security has been staggering. But the absence of reconstruction efforts might increase dissatisfaction to the point that insurgent recruitment would rise sharply. In Afghanistan a kind of middle course has been followed, with very carefully targeted civil affairs initiatives being undertaken in areas where security is reasonably good and where the rebuilding process will win over the affection and loyalty of the locals. It is hardly a perfect system; but the idea of waiting for the war to end before beginning the rebuilding process means, in practice, ceding the initiative in the influence campaign to one's enemies.

Strategists must consider the conditions under which these kinds of influence operations are most likely to achieve tangible results. Civil affairs troops never operate in a vacuum; these frontline "soldiers of influence" routinely face the whole spectrum of possible reactions. They may be greeted with open arms, as they were by the Kurds during and since the invasion of Iraq in 2003. While less open to them, Iraq's Shi'a population also proved willing to work to some extent with American (and British, in this case) civil affairs troops. Many Sunnis, on the other hand, viewed these humanitarian soldiers in much more openly hostile fashion.

Considering the Iraq intervention from a civil affairs perspective can give one a very good idea of how the course of the campaign unfolded: easily and with minimum force in the Kurdish north; more bumpily in the Shi'a south; and wretchedly in

the Sunni middle. The varying fortunes of influence practitioners in different parts of Afghanistan may also reveal the true
situation on the ground in that country. Thus while they aim
to influence others, our civil affairs troops may also provide
senior decision-makers with crucial knowledge that will influence our own views and actions.

Senior political and military leaders seem, all too often, to
be inattentive to this connection. For example, the invasion of
Iraq was cast in terms of "liberation"; yet the military campaign
caused untold damage to civilian infrastructure under the military rubric of shock and awe. Information strategists who worried about this contradiction (I was among them) suggested a
smaller, less destructive military campaign, using far fewer
troops and involving much less bombing. The Pentagon's more
traditional military thinkers, on the other hand, believed that
shock and awe would cow the Iraqis into submission. In the
event, the traditionalists won out in the debates over strategy,
despite Donald Rumsfeld's initial support for the smaller-scale
approach. They vastly outnumbered those of us on the opposing side, and Rumsfeld chose to accede, in large part, to their
preferred plan.

But the traditionalists' shock-and-awe operations kindled so
much resentment among Iraqis that, soon after the occupation
began, it fueled a bitter insurgency aimed at driving U.S. forces
out of their country. It was an uprising that could not be
quelled by strictly military means, though traditionalists would
assert that massive numbers of American forces—the figures
they used ranged from 250,000 to 500,000—might have tamped
down the violence. Those of us on the other side of this debate,
driven by the concern that greater presence would spark
greater resentment, called for significant force reductions quite
early on—before Paul Bremer dismissed the roughly 400,000
troops in the Iraqi military who could have served from the
outset as a force for continuity and security. Once this last vestige of indigenous order was demolished, the problem became
more complex and intractable.

At this point U.S. influence operations began splitting off from the military in the field. Instead of a close integration between counterinsurgent forces, civil affairs troops, and our information operators, the influence people began to go their own way, concentrating on a freestanding media campaign. This consisted of starting up and running a U.S. Arab-language radio station (Radio *Sawa*) and a television channel *(al Hurra)*, both of which were aimed at audiences within and beyond Iraq; and "purchasing" journalists to write pro-American stories about the occupation of Iraq. This latter endeavor soaked up about $100 million and caused something of a scandal when these blatant acts were revealed. Rather than producing a positive influence, these undertakings brought the United States international opprobrium for its actions in Iraq. And Iraqis themselves showed their disapproval: whenever they were polled, large majorities favored the immediate withdrawal of American military forces from their country. For example, in a major independent poll taken around the fourth anniversary of the American invasion, in March 2007, nearly three-fourths of all Iraqis favored a rapid end to the occupation.

Adverse developments in the information domain in Iraq had for some time been seriously eroding a more general level of international support for the global war on terror. Rumsfeld was aware of this problem and frank about it in his public assessment of the parlous state of our information strategy. In a speech given at the Army War College in March 2006, he put it bluntly: "If I were grading, I would say we probably deserve a 'D' or a 'D-plus' as a country, as to how well we're doing in the battle of ideas that's taking place in the world today." He went on to say that "we have not found the formula as a country for countering the extremists' message."

Rumsfeld's remarks at the Army War College beg the question of just what formula the United States was following in its influence operations. For the most part, American information strategy is driven by the notion of trying to convince Muslims that al Qaeda and its affiliates have "hijacked Islam." The problem with this approach is that the American president and other U.S. leaders are not authoritative or unbiased sources from whom Muslims are likely to take guidance about their religion. And to the extent to which friendly Muslim clerics are persuaded to speak out against the terrorists, they are listened to only by those of their co-religionists who are least likely to sign up for the jihad in the first place. Polling data suggest that the core al Qaeda message, which has to do with the overthrow of "apostate" governments and the restoration of a vast caliphate, is attractive at most to about 5 percent of the world's 1.4 billion Muslims. Even so, this represents a primary pool of some 70 million from which to draw on, a more than ample recruitment base for a movement that, at its height, has commanded only a few tens of thousands of members. Trying to defeat militant Islam by jawboning hard-core zealots will not work.

Among the first generation of al Qaeda extremists, religious fanaticism as a prime motivator was the exception rather than the rule. Thanks to the pioneering work of Marc Sageman, a practicing psychiatrist and former CIA field agent, we know that most of those who joined the cause during the crucial decade of the 1990s were from middle-class or better economic backgrounds. And a large percentage of these accomplished their higher education in non-Muslim countries. The second generation—those drawn to al Qaeda because of the images of outrages against Muslims that they view on the web—is not as well studied, but preliminary evidence suggests the newcomers too have decidedly middle-class origins.

The implication of this finding is that by focusing on religious issues in our influence strategy, we may have missed the target: average Muslims who simply oppose American policies and actions. How can influence operations be redirected to engage this quite different demographic group? Almost certainly not with U.S.-controlled radio and television broadcasts, or paid-for editorials in the press. But we could gain true influence over those who are motivated by opposition to our policies by amending these policies in ways that would tamp down militant fervor. At a strategic level, this would mean paying attention to al Qaeda's demands for the withdrawal of U.S. forces from Muslim lands, and for taking a more neutral stance on the Israeli-Palestinian dispute. In the wake of 9/11, we quietly removed our forces from Saudi Arabia; but the long, bloody occupation of Iraq has proved a severe irritant and a real source of recruitment for jihadists.

On the diplomatic front, the continued strong U.S. alignment with Israel provides yet another reason for zealots to join the jihad. Contrary to the belief that only closer U.S. engagement in the struggle over Palestine will help reduce support for terrorism, our involvement as a strong partisan of the Israeli cause actually foments more anti-American anger. Given the intractability of Arab-Israeli conflicts—which have grown worse in the wake of fissures among Palestinian factions—it seems poor policy to try to erode sympathy for terrorists by linking this goal to the even more difficult problem of Palestine. Stepping back from direct involvement and adopting a more clearly neutral stance—even to the point of eliminating military support for Israel—is the indicated policy path. Israel is by far the strongest military power in the Middle East anyway, and does not need American arms or security guarantees. Yet it is the very closeness of the relationship between Israel and the United States, particularly the tight military-to-military ties, that may be the most significant impediment to our efforts to influence Muslim mass publics favorably.

At the strategic level, it thus appears that our prospects for mounting successful counterterror influence operations will remain dim, at least until U.S. forces leave Iraq and American diplomacy toward Israel appears less like unquestioning advocacy—two areas where we can retrench without abandoning our core strategic interests. And there is one other area where we might adjust our approach to influence operations in ways that could reduce Muslim youths' desire to sign up for the cause. This would be in the realm of ethics, where strict adherence to the formulations of classical "just war" doctrine could improve our own behavior, so that our actions would provide less grist for the terrorist propaganda mill.

*

Since antiquity, two of the most important elements of military ethics have involved injunctions to maintain the immunity of noncombatants, and to treat mercifully those who surrender or are captured. Unfortunately our military campaign in Iraq has provided an enormous amount of material—most of it consisting of stark video images—to our enemies suggesting that we have engaged in serious violations of these ethical precepts that are so central to notions of waging war in a just fashion. With regard to the immunity of noncombatants, for example, our shock-and-awe aerial bombing, along with later rules of engagement that allowed for air attacks on suspected insurgent safe houses, have resulted in the killings of some tens of thousands of innocent Iraqi civilians. Photos of the degrading abuses at Abu Ghraib prison, not to mention at other U.S. detention facilities around the world, have also kindled a sense of outrage that must certainly have spurred jihadi recruitment over the past several years.

Without doubt, the terrorists' own actions surpass by far even the most problematic U.S. military excesses in the war on terror. But the evil done by others is no excuse for lowering our own ethical standards. The central point of ethics, particularly in wartime, is to provide a guide for one's own judgment and conduct regardless of the errors or outrages committed by others. It seems clear that much of the ferocity of American military campaigns in the wake of 9/11 grows out of rage at our having been violated by these attacks. While our retaliatory behavior is totally understandable, we must recognize that such a response pattern only feeds the beast of terrorist recruitment. True influence over those who think about supporting or joining the jihad can only be achieved once we have mastered our own anger and can focus our revulsion where it belongs: on the terrorists. And this process can begin only when our military, from senior officers to private soldiers, recognizes that their own behavior is perhaps the single most important element in any influence operation.

This is certainly true of military campaigns in the field; but it is equally true of detention and interrogation policies. Here, aside from the deleterious effects of skirting, sometimes flouting, the Geneva Convention, U.S. military and intelligence elements have missed important opportunities to achieve influence over and gain valuable information from detainees. The basic problem has been the strategic choice—made when the first groups of prisoners were arriving after the toppling of the Taliban—to pursue a hard, coercive approach to prisoner treatment. Many excesses followed, including what can only be called torture, and sometimes led to wrongful deaths. This approach also inadvertently helped foster a strong resistance among detainees, who have divulged little useful information over the years. If they had, our war on terror would have gone much better than it has. The coercive approach, driven by 9/11 rage, old habits of mind, and a perceived pressing need for quick results, has for the most part failed miserably.

But it is not too late to reverse field. From the outset, many voices in the military—quietly joined by some in the law enforcement community—argued for a more persuasive approach to the detainees. They wanted something much closer to the police ideal of respecting rights while still imposing psychological pressure, and perhaps even using deceptive tactics. For example, this might consist of employing classic "prisoner's dilemma" techniques, convincing the recalcitrant that some of his fellow prisoners were already talking, even if they weren't. A little of this was tried; but such methods were drowned out by the drumbeat of abusive behavior that unwittingly did so much to harden detainees' resistance to U.S. interrogators.

As I have pointed out to senior military intelligence officers, U.S. troops themselves have proved the point that the persuasive approach is worth trying. During the Korean War, for example, American soldiers taken prisoner were initially kept under the control of the North Koreans. Treatment was uniformly brutal, and the captives soon banded together to resist their tormentors' calls that they sign documents denouncing the United Nations cause in Korea. But after China's entry into the war—after Gen. Douglas MacArthur's decision to send his forces farther north, despite Beijing's warnings—the Chinese took administrative control of most American prisoners. And soon a very different sort of game was afoot. Treatment became less harsh, interrogations became more like intellectual cat-and-mouse games.

The Chinese goal was to win any small concession, such as to have a prisoner admit that "killing civilians with aerial bombing is wrong." Once this was done, interrogators would gently lead the captive to another, more expansive statement. Over a period of months they shifted the prisoner population from generally resistant to, in many cases, openly compliant, with some prisoners willingly recording denunciations of the UN operations in Korea. The United States viewed this process as brainwashing, a frightening concept depicted outlandishly—but dramatically and effectively—in John Frankenheimer's classic film *The Manchurian Candidate*. In fact the Korean War detainees were subjected to the skillful, effective application of persuasive interrogation techniques that used the core psychological principle of "commitment and consistency." The idea is that anyone who has admitted to even a small transgression may be convinced, bit by bit, to admit to more. And then more again, because the need to act in ways that are consistent with one's previous behavior is one of the most basic human impulses.

*

While deceptive techniques are commonly used in police-style interrogations—with questioners often implying that they know things they really don't—and could be used more effectively with terror war detainees, deception could be even more broadly employed in influence operations. There are ways to do this without misleading the American public, because these deceptions would not be played out in the mass media. Instead they would be conducted in clandestine settings, where terrorist cell members would be confronted with the possibility that fellow jihadists might actually be infiltrators working for the Americans. Or perhaps the criminal gang that is supplying the terrorists with materials or information is really in league with counterterrorist elements.

Because today's terror networks are open systems, as the stories of so many of their recruits have proved, and are relatively easy to join, all sorts of deceptions are possible. For example, a group of young men who join the jihad together may actually be infiltrators, working for counterterrorist authorities, either for idealistic reasons or for pay. The networks themselves, to the best of our knowledge, do comparatively little vetting of recruits, relying instead on the recommendations of current network members. Terrorist data miners do seem to be demonstrating some ability to check out the recruits by virtual means, but their capabilities can be easily overcome by our "cover" systems. It would not take many infiltrators to cause a huge disruption of the terror networks, given their connectivity and the likelihood that even localized damage would create ripples throughout the entire organization, where bonds of trust would now be undermined.

It might even be possible to achieve great influence in the absence of *any* actual infiltrators, as long as the terrorists believed that some of their fellows were operating against them. This ruse could work especially well in cyberspace, where money could be moved about, or suspicious messages from trusted operatives to "outsiders" could be planted. A whole host of possibilities can be conceived for this kind of divisive influence operation, whose main thrust would be to undermine bonds of trust. Even before the rise of the web and the internet, this kind of operation was used with considerable success. Two decades ago the Abu Nidal Organization (ANO), the al Qaeda of its time, was gravely damaged by an operation that led Abu Nidal to believe that his own people were stealing from him. In the event, he liquidated more than a hundred of his own operatives. His other minions were so demoralized that many of them ran off, and the ANO was never itself again.

Now is the time to rekindle some of this trickery. Whether infiltrators are real or simply conjured up, they can sow doubt in the terrorists' minds, among their leaders and within the ranks. The likely consequences would be waning recruitment and desertion among those already serving the terrorist cause. Further, this initiative could be pursued in the real world or the virtual world. In the latter domain, even a false hint that terrorist communications on the web and the internet were being tracked might drive them out of cyberspace, with crippling effects on their global networks' basic functions. A successful deception of this sort would make for an ultimate influence operation, the benefits of which would far outweigh the trickle of actionable intelligence currently gleaned by surfing websites frequented by jihadis.

Real or pretended, infiltration is not the only kind of deceptive influence operation that may be mounted without misleading the American public. At a strategic level, a common *ruse de guerre* is to plant or allow extremely sensitive information to fall into the enemy's hands, convincing him that a particular action is impending when the reality is something quite different. The most spectacular case of this sort was the World War II "man who never was," a corpse outfitted as an Allied officer carrying plans and correspondence pointing to an invasion of Sardinia—when the real target was Sicily. My own experiences in this field have confirmed, time and again, the value of the notion of allowing adversaries to "find" useful materials seemingly through their own efforts. And the process need not involve planted corpses. In the war on terror there are many other ways to employ "planted information" deceptions.

Insurgents who listen in on U.S. military radio traffic, for example, can be misled by messages crafted with interception in mind, or by sharp increases or drops in communications activity. Terrorists and insurgents have long used this tactic against our forces, and al Qaeda operatives have become masters of the use of "chatter" to deceive. Other tactical deceptions may be completely low-tech. A telling instance of this sort of influence operation was played out in the field (in a place that cannot be specifically named) by a special forces officer who had been a student of mine. He had too few resources to guard all the possible infiltration routes his enemy might be using, so he grabbed a mannequin from a bombed-out store, dressed it in Kevlar helmet and combat fatigues, and positioned it with binoculars on a mountaintop overlooking a particular pass. In the days and weeks that followed, insurgent traffic on this route dried up completely; and radio intercepts heard the enemy advising his fighters to stay away from that pass because "the Americans watch it constantly now." Sometimes old-fashioned methods work best.

Aside from a few small, very "black" units and some opportunistic trickery in the field, deception is becoming something of a lost art in the U.S. military. Concerns about breaking the rules—even implicit ones—cannot wholly explain the decline of deception. More likely it has fallen prey to such notions as "overwhelming force"—the Powell Doctrine—and "shock and awe." We seem to have bought into the belief that influence operations are weapons-driven rather than based on the articulate expression and clever dissemination of creative ideas. This is simply tragic. As my colleague Barton Whaley, perhaps the world's leading expert on military deception, has observed, even a small investment in efforts to mislead one's foes has, throughout history, generally achieved very high returns. Brute force has gained little traction against terror networks over the past several years. The time has come to employ more guile.

*

If doubt remains about the importance of influence operations, one need only look to the extensive use of cohesive and divisive psychological operations, as well as to the many deceptive practices, of our insurgent and terrorist adversaries. It often seems that their battle doctrine is weighted far more heavily on the side of information than on physical destruction. In the years since 9/11 (I am writing in late 2007), al Qaeda and its affiliates have mounted only a handful of successful major operations: bombings in Bali, Madrid, and London. Some other plans for big attacks have been preempted, in Singapore, Morocco, London (a few times), and the United States. And even though al Qaeda was able to mount a series of smaller "wave attacks" in places like Saudi Arabia and Turkey, and has struck at U.S. forces and fomented civil war in Iraq, the main point is that the terrorists have serious limits to their physical capacity for mounting field operations. Their networks have to some extent compensated for this with skillful influence operations.

For one thing, al Qaeda has, with limited physical resources, pursued a kind of cost-imposing strategy against the United States. By presenting itself as capable of attacking anywhere, anytime, al Qaeda has induced us to make huge security expenditures and strained our large military to the breaking point. This effect is at the heart of the whole notion of influence operations; and historians will no doubt one day see al Qaeda's performance in this field as nothing short of spectacular. It is already appreciated by some, as the American scholar John

Mueller has noted in his incendiary critique, *Overblown*. It will soon be acknowledged openly by even more specialists in this field.

The reason that al Qaeda's influence operations have been so effective, I believe, is that they are well suited for exploiting our own "scaling problem." They can mount just a few operations and yet be able to count on the Americans having to respond in costly, balky ways. For the U.S. military comes in division-sized chunks that form elements of even larger interservice expeditionary forces, in part because this is the scale at which our military leaders prefer to operate. And this preference itself seems to grow out of the belief that large forces can win decisive battles quickly and with fewer casualties suffered by our troops, thanks to their overwhelming strength. This approach is thought to be necessary because of the military's near-religious belief that the American people have no stomach for casualties.

This belief persists despite a large body of evidence—mostly polling data from wartime surveys, including some during the Vietnam years—that shows quite convincingly that American support for military interventions often persists despite losses. As John Mueller has put it about American mass opinion and its influence on our leaders: "Once troops are engaged, as discovered in such unpopular armed conflicts as the War of 1812 and Vietnam, it is difficult to generate the political will to back away." As to detailed data analysis of public opinion in wartime, Eric Larson has shown convincingly that sensitivity to casualties greatly depends on perceptions of the worthiness of the cause. That is, as human costs mount, a highly questionable intervention is more likely to suffer loss of public support than one deemed just or necessary. Even an ambiguous conflict like Vietnam shows some kind of staying power among the mass public. As late as the end of 1970, after five years of fruitless fighting, more than half of all "high-knowledge respondents" who identified themselves with both major political parties wanted either to keep on fighting as we were—while continuing negotiations—or to escalate the war.

Despite this evidence, senior generals continue to believe that a bloody, protracted fight necessarily leads to loss of public support. In fact all the data show that in failed military operations, it is an inability to win battles that erodes support over time, not the mass public's allergy to casualties. Based on their misconceptions about the resilience of public support—and an illusory but powerful belief in the media's anti-war biases—our military leaders lobbied hard for sending twice as many troops to Iraq as actually have gone; and in the years to come their mantra will be that we must never again go to war with "insufficient troops." Even an updating of the old fiction about the public's "stab in the back" of the military—the so-called Vietnam Syndrome—has reemerged as the "Iraq Syndrome." But all the opinion polls show that the same pattern of public belief that has persisted throughout our history continues, and that we did not flounder in Iraq due to lack of sustained public support. Instead our protracted military fumbling in the face of an innovative insurgency eventually undermined public support.

Yet the turn of mind in the military is still very much toward the notion of "bigger is better" in the use of force. And this mentality has played right into the hands of the terrorists' battle and influence strategies, especially in Iraq. Our adversaries will continue to seek to foment irregular, protracted conflicts, in response to which the Americans will, they hope, respond with large forces and the heavy, often indiscriminate firepower that comes with them. Inevitably such expeditionary forces will inflict the kind of heavy collateral damage that alienates the very populations that U.S. troops are trying to win over. If Iraq is a model of the things we ought to avoid, for the terrorists it is the prototypical conflict they would hope to replicate in other theaters.

We do have a way out of this trap. It lies in cultivating a willingness to "go small" and to rely more on influence operations than on kinetic, explosives-oriented attacks. For all the U.S. military resistance to this notion, one of the most articulate arguments in favor of it has come from British Gen. Rupert Smith. He argues that military victories are unlikely to be gained in the absence of campaigns that have fully integrated all aspects of the domain of influence operations. He carefully qualifies his position, observing that "there is still utility in military force, *provided it is applied correctly to support the winning of the clash of wills.*" For General Smith, a natural progression would be to see a decline in the prevalence of mostly "kinetic" field operations and a rise in those undertakings in which influence-oriented elements will lead. In all cases, though, it is clear that he would like to see a new kind of "combined arms" approach, one that explicitly and skillfully knits together the informational and military initiatives.

Interestingly, the field campaigns of recent years in which U.S. forces have achieved most success on the ground have been those where sharp constraints were imposed on the scale of military operations. In Afghanistan in the fall of 2001, we had to take down the Taliban quickly, but moving a whole field army to that landlocked country would have required transit permissions and would have taken many months under the best circumstances. Instead just 11 special forces "A-teams" and a sprinkling of air force special tactics soldiers were used in the campaign that toppled the Taliban in a few months—about 160 sets of "boots on the ground." They routinely deceived the enemy about their strength and location, and used skillful cohesive psychological tactics to hold together the Afghan fighters they were leading into battle. And the support for their intervention persisted long after this campaign. Even though the Taliban still make mischief, the situation has remained largely controllable at very modest cost—in large part because of the successful influence operations that have been woven so tightly into the fabric of this intervention.

Another successful instance of a tiny military endeavor that has relied heavily on influence operations is Operation Enduring Freedom / Philippines (OEF/P), the effort to counter the al Qaeda–affiliated Abu Sayyaf Group and the separatists of the Moro Islamic movement. This time the constraint on a large U.S. military intervention was imposed by the Philippine government itself, so the American presence has been strictly advisory. And it has relied heavily on cohesive psychological operations designed to maintain loyalty to the central government in Manila while undermining support for the terrorists on Basilan and other southern Philippine islands. Other, more sensitive information operations have also been employed, about which more cannot be openly written. But it should suffice to note that, in a campaign in which the American contribution has been sharply limited to influence operations, we have seen an enemy driven back in disarray and kept on the run. Between our advisers and the armed forces of the Philippines, something like a model of small military actions and aggressive influence operations has emerged, one that should be replicated elsewhere.

In at least one other important situation, our principal reliance on influence rather than on bombardment or invasion has made a big difference. The setting here was Saharan Africa, principally in remote territory on both sides of the Algerian-Chadian border. The target was another al Qaeda affiliate, the "al Parra" organization that had been causing much mischief. Again American involvement had to be quite limited, in this instance to providing intelligence, some logistical support, and deceptive information operations. The details of the destruction of al Parra must also remain veiled; but the end result was that a clever deception helped place the group in a gravely compromised position, from which it could not extricate itself. This was another triumph for influence operations that were skillfully integrated into small-scale military actions.

Each of these successes featured a blending of military and information operations, and a willingness to work with others and to cede overall control to them in the prosecution of these campaigns. In essence these initiatives were our first serious forays into the process of building our own networks to fight the terror networks. Successes like these should provide a strong hint that the "bigger is better" school of thought is hardly likely to win the war on terror; our enemies can slip these heavy punches all too easily. Today it seems that the glimmer of hope offered by these campaigns is encouraging a deeper appreciation of the value of influence operations, especially in the context of fighting terror networks. An antidote has begun to emerge to the simple reliance on brute force and the habit of mind toward a "new American militarism," about which the soldier-historian Andrew Bacevich has warned so eloquently. In the realm of covert action—so dangerous because of what the scholar John Prados calls its "seductiveness"—influence operations may provide an alternative to hazardous escapades or mitigate their risks.

With the emergence of two network warfare commands—one in the navy, the other at the Strategic Command—it is clear that some steps are being taken toward reducing our reliance on traditional physical force and blending in a greater use of influence operations. For now, both these military commands are far too fixated on cyberspace-based operations. But they do at least speak to an institutional interest in becoming more adept at "netwar," a vision of an emerging form of conflict empowered by the network form of organization. The need to understand and master this concept will prove crucial to winning the war against al Qaeda and other conflicts to come. It is considered in detail in the next chapter.

CHAPTER SEVEN

A New Course of Study: "Netwar 101"

SINCE THE ONSET of what the Pentagon occasionally calls "the long war" on terror, there have perhaps been no two words more commonly used to describe our adversaries than "terror networks." These words suggest shadowy cells dispersed throughout the world, relentlessly pursuing their common goal of undermining American security interests and able to stay on task with little overt control from any sort of high command. The organizational structures that distinguish these groups as networks have three fundamental forms: hubs, where one central node connects to many "spokes"; chains, good for moving people, money, and arms; and areas in which all members are connected to one another. Mohammed Atta, for example, was a hub for the 9/11 attackers. The "ratlines" that foreign fighters have followed into Iraq are classic chains. And the infamous "Hamburg cell" of al Qaeda was exemplary of the many terrorist network nodes where all members are in contact with one another. In practice, most terror networks exhibit hybrid designs that often feature skillful blends of all three of these fundamental forms.

The network form of organization, which has proved so attractive and useful to terrorists, has also impelled them to pioneer new modes of confrontation and conflict; for even though their networks are magnets for smart, tough, dedicated operatives, it would be suicidal for the terrorists to try to take on their betters by traditional means. They are simply too few in number and too lightly armed. For example, at its height al Qaeda has probably had no more than a few thousand fighters in the network's core groups—about as many individuals as carry rifles in an average American infantry brigade. And when the new generation of recruits—the largely unskilled one that fills out the ranks of their self-depleting kamikaze-style suicide squads in Iraq—is included, the numbers don't grow much. Even including Iraqi insurgent network allies, or resurgent Taliban in Afghanistan, the total numbers of combatants al Qaeda can field wouldn't so much as fill out one U.S. division.

In order to engage their much bigger and far more heavily armed opponents with some hope of success, al Qaeda and affiliated terrorist and insurgent networks have had to craft a new way of war—"netwar," to be precise. This is a term that my RAND Corporation colleague David Ronfeldt and I introduced in the early 1990s to describe the manner in which we believed networks would fight.

We reasoned that instead of massing forces, which has been the goal of most militaries throughout history, networks would become adept at dispersing their numerous small units in many locations. This would benefit both defense and offense, for such a loose deployment scheme would make them harder to find and destroy while at the same time allowing them the opportunity to mount swarming attacks in many different places. In an age in which ever more destructive power continues to migrate into the hands of small groups—think of the damage just nineteen al Qaeda fighters achieved on 9/11, or what a terrorist cell armed with nuclear weapons might do one day—the netwar approach seems ideally suited to their needs.

Ronfeldt and I reasoned that this kind of warfare was coming, and that the only effective way to counter it was for our military, intelligence, and law enforcement elements to develop nimble networks of their own in the fight against the terrorists. It was, we thought, very much like the situation in the blitz-krieg era some seventy years ago, when military experts concluded that "the best way to fight a tank is with a tank." Now, we thought, "It takes a network to fight a network." Yet in all the years since we first fielded this concept for the Department of Defense, terrorists, criminals, insurgents, and even militant social activists have consistently shown a greater grasp of netwar principles than the U.S. military, and much more willingness to employ them in practice. Hence the need to continue to reiterate—ad nauseam, it sometimes seems—a kind of primer in network-age warfare for both senior leaders and field operatives. "Netwar 101" is what I have called this effort to raise the group consciousness of the U.S. military, first by analyzing cases of networks in battle, then by identifying the organizational, doctrinal, and strategic implications of this new phenomenon.

Over the past two decades there have been abundant examples of netwar. Among the first was the rise of a skillfully (but not centrally) coordinated network of nearly three hundred small drug operations in Colombia in the wake of American-led efforts that had resulted in the killing or capture of the leaders of the Medellín and Cali cartels. These new networks of small operators had no commander-in-chief, but they shared the common goal of producing and distributing their product, and they enjoyed secure means of communication provided by couriers, encrypted phones, and web and internet links. Soon more cocaine than ever before was making its way to the United States, and the Colombian networks had begun to forge new ties with increasingly aggressive Mexican networks that initially had specialized only in transshipping drugs.

Against this rising tide of drug networks, the American response, the multibillion-dollar "Plan Colombia," has continued to focus on targeting "leaders," despite the fact that the networks don't rely on one or a few bosses to run the show. As you might imagine, this strategy has not worked at all. To be sure, there are other elements to the costly counterdrug plan (such as encouraging crop substitution and using herbicides to eradicate crops), but the networks have just as easily outflanked these. For example, to get around aerial spraying of their fields, the drug networks quickly shifted to interplanting coca among legitimate crops. Now Colombian troops must find these fields, then go in and pull out the coca by hand, an exceedingly slow process that leaves them at risk of being attacked while they are at work. Most troubling of all is that the new Colombian model for the cocaine business, based on the formation of many small but highly networked operators, is largely the one being followed today by drug rings from Afghanistan to Southeast Asia and beyond. If there is ever to be hope of winning the "war on drugs"—which we have now been waging formally for more than thirty years—it undoubtedly lies in our willingness and ability to learn more about how to undermine networks.

Around the same time that drug operators were becoming so fully networked, insurgents in various areas of the world also began to shift toward far more dispersed and "decontrolled" organizational forms. Sometimes this process was unwittingly helped along by their opponents who, like the United States, were single-mindedly focused on knocking out enemy leaders. For example, in Chechnya, the breakaway Russian republic, Muslim militants saw their leader Dzhokar Dudayev tracked, targeted, and killed by Russian forces early on in their attempt at armed secession, which ran from 1994 to 1996. After Dudayev's death, however, the Chechens relied much more on operations of small fighting cells of no more than twelve to twenty militants each, bonded together by tribal and clan-based social ties, and given little direct tactical oversight. In 1996 a force of just several thousand insurgents, organized in this loose fashion and interconnected mostly by runners and a clever mix of short-range and shortwave radios, drove a far larger Russian force from their country.

They did so in pitched battles featuring swarming attacks coming from all directions, not just classical hit-and-run guerrilla raids. And they succeeded despite the fact that the Russian forces were replete with artillery, tanks, and attack aircraft while the Chechens' heaviest weapons were rocket-propelled grenades (RPG). Even though the insurgents sawed off their gun barrels to improve RPG velocity—the better to penetrate tank armor—they were still terribly outgunned. They shouldn't have won, but they did. And the fact that the Russians came back smarter the second time, and have operated more effectively (and been far more brutal) against the Chechens, takes nothing away from the amazing initial campaign by the insurgent networks in 1996. With little or no regularly functioning central command structure, in small numbers and fielding only light weapons, they defeated one of the world's great militaries in direct battle. This was a quintessential case of netwar.

Other netwars have appeared since then, none more haunting than the Iraqi insurgency, which began in earnest in August 2003—a little more than four months after the beginning of the American military occupation—and continued unabated thereafter. The insurgents had no real central leadership, as proven by their persistence after such losses as the capture of Saddam Hussein, the killing of his sons, and the death of the leading terrorist Abu Musab al Zarqawi. Further, al Qaeda fighters were always fairly few in number, and the other rebels were so seriously divided along ethnic and religious lines that a civil war would soon break out. But all the insurgent organizational structures—more the Sunni than the Shi'a, however—emphasized both creating dense interconnectivity between trusted members and allowing great autonomy of action for individual cells. These were the core attributes that gave the insurgents the ability to wage a protracted contest against the better-armed Americans for control of Iraq.

It turned out to be a struggle that became a quagmire for U.S. forces. By the fall of 2006, most Americans simply wanted it to end. Late in the game (in 2005), Donald Rumsfeld finally began referring publicly to the conflict as a netwar—thanks to a letter from RAND Corporation president Jim Thomson that pointed out the networked nature of the conflict. Thomson put it this way: "The Iraq insurgency demonstrates the closest man- ifestation yet of 'netwar,' which is characterized by flatter, more linear networks rather than the pyramidal hierarchies and command and control systems of traditional insurgent organi- zations." This was clearly an epiphany for Rumsfeld, whose own view of military transformation had until this point been governed by technology-oriented issues. As he put it in his sem- inal article on the topic in 2002, "we must begin shifting the balance in our arsenal between manned and unmanned capa- bilities, between short- and long-range systems, between stealthy and non-stealthy systems, between sensors and shoot- ers, and between vulnerable and hardened systems." Rumsfeld made no explicit mention of networking at all, save for a nod to the Afghan campaign, which featured an ability to "communi- cate and operate seamlessly on the battlefield."

Soon after the Thomson letter, Rumsfeld was aggressively encouraging the use of more networklike small-team tactics against the insurgents, to replace the "overwhelming force" ap- proach that had dominated U.S. conduct of the campaign. But for the most part the Pentagon demurred, taking the position that our Iraq policy was failing because Rumsfeld had not sent enough troops to the fight in the first place. This was a point of view that senior generals knew would win traction with elected officials of both parties, and with a broad spectrum of the mass public. And so Rumsfeld's belated call for change initially went unheeded, and he was sacked in the wake of off-year elections that had seen anti-war rhetoric help the Democrats regain control of both houses of Congress. But the shift to the networked "outpost approach," coupled with outreach designed to network with friendly tribes and former insurgents, suggests that the netwar paradigm was finally adopted in Iraq by mid-2007.

The experience of netwar in Iraq suggests that yet another key element in this new mode of conflict is the manner in which even a small degree of violence can have disproportionate perceptual effects. Netwar has a postmodern quality, one that takes advantage of the tendency in our time to view the actual fighting in any conflict as a backdrop to the more important "battle of the story" about why the war is being waged in the first place. In this regard, a small, steady trickle of casualties is all that is needed to provide a daily reminder of the "sharp practices"— and some of the outright misrepresentations—that helped sell the war to the American public in the months before the March 2003 invasion of Iraq. For his part, Rumsfeld seemed to be aware of this issue early on, concluding his article on military transformation with a cautionary note along these lines: "And finally, be straight with the American people. Tell them the truth. . . ."

The point is that "influence operations" are likely to play a major role in the outcome of any netwar and therefore must be closely coordinated with military actions in the field. In more traditional terror campaigns, occasional violence is done with a single-minded focus on gaining attention rather than on shaping a battlefield situation. In Iraq the insurgents went well beyond this simple signaling approach to terror. Instead they somehow created a full campaign in which a drumbeat of regular acts of violence was used to wield powerful influence over other Iraqis, the American public, and even world opinion. The insurgents did a better job than U.S. forces in achieving a high degree of integration between the use of force and the effects of their influence operations.

But being more attentive to the role of information could not guarantee that a nation would defeat a network in any given conflict. One need only look to the Israel-Hezbollah War that was waged during the summer of 2006. This was one of the first conflicts to erupt explicitly between a nation and a network. In this instance, Lebanon the nation-state was more an arena than an active combatant—despite the fact that Hezbollah had a formal position in the Lebanese government at the time and still does at this writing (late in 2007). The conflict was precipitated by a Hezbollah raid on an Israeli outpost that resulted in the killing of several Israelis and the capture of a few soldiers. Israeli leaders saw this action as a *casus belli,* one that gave them a justifiable context for the war, and the Israeli Defense Forces (IDF) soon began a vigorous campaign to destroy Hezbollah's combat capabilities.

Deploying more than 100,000 troops, including heavy armor and artillery, and hundreds of advanced ground-attack aircraft, the IDF advanced into southern Lebanon with the aim of killing or capturing Hezbollah fighters and destroying their stores of missiles. Beyond the immediate battle area, which ran some twenty to twenty-five miles from Lebanon's southern border to the Litani River—that is, in the area where it runs parallel to the border, before turning northward—the Israeli Air Force waged a relentless strategic bombing campaign that struck at targets throughout all of Lebanon. To disrupt Hezbollah's central command and control, cell-phone towers were targeted, and supply routes were broken up with strikes against virtually every bridge leading to the battle zone.

Against this might, Hezbollah fielded perhaps as many as three thousand fighters, all organized into small teams—much like the Chechen squads of twelve to twenty fighters that had defeated the Russians ten years earlier. This gave Hezbollah many more units of maneuver than the Israelis, whose principal ground operations—aside from a handful of small, deeply infiltrated "spotter teams"—were undertaken mostly by units comprised of at least several hundred soldiers. Hezbollah had taken the precaution of prepositioning missiles in hidden sites all across the battle zone, so Israeli efforts to disrupt the movement of weapons southward was preempted. So were Israeli attempts to disrupt Hezbollah's command and control with aerial bombing, as the small networks of fighters were prebriefed on the locations of weapons caches—the overall arsenal probably totaled about thirteen thousand missiles and rockets— throughout an area that had been subdivided into seventy-five "military zones" before the war. All the teams had to do was unearth the weapons, move to nearby firing sites when necessary, launch them, and move on. "Shoot and scoot," if you will. No stream of orders from a high command was necessary. Just aim south to make sure the rockets fell on Israeli soil.

In the event, the network fought well. Hezbollah's forces launched some two hundred missile weapons on the first day of the war, and more than two hundred on the last day of the fighting just over a month later. And when the Israelis realized that their air campaign was failing, the ground forces they unleashed were met not by guerrilla hit-and-run tactics but by a swarm of small Hezbollah teams, fighting them head on, much as the Chechens had done against the Russians in 1996. Interestingly, the "exchange ratio" in these firefights was very nearly even, with each Hezbollah casualty coming close to being matched by an Israeli. By the end of the war the Israelis had indeed killed nearly a thousand Lebanese versus just a few hundred lost on their side, but most of the deaths were suffered by Lebanese civilians who had been caught in the aerial bombing.* And this in turn hurt the Israelis in the "battle of the story" about why and how the war was being waged. In-

---

*A well-placed source outside the U.S. military and intelligence communities told me that Hezbollah held 183 funerals for fighters killed in direct battle with Israeli troops.

deed, much of the world came to view the Israeli use of force as disproportionate.

What's more, a majority of Israelis felt that the IDF had lost the war, even though about 90 percent of the public had supported an air-only campaign against Hezbollah, the very strategy that resulted in so much international opprobrium being heaped upon Israel. In the wake of this conflict, the high-level Winograd Commission was appointed to determine what had gone wrong, and delivered a scathing report on Israeli military performance during the conflict. The military chief of staff who had masterminded the campaign (air force Lt. Gen. Dan Halutz) felt obliged to resign. More than anything else, the war shook Israeli self-confidence. Hezbollah missile attacks on northern Israel had inflicted little real damage—just a fraction of that done by the bombing of Lebanon. But the conflict in the summer of 2006 was yet another piece of evidence suggesting that Israel was having a hard time dealing with a nettlesome network. Hezbollah had withstood the Israeli occupation of southern Lebanon for years, beginning in the 1980s, and finally drove the IDF out in 2000. Six years later the terror network had once again slipped all of Israel's heavy punches and managed to deliver more than a few of its own. For a country that had been defeating Arab national armies regularly since 1948, the inability of the IDF to defeat this Hezbollah network struck a real nerve among all Israelis.

It should strike a chord in American strategic thought as well, given our own difficulties in grappling with terror networks. But it hasn't, as the American military is, for the most part, reluctant to learn from others' experiences. The comment I have most often heard about the Israel-Lebanon War of 2006, including from a range of our general officers, is that "We would never have done it like that." Perhaps not. But the way the United States has sought to grapple with networks has been, with few exceptions, by mostly conventional military means, along with a mania for hunting down "leaders" of an organization that can function quite well without much high-level direction. And we have continued to pursue our well-worn paths despite the fact that our experiences of the past several years suggest the urgent need to think in terms of netwar, to recognize that the hallowed principles of war have been affected by the emergence of the network. Our reluctance to make this intellectual leap imperils us the most.

*

The greatest problems bedeviling American efforts to confront and defeat hostile networks are conceptual. And the most prominent of these is the apparent unwillingness to understand the networks themselves. Instead of being seen as autonomous entities, terror networks have, all too conveniently, been viewed by U.S. leaders as wedded to nation-states. Thus in the first great conflict between nations and networks, which has been under way since September 11, 2001, we have been trying to defeat the networks by going after other nation-states.* More than any other reason, I believe, this is why we invaded Iraq. Our security establishment and senior elected leaders all think in terms of nations, not networks. We are constrained by old habits of mind, which in this case have deep roots in the general history of armed conflict.

During most of the period since the rise of modern nation-states about five hundred years ago, wars have been waged principally by states against other states. It has been logical for leaders to think in terms of confronting nations rather than networks. To be sure, in earlier eras there were occasional campaigns against bandits, pirates, smugglers, and other kinds of raiders. And Britain and other colonial powers did accumulate some experience in "small wars" during the nineteenth century. But the vast majority of fighting for the past half-millennium

*Osama bin Laden and his affiliated networks began attacking us earlier than that, but it was only in the wake of the strikes against the World Trade Center and the Pentagon that we awoke to the reality of the terror war.

took place between recognizable nations. Even the early American experience in combating the Barbary pirates was ultimately framed in terms of interstate warfare and featured an expeditionary force launched with the idea of effecting "regime change" in Tripoli, the source of so many of the depredations against American trade. When President Thomas Jefferson chose to negotiate a peace treaty with Barbary, it only put off the day when Britain's Royal Navy would have to bombard the pirate ports, and then post-Napoleonic France would be urged to invade Algeria, taking over this country and eventually controlling its neighbors as well in order finally to quell the nettlesome networks operating from their shores. Alongside the profusion of small colonial wars of this sort were the several conflicts waged throughout the world among states, quite often between the great powers themselves, culminating in two world wars.

But over the past fifty years a fundamental change in warfare has manifested itself, as most conflicts have erupted not between nations but among factions within states. Sometimes these wars have spilled over and involved other countries; but the underlying dynamic driving conflict since the 1950s has been internal. Of approximately thirty wars now going on in the world, only one clearly began as a war between states: the American invasion of Iraq. Even this conflict quickly morphed into a civil war as well as an insurgency against an occupying force. To some extent Palestinian resistance to the Israeli occupation of the West Bank and Gaza might also be construed of in terms of classical international conflict—except for the fact that the Palestinians do not represent a recognized nation-state. And ongoing struggles between the Palestinian Fatah and Hamas factions clearly fall under the rubric of internal war.

Beyond Iraq and Israel, today's wars are all quite obviously internal.* From Colombia to Sudan, Somalia to Sri Lanka, and

---

*The continued fighting in Chechnya, a republic of Russia, is also an internal conflict, though the Chechen goal is clearly to win independence—a goal of many other insurgents around the world.

on to a host of other conflicts, the combatants are usually highly networked ethnic elements within these countries, striving bitterly against each other. Often their hope is to win independent statehood, as has been the goal of Kurdish rebels, for example, for many generations. Sometimes the aim of a rebel group is simply to achieve a more equitable distribution of societal resources, as is certainly the case in the Darfurian uprising against the central Sudanese government's policies. Undoubtedly some of the motivation for Sunni insurgents in Iraq has been to position themselves for a better political and economic arrangement in post-Saddam (and, eventually, post-American-occupation) Iraq. The vast majority of the world's violence is now being perpetrated by networks of substate factions rather than the nations themselves.

Almost all these networks are fighting in unusual ways, ranging from insurgent operations that follow the lines of classic hit-and-run guerrilla warfare to assassinations, kidnappings, and acts of sheer terror. The Tamil Tigers, the ethnic group rebelling against the Sri Lankan government, has adopted widespread suicide tactics on the battlefield. Many Tamil fighters keep vials of cyanide around their necks, an adornment that symbolizes their deep commitment to the cause of independence for their people. The Tamils and many other insurgent networks have thus been pioneering a way of fighting that flows from their organizational form: netwar, which is characterized by there being a common goal but little central control, and by fielding small fighting units so that there can be many of them.

How different this situation today is from the dawn of our own rebellious republic, when George Washington did his utmost to ensure that the Continental Army emulated European military organizational forms and was relentlessly drilled in the most conventional tactics of the time—"massed volley fire" at very short range. Washington may have been leading an insurgent movement, but he wanted to wage war in the most

conventional way possible. Contrary to the stereotypical view
of the British Redcoats lined up in close order while our dispersed snipers simply picked them off, the "thin red line" more
often than not squared off against an equally thin blue line of
Americans.

Washington had to face sharp internal criticism of his preferred approach, especially because he won so few battles in
this manner. Maj. Gen. Charles Lee was perhaps the most articulate proponent of an irregular approach, arguing that, as
the historian Russell Weigley has summed up his point of view,
"a war fought to attain revolutionary purposes ought to be
waged in a revolutionary manner." Washington would have
none of this, however, and refused to be diverted from his goal
of creating a conventional army. In the end, though, Charles
Lee and those of like mind seem to have won out, as the outcome of the Revolution was decided in an unconventional campaign conducted mainly by small units in the South, most
notably a network of irregulars fighting with Francis Marion,
the "Swamp Fox," and other hit-and-run outfits that worked in
conjunction with a small regular force under the command of
Nathanael Greene. This skillful blending of raiding forces and
regulars wore down British Gen. George Cornwallis's army and
impelled him to fall back on Yorktown—where he was trapped
by the timely appearance of a French blockading fleet and
forced to surrender. Yes, George Washington did march his
forces down from New York to Yorktown to conduct the siege,
and the French naval force under the command of the Comte
de Grasse did remove any hope of escape by sea. But Cornwallis would never have found himself trapped in Yorktown had it
not been for the exhausting failure of his attempts to come to
grips with the irregulars.

These happy results for the networks of early American
fighters had little lasting effect on the U.S. military, which
quickly returned to the comfortable track of emulating the Eu-
ropeans—especially the thought and practices of Napoleon

Bonaparte and his principal interpreters. Americans had a particular admiration for a Napoleonic staff officer, the Baron Antoine Henri de Jomini. His great study *The Art of War* was replete with axioms and principles and was widely studied by officers on both sides in the American Civil War. In their preface to the 1862 English edition of Jomini's book, the West Point translators went so far as to say, "General Jomini is admitted by all competent judges to be one of the ablest military critics and historians of this or any other day."

Both sides in the Civil War tried to follow Jomini's principles of offensive warfare, mass, and maneuver, among others, none of which really bore on issues of irregular warfare, and none of which worked as intended in a conflict that saw more than a million troops engaged in a theater of operations as large as Western Europe. Rifles and artillery, as well as rail and telegraph, undermined many of Jomini's formulations. It seems as if Abraham Lincoln was the only leader who saw clearly the need to diverge from strategic dogma. Lincoln consistently urged his generals to distribute their forces in a "cordon offensive" rather than to mass as many of them as possible in one place, in search of a single decisive battle. The president eventually prevailed over his recalcitrant generals by finding some soldiers who were amenable to his ideas (notably Grant, Sherman, and Sheridan). Despite Lincoln's having prevailed in the strategic debates during the Civil War, Jominian thought retained its appeal. Its principles soon returned to prominence and have become the most important guide to American strategy ever since.

Military innovation was thus stifled, and notions of irregular warfare went into almost total eclipse until the Vietnam War. A brief rebirth of unconventional thought occurred during U.S. counterinsurgency operations in the Philippines from 1899 to 1902; and the Marines operating in the Caribbean and Central America during these years, and on into the 1920s and 1930s, showed an aptitude for irregular warfare as well. But the insights from these smaller conflicts were quickly discarded as the United States became involved in the world wars and, soon after, Korea.

Early in the 1950s, as the Korean War wound down, the cold war accelerated, and the atomic bomb was fast becoming a principal element in the arsenal of our chief adversary, the Soviet Union, there seemed to be a reawakening of latent American capacities for irregular warfare. Army special forces (SF) were created and fielded during these years, with the idea of having their twelve-man "A-teams" lead European partisans in a fight to be waged from behind the lines in areas overrun by Soviet forces in a future war. The opportunity to fight in this way never arose in Europe, but SF soon found much to do in Southeast Asia. U.S. combat involvement in the Vietnam War began with many SF teams helping mount an indigenous resistance to the advancing North Vietnamese army. The Marines soon showed that their institutional memory was intact, rekindling the small-unit capabilities and concepts of an earlier era in their "combined action platoons" (CAPs). With these units they enlisted and empowered the South Vietnamese people who, with Marine support sometimes as small as just a squad of eight to ten, secured a swath of the coast and quite a ways inland as well. The Marines also often operated unconventionally at the platoon level (forty to forty-five riflemen), mounting repeated raids from the sea on Vietcong units. In the process of doing so they created a largely pacified coastal zone that ran virtually the entire length of South Vietnam. All this was accomplished with relatively small numbers of troops and in a highly networked fashion, especially as ground forces were directly linked to Marine pilots accustomed to "putting the 'close' in close air support." But all too soon the Pentagon, which had been fighting a war of ideas about the idea of *this* war, shifted to a "big-unit" approach. And soon all went awry, with tragic end results.

Curiously, the war against the terrorists has followed a similar path. The first strategic steps the United States took were nimble and highly networked—out of necessity, as this was the only way to invade Afghanistan quickly and with any hope of success. The result was remarkable, achieved in conjunction with airpower, as already noted. But it sparked a debate that has raged ever since. A few analysts—I among them—have argued that this campaign changed the nature of war in our time. The majority, however, see the campaign, in the words used by the military historian Stephen Biddle, as "surprisingly orthodox"—though they also see it, seemingly contradictorily, as an anomaly rather than as the kind of operation that could be regularly repeated in other settings. Given that, even when friendly Afghan allies are included, the offensive was mounted with fewer than a third of the total number of Taliban and al Qaeda fighters in the field against them, the argument for the orthodoxy of this campaign grows somewhat strained. Traditional military doctrine usually calls for a numerical superiority of three-to-one at the point of contact in order to mount an offensive with reasonable expectations of success.

An important middle ground in the evaluation of Operation Enduring Freedom was staked out by the defense analyst Michael O'Hanlon, who described the Afghan campaign as a "flawed masterpiece." Flawed because of the unwillingness of U.S. military commanders to set down some troops at the outset of the campaign—say, from the Ranger regiment, or elements from the Tenth Mountain Division—in a blocking position at Tora Bora so as to prevent Osama bin Laden's escape with his own cadres and his Taliban allies. O'Hanlon is absolutely correct about this. A true netwar approach to the campaign would have considered the entire battlespace from the outset, and thought in terms of being able to position our forces anywhere we wished in the area of operations. Instead our thinking was far too linear, and the Tenth Mountain did not deploy to the vicinity of Tora Bora until early in 2002—in the

Anaconda operation—just a bit too late. A flawed masterpiece yes, but still a quite remarkable campaign.

One of netwar's defining characteristics is its nonlinearity, which places a real premium on the ability to engage in lateral or multidimensional thinking. Had such an interdicting move been made in Afghanistan, it would have been "difficult and dangerous," as O'Hanlon notes. "Yet, given the enormity of the stakes in the war, it would have been appropriate." O'Hanlon also showed a keen sense of network warfare when he observed of our command and communications systems that the "networks were not always fast enough, especially when the political leadership needed to intercede in specific targeting decisions." Still, despite its flaws, the Afghan campaign offered a glimpse of a radically different approach to the future of conflict. It is a troubling, disruptive view of things that imperils our long-standing beliefs about military doctrine and implies that the way we invest our resources, organize our forces, and conduct our battles may be in dire need of an overhaul. Yet there remains sharp, sustained resistance to this idea.

*

The evidence for what Martin van Creveld has called "the transformation of war" is overwhelmingly apparent to us now. Two decades ago, in his book of the same title, he was being predictive to a significant degree. But van Creveld's more recent review of the past century of conflict relies much less on prescience than on an exceptionally insightful analysis of events— from World War I right up to Iraq—that fully bears out his initial idea about the major shift in the nature of war. Yet the recent American effort to understand armed conflict, based on our own military experience, has nonetheless been quite mixed and confusing. This has been unquestionably the case since the first glimmerings of our involvement in Indochina more than

fifty years ago, and proceeding on to counterinsurgency operations in Iraq. As I have pointed out, a major reason for our
difficulty in grasping the nuances of warfare against networks
lies in the roots of our own strategic culture. In particular, our
overemphasis on preparing for war against traditional enemies
and the use of conventional tactics have not served us well. But
there are two other factors at work: the mesmerizing effects of
technology and the ineluctable pull of the so-called principles
of war. Together with our nation-oriented mind-set, these factors have conspired to hamstring the war on terror, and they
threaten to undermine hope for American military reform.

On the technology front, netwar as a concept has been co-
opted by computers. The best evidence of this is that the two
entities created by the Department of Defense with "netwar" in
their names are almost completely focused on "computer network operations" (CNO). The navy has a network warfare command (NETWARCOM) in Norfolk, Virginia, led by a three-star
admiral and dedicated almost entirely to ensuring smooth, secure information flows. The Strategic Command (formerly the
Strategic Air Command, the famous SAC) in Omaha, Nebraska,
also has a network warfare operation, currently under the command of a one-star (brigadier) general. This organization too is
all about information security—though it has begun to think in
more proactive terms about the offensive aspects of computer
network warfare against our adversaries. For both these commands, "network warfare" is mostly about information systems
and cyberspace-based operations.

Over the past several years I have attempted to change this
perception, and leaders in Norfolk and Omaha do now acknowledge that network warfare includes an understanding
of how opposing networks fight, and calls for us to build our
own networked units to engage them. But today the major emphasis is still on computers. I am repeatedly told, "We'll get cyberspace right first, then move on to the other [aspects of
netwar]." Meanwhile insurgent networks ran rings around our
forces in Iraq—at least until our shift to the "outpost strategy"

in 2007—and nodes in the al Qaeda network have continued to surface throughout the world.

According to the U.S. government's official statistics, acts of terror (that is, attacks on innocent civilians) rose from just over three thousand in 2005 to more than fourteen thousand in 2006. And almost half the attacks in 2006 took place in Iraq, where the U.S. military is the most heavily deployed, suggesting that these forces can be better used. Surely it is possible to improve our military's performance by sharing more information swiftly and distributing it widely. But we can achieve this benefit only if we redesign our organizational structures so that they can make maximum use of such information flows.

If not, and if existing hierarchies remain undisturbed, the problems of effectively processing or structuring information inflows will prove insurmountable. Perhaps the best example of this problem was provided by the army a decade ago, in its "Force XXI" exercise. In this instance the entire experimental force was fully digitized, creating an absolute cascade of information, both about friendly positions and possible enemy movements. But because no new organizational structures were introduced, the old hierarchical chain of command was swiftly overwhelmed with data and the force in the field was crippled. This is what happens when new technology is simply grafted onto existing organizational structures. Conversely, when new organizational designs arise to take advantage of new technologies, the results can be stunning. In the case of World War II–era German blitzkrieg, the relatively new weapons technology of the tank was best suited to concentration in a few armor-heavy divisions, rather than being parceled out in small numbers to all divisions, as the French army did. Skillful organizational redesign gave the Germans their advantage at the outset of the war. As in modern architecture, so it is in war: form should follow function.

The other major obstacle for the U.S. military in building a capability for network-style conflict is its unswerving devotion to the canonical principles of war. From the dawn of American strategic culture, when George Washington strove to emulate classical European military practices, the ideas of mass, unity of command, and simplicity have dominated among our leaders in and out of uniform. To be sure, the other six concepts that make up the best-known set of principles, those articulated by the Baron Jomini and succeeding generations of classical strategists, have not been ignored. These are: the objective, the offensive, economy of force, maneuver, security, and surprise. But it is the inevitable triumph of mass that animates, for example, the doctrine of "overwhelming force" associated with Colin Powell. And it is an unwavering belief in the power of centralized leadership that fosters hierarchy and such stark phrases as President George W. Bush's "I am the decider!" The mania for simplistic strategic formulations is also evident in General Powell's public statement before Operation Desert Storm in 1991, about how the Iraqi army would be defeated in that campaign: "We're going to cut it off, then kill it." George Bush's oft-repeated formula for defeating terrorism—by spreading democracy—is yet another testament to our devotion to simplicity.

But in an age of netwar, overwhelming force is not only unnecessary but almost useless against a dispersed foe. Israeli forces vastly outnumbered and outgunned their Hezbollah opponents in Lebanon during the summer war of 2006, but those numbers made no difference to the network. Hierarchical decision-making is achingly slow, and far too balky to catch up with nimble networks, as the meager results of the first seven years of the war on terror suggest. And if terror networks have far fewer fighters than the armies of even small nation-states, what seems clear is that the netwars they wage are complex, dispersed, and nonlinear. The Israelis learned this in Lebanon, and we have learned it in Iraq. Warfare is no longer simple, and to persist in treating it as a simple or straightforward phenomenon is to court disaster.

Even the other six traditional principles of war that our military cleaves to become problematic when viewed fron the perspective of netwar. The "objective," for example, seems related to simplicity, as it implies winning by pursuing one very correct goal. But dispersed networks cannot be defeated by one blow; they are truly "flat" organizations, in the business sense, which can continue operating despite losses suffered in any one area. In turn, networks, by virtue of their dispersed and autonomous nature, allow for the pursuit of several objectives simultaneously. And they are able to take the offensive far more easily and broadly than a hierarchically organized armed force could ever hope to. The same is true in areas of security and surprise, where the stealthy nature of networks conveys inherent advantages over their far more visible conventional opponents. Needless to add, this almost surely means that networks also have the edge in maneuverability, as well as in their ability to achieve much with little expenditure of funds and fighters ("economy of force"). The 9/11 attacks on America—as well as earlier ones—prove this point, given that al Qaeda caused so much disruption in return for the modest investment of nineteen fighters and perhaps $300,000.

American fixation on technological solutions, and our single-minded devotion to principles of war that are either ineffective against networks or convey an advantage to them, have gotten us into a deep hole. Can we climb out? Yes, if we are willing to embrace networks, and if we begin waging a netwar of our own, guided by new emerging principles. One of these principles is that when fighting a network, it is crucial not to attack too soon, because the hardest task lies in knowing how many bodies are in the network and where they are. If old-style thinking prevails, as it has so often recently, the more that is destroyed, the less will be known about the remainder of the network. Patience is essential in gaining the intelligence needed for waging a netwar campaign. It is necessary to wait and watch long enough so as to be able to strike with heavy effect. Patience is perhaps the most difficult virtue for us to cultivate. Still, it is the most necessary, because, as Donald Rumsfeld noted in a speech to the Council on Foreign Relations during his last year as secretary of defense, finding the networks is the most difficult task and the one for which we are most poorly prepared. He put it this way: "If you think of the task that the military has, it's to find the enemy, it's to fix the enemy in time that you can do something about it, and finish. We have overwhelming ability to finish. We are light on the ability to find and fix." This "lightness" is caused by hierarchical "heaviness" in our fifteen separate intelligence agencies, which need to be more highly networked.

Two other emerging principles center on the need to distribute one's forces in smaller and more numerous detachments, and to decentralize decision-making in order to empower them. In Iraq the shift in early 2007 away from a few super-sized forward operating bases to a dispersed network of small outposts—more than fifty were established in Baghdad alone—was a sign of recognition of the utter futility of trying to apply "overwhelming force." Further, in May 2007 authority was granted down to the level of lieutenant colonel to negotiate local deals with insurgent and tribal leaders, making it easier to turn them against al Qaeda and greatly increasing the counterinsurgent network's capacities. But this shift came several years too late, for the campaign in Iraq was by then suffering from many other problems, not least the insurgents' great advantage in influence operations—over the Iraqi people, world observers and average Americans, and most of the political elites that govern us.

For an example of the more timely practice of netwar techniques, one can point to the initial success of the campaign in Afghanistan in the waning months of 2001, when a small network of fewer than two hundred U.S. special forces soldiers worked closely with indigenous insurgents opposed to the Taliban and achieved much at low cost. Even though the fighting has continued in Afghanistan, the societal situation is far better there than in Iraq, and the cost of fighting the Taliban and al Qaeda cadres operating from their safe haven inside Pakistan remains but a fraction of the blood and treasure expended so fruitlessly in Iraq. Just as important, the context of this conflict remains favorable, as the continued American intervention is widely accepted, even to the point of having large contingents of NATO forces still deeply involved in counterinsurgent operations. In all these respects, the Afghan campaign reflects a far more positive example of our practice of netwar than does Iraq. The puzzle, of course, is why shifting to more of an Afghan model was resisted for so long as the situation unraveled in Iraq.

As heartening as the lessons from Afghanistan may be—and the signs of our finally appreciating the network dimension in Iraq too—it remains crucial to recognize that our opponents do not think solely in terms of waging war in a few countries. In a very real sense, networks know no territorial boundaries. Al Qaeda operates in sixty countries and in recent years has been involved in mounting or fomenting terrorist attacks across a swath of the world ranging from Morocco to Mindanao. Their level of activity has continued to grow. If terror networks are allowed to stay on their feet long enough they will obtain nuclear or biological weapons, making a mockery of our retaliatory threats: a global network has no "homeland" that can be held hostage for its good behavior. In short, there is no "mutual assured destruction" when a nation comes up against a nuclear-armed network. Further, networks will have many alternatives to the use of missiles as delivery systems, implying that continued investment in ballistic missile defenses is misplaced.

For all these reasons we should feel right now an exceptional sense of urgency about the need to defeat terrorist networks. This contradicts the notion of pursuing a "long war" against them; time is not on the side of nations in the struggle against networks. Thankfully there are some signs that thoughtful analysts have "cracked the code" of netwar, and that their views are increasingly being heard in the right places. For example, the counterterrorist expert John Robb, in his *Brave New War*, eloquently captures the essence of the kind of conflict waged by widely dispersed but networked cells of "global guerrillas" that is nonlinear, aimed at "systems disruption," and employs "swarm tactics." Robb goes beyond merely sounding the alarm; he offers a vision of how we might prevail against these enemies by learning from and emulating their most effective organizational and doctrinal innovations. His call for a quality of "dynamic, decentralized resilience" is highly consistent with the netwar paradigm.

Another important voice is that of former Senator Gary Hart. In *The Shield and the Cloak* he addresses both the issue of reshaping the military (our "shield") along nimbler, more networked lines, and argues for creating a network of allies (a "cloak") that will routinely share sensitive information in timely, targeted ways. Marine Col. Thomas X. Hammes rounds out this trio. In *The Sling and the Stone* he makes the crucial linkage between netwar and the more popularly accepted notion among military officers and policymakers that we are today experiencing an era of "fourth-generation warfare" (4GW). For Hammes, the two concepts are basically the same. What makes 4GW distinct, he argues, is its reliance upon the network form of organization. As Hammes sees it, "netwar, also known as fourth-generation war, or 4GW, is the complex, long-term type of conflict that has grown out of Mao's People's War." Later on he points the way to learning how to fight in this fashion: "In contrast to simply maintaining and marshaling massive assets to destroy enemy targets, 4GW, or netwar, requires the governments to focus the intellectual capital of our people." So far, the U.S. military's senior leaders have been slow to heed this message, but it has begun to resonate with younger officers.

Robb, Hart, and Hammes have improved awareness of the challenges in a time of war against networks. And in this awareness lies our greatest source of hope for progress and greater military effectiveness. But I am haunted by Hammes's urging that human capital lies at the heart of our ability to wage netwar. It seems that we might get everything else right— organization and doctrine, technology and strategy—and still lose if our warriors and strategists lack the suppleness of mind needed for this new kind of conflict. This puts considerable weight on the social context of the U.S. military today. As discussed in the chapter to follow, the social arena has been the only one in which the armed forces have, with some important exceptions, embraced radical change. The irony, however, is that a number of the most salient shifts in military society over the past few decades may have produced harmful overall effects. They may impair our ability to wage netwar and thereby reduce our military's chances of winning the war on terror.

CHAPTER EIGHT

Social Change and the Armed Forces

IT IS CURIOUS that American military leaders, so resistant to organizational redesign or doctrinal innovation, have some-times embraced radical social change. This malleability in so-cial matters first manifested itself seriously in the area of race, where the segregation of African Americans into separate units had been the rule from the Civil War through World War II. But the dam burst in postwar America, with full integration of the armed forces instituted by President Harry Truman in a 1948 executive order, then implemented during the Korean War, a change the military accepted without serious resistance and strove to make successful. While racial tensions continued to play out over the next few decades—especially on naval vessels during the Vietnam War, where some near-mutinies occurred—in the main the U.S. military has now had an admirable record on race for more than half a century. In this respect the armed forces provide a good example for American society as a whole.

Colin Powell stands as the prime example of the openness of the system to advancing minority officers, moving up as he did from second-lieutenant to four-star general and chairman of the Joint Chiefs of Staff, not to mention his later leap to secre-tary of state. And Powell is hardly an outlier, as the ranks of general and flag officers are today replete with minorities. Their success in reaching the highest ranks of the American military compares very favorably with the comparatively lower accession rate of African Americans, Hispanics, and others to the senior or chief executive levels in the largest public corporations, or of major partners in leading law firms. Far below the highest ranks in the military, a day-to-day camaraderie may be found between the races among enlisted service members and at the junior officer levels. This extends to their families as well, who often live together in highly integrated housing enclaves, providing a beacon of hope for the larger American society about the prospects of eventually ending racial bigotry. In terms of race relations at least—extending beyond African Americans and including those of Asian, Hispanic, and other heritages—the military seems to have gotten things right.

Progress has moved more slowly with regard to the second great area of social change: gender. Women gained full equality as service members in 1948, at least in formal institutional terms. Practically, though, their acceptance has been fitful at best. Witness the Women's Army Corps (the WACs), which was not fused with the regular army until 1978, a thirty-year lag. Today, despite many decades of stop-and-start experimentation, the "combat arms" in all the services remain largely male preserves. This is especially the case in ground combat units, where the principal fear is that women cannot carry their full share of the load, literally or figuratively. Yet women fly planes under fire all the time and, in an era of insurgency and other forms of irregular warfare, where there may be little distinction between front and rear areas, many of the military's more than 200,000 women (roughly 1/7 of total active forces) routinely go in harm's way. And the threat of harm is not posed only by the putative "enemy."

It turns out that women are also sometimes imperiled by their male comrades, who have victimized them by shunning, hazing, or perpetrating one form or another of sexual harass-ment, exploitation, or predation. When women first began ap-pearing on ships serving long deployments, for example, their vessels sometimes returned to home port with many of them pregnant. This "love boat" phenomenon has diminished over the years but hasn't disappeared. And it isn't limited to ships, as shown just a few years ago in the case of Army Specialist Lynndie England, a female guard involved in the abuses at Abu Ghraib prison in Iraq, who was impregnated by another guard serving with her. Beyond these willing liaisons, though, there is also a troubling undercurrent of sexual violence toward women, ranging from rape to abusive and degrading behavior, such as chaining women students to urinals at the naval acad-emy in Annapolis just a decade ago.

Official policy seeks an increasing role for women in the military, a goal embraced by senior admirals and generals—yet a kind of one-sided battle of the sexes continues to gnaw at the integrity of the services. This struggle sometimes seems to worsen in various ways, as shown by the numbers of sexual as-saults reported by the Pentagon, which in 2005 jumped to 2,374, a sharp rise from the 1,700 reported in 2004. Since then this figure has declined slightly, but the overall numbers of in-cidents of sexual and other violence against women remain alarmingly high.

Despite the problems posed by placing women in combat roles, and their continuing vulnerability to sex offenders, in the years ahead they will undoubtedly continue to chip away at the barriers that have made it so difficult for women to rise to the highest ranks. Even if infantry platoons remain a last bas-tion of male exclusivity, there are many other combat special-ties in which being a man is no longer a bona fide occupational qualification. This is an age of smart weapons that can strike with precision from a distance, and the finger on the trigger can just as easily belong to a woman or a man. The problem of sex crimes against women service members is treatable with the unwavering pursuit and punishment of offenders, and an equal determination by senior leaders not to be sidetracked from the goal of allowing women to serve their country, both in battle and in noncombat military occupational specialties.

Beyond race and gender restrictions on service, which have given way in varying degrees, the only area where resistance to social change has been successfully sustained has to do with sexual orientation. The U.S. military has long opposed the integration of gays into the services, and the "don't ask, don't tell" compromise negotiated between Colin Powell and Bill Clinton in 1993 has, for the most part, been used in practice to weed out gays whenever they are detected. In addition to the visceral opposition many straight service members express toward the prospect of being in close contact with gays for extended periods in the field—and concerns about the possible damage to military cohesion and combat effectiveness—the attitude toward gays also has a strong overlay of religion-based antipathy.

The U.S. military is currently populated with large numbers of self-defined "evangelical Christians," who tend to view homosexuality primarily in biblical terms, as an "abomination." They constitute some 40 percent of the total active-duty force today (with evangelicals also accounting for more than 60 percent of the chaplain corps), even though the number of evangelicals in the overall American population is only 14 percent. Many Catholics and mainline Protestants also have quite negative views of gays, and they bring the numbers of self-professed Christians in the service to more than 75 percent. In short, the military social environment is a forbidding one for gays.

Senior officers, loath to countenance any social experiment that might undermine unit cohesion in battle—and in many cases having an anti-gay religious perspective themselves—have thus felt the need to prune out gays wherever and whenever possible. This is a dynamic that shows every sign of staying with us for a long time, as concerns about possibly undermining combat effectiveness will continue to trump notions of social equity. The problem will no doubt linger long after women are routinely holding combat commands. Meanwhile gays will nevertheless find themselves able to serve unobtrusively in many military settings, and they will probably move steadily into more and more areas of specialty, particularly as homophobia continues to decline among our troops who, according to polls, are concentrating more on their colleagues' operational skills than their sexual orientation. But, as with women service members, gays will undoubtedly face the greatest obstacle in joining frontline combat units.

Interestingly, the "weeding-out process" in combat units is not always driven by antipathy toward gays. Over the past several years, and especially in the wake of the unpopular occupation of Iraq, many service members have outed themselves. In the army and Marine Corps, just an individual's admission of homosexual preference has started the bureaucratic wheels turning toward separation from these services. The air force has been less eager to root out such cases, treating them at times more like instances of conscientious objection. That is, the air force has occasionally placed the burden of proof on the gay service member, demanding considerable documentation of the claim of homosexual orientation. The navy falls somewhere between these approaches. In other words, there has developed a "gay card" that some—who perhaps aren't even gay—would seek to exploit as an easy way out of the hazards of service. This is an odd twist to the military's thorniest social problem, and yet another reason to jettison the "don't ask, don't tell" policy in favor of openly allowing gays into the services while keeping them from some key units in order to avoid undermining cohesion among combat troops. This is a policy adjustment that all sides ought to be able to accept.

Another important aspect of social change in the military, also driven by religious sensibilities, has to do with Islam. Simply put, the U.S. military has precious few observant Muslim service members—just over 3,000, all told, in a total active duty

force of more than 1.3 million.* Only a tiny fraction of these
have skills in Arabic or other related languages, because most
adherents of Islam in the U.S. military are African Americans
whose first (and often only) language proficiency is in English.
Lack of linguistic skill and cultural awareness in this area has
proved to be a real handicap, given that the United States has
found itself deeply involved in conflicts where we have either
fought against or tried to protect Muslims since 1990, when
Saddam Hussein invaded Kuwait. In that war we opposed
some Muslims while trying to liberate others, and were allied
with yet more (from Saudi Arabia, Egypt, Syria, and the United
Arab Emirates, among others).

Beyond Operation Desert Storm, we soon found ourselves involved in protecting Muslims while fighting their
co-religionists in Somalia, then later helped Muslims in Bosnia
and Kosovo in their struggles against the Orthodox Christian
Serbs. Of course, the "war on terror" that began in 2001 pitted
American forces against a global insurgent network run by
Muslims, and has since featured extended campaigns in
Afghanistan and Iraq, two of the world's forty-four Muslim
countries. But many of our allies in this war are Muslims too,
so the situation hardly reflects the phenomenon that Harvard
professor Samuel Huntington began calling, more than a
decade ago, a "clash of civilizations."

Even so, we could be doing much better in making social
connections with Muslims. One large step in this direction
would be to bring more Muslims into the U.S. military. Here
again, as in the case of race relations, senior leaders are em-
bracing a major social shift: they are energetically pursuing the
recruitment of more Muslims. To date, though, they have had
precious little success. Still, the sustained attempt to bring

*Muslim advocacy groups suggest that the true number is closer to fifteen thou-
sand, the discrepancy being accounted for by service members who fear to acknowledge their faith openly due to concerns about persecution.

more Muslims into the military is a clear sign of willingness to accept, even engineer, a significant social shift in armed forces that have been self-defined largely along Christian lines.

The likelihood is that the numbers of Muslim service members will not grow explosively, though our conflicts with Islamist extremists will probably continue for years to come, as will our deployments in various Muslim countries. So if the prospect of getting more Muslims to join the military is unlikely, an alternative answer may be to deepen all service members' understanding of Islam. Some of this education goes on already, but far too little, as most leaders would admit. And frankly, it's difficult to impart such cultural awareness service-wide, so there will also have to be more attention to such basic guides to behavior as the laws of war.

Deeper respect for and understanding of the principles of the immunity of noncombatants, the rights of those who have surrendered or been captured, and the requirement to use force proportionately rather than excessively should be encouraged. These are some of the key components of millennia-old "just war" theory and should form the core of a body of ethical instruction that can compensate for some of our chronic deficits in cultural understanding. In short, you don't have to be a Muslim to know not to mistreat one.

*

For all the importance of equity issues that attach to matters of race, gender, sexual orientation, or even religion, perhaps the most significant process of social change in the U.S. military began more than thirty-five years ago when the draft was abolished. The emergence and persistence of the all-volunteer force (AVF) has fundamentally changed the character of the U.S. military as a social institution. Even though the modern draft applied only to the army,* the AVF has led to a sharp decline in the

---

*A significant exception occurred during the Vietnam War, when about one in twenty-five draftees were told they would be placed in the Marines rather than the army.

number of Americans at higher socio-economic levels who have served in the military. The most dramatic example of this is provided by the observation of the eminent sociologist (and draft supporter) Charles Moskos, who has compared military service rates between Princeton graduates in 1958 (when he graduated from Princeton) and 2006. The contrast is startling. Half a century ago, in the midst of the draft era, more than 400 of a graduating class of 750 men had already served or would soon go on to do so. In the 2006 graduating class from Princeton, only nine entered the military, of roughly 1,100 men and women. Princeton hardly stands alone; its experience is now the norm. Those who are far better off are far less likely to form a bond with their countrymen based on the shared experience of military service.

Is this bad? Some would say not, reminding us that "America has no tradition of a draft absent an ongoing war, hot or cold . . ." But this formulation mistakenly neglects the point that Americans have routinely resorted to conscription to fill the ranks of their armies in periods of conflict, from the bloody Civil War to the brooding cold war. To refrain now from employing a draft, during what many hawks call "the long war"— so named to galvanize and sustain support for the effort—is actually a deviation from our long-standing historical pattern. When the United States has found itself in major wars or other protracted forms of conflict, its leaders have regularly relied on conscription.

Even so, it is important to note that, in this era of unconventional warfare, there is little need for massive numbers of troops. Military needs could be met with modest calls each year. A new draft would not have to be universal but could be tailored to specific needs. As a hedge against the reemergence of major, protracted conventional war, more draftees could be brought in for shorter periods of active duty, after which they would remain in a large, capable reserve. This shift toward a smaller regular force and a larger reserve was first argued for by former Senator Gary Hart, before 9/11; but it is important to note that he was not calling for the reimposition of the draft. A further point to keep in mind is that those individuals today who wish to revive conscription as part of a larger requirement for "national service" for all youth—in the armed forces or in other areas of public service, as Professor Moskos has called for—should be distinguished from those who may simply wish to see the return of military draftees. Those who favor the draft simply want to fill army ranks; "national service" advocates hope to instill an ethic of public service into future generations.

Critics of selective service have focused their attention on the many inequities of a system that once allowed a variety of deferments and exemptions that proved difficult to apply fairly. They fail to note that these problems were addressed, and that the last years of the draft saw it far more evenly administered, principally by removing most deferments and relying on a birth-date lottery system for setting the order of preference among draftees.

No, the draft didn't die because of intractable problems associated with administering it. It was ended because of the unpopularity of the Vietnam War. There was no way the American people would continue to support conscription if it meant supplying more fodder for a conflict that most Americans opposed and that all Americans could see was being lost.

It was not only opponents of the Vietnam War who wished to end the draft. The military itself became a major proponent of the shift to an all-volunteer force, the idea being that an increasingly "hollow army" of disgruntled conscripts could be replaced by a new army of long-term professionals with finely honed skills. This became something of a mantra, so much so that a mythology emerged about the poor performance of draftees in battle. This view was imbibed and repeated by many in the officer corps, and even accepted by Donald Rumsfeld, who on one occasion when he was secretary of defense was made to apologize publicly for his disparaging comments about the performance of conscripts.

The fact is that draftees have generally fought with great distinction in many American wars, including in Vietnam, where studies by the army's own Center for Military History praise their performance. But the great unpopularity of the Vietnam War, and resistance to the conscription of young men to serve in it, afforded an opportunity to deflect attention away from the fact that senior American generals were conducting the conflict in less than effective fashion—trying to win a guerrilla war by applying huge amounts of conventional force. And so the simultaneous end of the draft and of our involvement in Vietnam were seen as signs of hope that a better kind of soldier would emerge from the ashes of defeat.

Aside from their willful failure to learn the lessons of Vietnam, and their related treatment of draftees as scapegoats, generals and many senior policymakers have at least one other major reason for avoiding conscription: the prospect of privatizing a considerable amount of military activity, from food service to special operations, might prove extremely efficient. If you can hire out for so many of these functions, at much lower cost, why would you want to return to having generations of conscripts sitting around peeling potatoes? Donald Rumsfeld, a highly successful businessman before returning to the Pentagon in 2001, was a major proponent of outsourcing. In Iraq, he oversaw an occupation in which the number of contractors in the country generally exceeded 100,000—engaged in activities from burger flipping to trigger pulling—not all that many fewer than the total number of serving troops on the ground.

This shift toward private-sector militarization is certainly reasonable. After all, mercenaries, seagoing privateers, and freestanding companies have a long history of military effectiveness. Swiss soldiers, who would hire out quite freely, were the best infantry in Europe during the late Middle Ages. Elizabeth I's irregular "sea dogs," led by Drake, Frobisher, and Hawkins, gave England the ability it needed, just in time, to withstand the threat from sixteenth-century imperial Spain.

And so on. Even in our time, the South African mercenary company Executive Outcomes showed its worth by heading off a looming genocide in Sierra Leone—with fewer than two hundred of its commandos deploying to the theater of conflict. No one can deny the many successes of privatization. But the troubling failures and overreaching of mercenaries, which also are part of the historical record, should give pause. Yes, there may be a place for this kind of outsourcing, but only under the most rigorous policy control. And only as an adjunct to, rather than as a substitute for, a highly competent, ethically healthy, and politically neutral standing national force.

Political neutrality is a somewhat troubling aspect of the era of the AVF. Over the past thirty-five years the political affiliation of service members has sharply skewed in the direction of the Republican party, in the officer corps in particular. Before the end of the draft, only a modest plurality of officers identified themselves as Republicans, with roughly equal numbers of Democrats and independents rounding out the remainder. In recent years more than three-fourths of all officers have identified themselves as Republicans, though officers who represent racial minorities retain the more even distribution pattern of the draft years, as do enlisted personnel and noncommissioned officers. The numbers of self-identified Republicans in the military do seem to have declined in 2005–2006, probably because of growing war-weariness over the Iraq conflict.

In any event, the "red shift" in political identity among the officer corps over the past few decades suggests that senior military leadership has been more likely to support the policies of the Republican party—a point reinforced dramatically by President George W. Bush with his repeated use of audiences of enthusiastic soldiers as the backdrop for speeches on some of his more controversial wartime policies (for example, the need to "stay the course" in Iraq, or later to support a "surge" to escalate our military effort). Indeed, the whole notion of supporting the troops—which can always be counted on to enjoy bipartisan consensus—has become conflated with support for specific policies. Political opponents of a particular policy have had to run the risk of being pilloried for failure to "support the troops."

In this area it seems that the American military has gone far afield from the example of political neutrality set by Gen. George C. Marshall, the army chief of staff upon whom President Franklin D. Roosevelt depended so heavily during World War II. Marshall had a great admiration for Roosevelt, but for all his devotion to the president, General Marshall refused even to register to vote while he was on active service. Given his position in the military, he thought such participation might constitute a conflict of interest. Even years later, when he served in a cabinet-level position, he refused to become involved in partisan behavior. One of his biographers, Forrest Pogue, summed it up very succinctly: "He would not even vote, and when no longer in uniform he still refused, as Truman's Secretary of State and Secretary of Defense, to contribute to the Democratic party campaign funds, speak at party meetings, or in any way lend his name or support to politicians seeking office."

General Marshall may have taken his impartiality to what seems today an extreme degree, but his position on this issue speaks to the deepest traditions of politically unattached professionalism in the American military culture. And while it is unrealistic to call for today's officer corps to abstain from partisan political activity, much less from voting, there is still much room for movement away from the degree of politicization the military has experienced since the end of the draft. There can be no better guide to a military professional's behavior than the example set by George Marshall, who remains an iconic figure, even to this latest generation of officers.

That Marshall's example of keeping his "professional distance" from politics is still relevant can be seen in light of several instances of inappropriate influence on assessments and decisions in recent years. Perhaps the best-known situation arose in the months preceding the 2003 invasion of Iraq, when a number of political appointees in the Pentagon made it clear to serving officers in the undersecretariat for intelligence that they believed the threat posed by Saddam Hussein was actually much more serious than was being acknowledged by the various intelligence agencies. Soon a special new intelligence report was prepared—with the military's imprimatur—that dissented from the rest of the intelligence community's considered views and, among other things, exaggerated both the status of Saddam's weapons programs and his links to terrorist groups like al Qaeda. While this report had a great deal to do with the fateful decision to invade Iraq, other, lesser-known instances of politicization of the military have arisen over the past decade or so. A particularly notable case had to do with policymaking on ballistic missile defense—where Pentagon assessments of the efficacy of this system tracked very closely with administration preferences, despite questionable test results. Whether the consequences are an unnecessary war or billions for pet defense projects, undue politicization of the military has had serious consequences. The "Marshall metaphor" is as needed now as it ever was.

Any effort to "depoliticize" the military will run into the complicating factor that officers who self-identify as Republicans are also likely to describe themselves as devout Christians (the same ones, no doubt, who so strongly oppose the integration of gays into the military). While there are solid reasons to discourage the overt politicization of the military, there is no similar imperative to curtail individual religiosity. Indeed, the reverse should perhaps be true. A strongly spiritual nature is often the cornerstone of courage in battle and a balm for the physical and psychic wounds that often come with practicing one of the world's oldest, most complex, and most dangerous professions.

In policy terms, this politico-religious linkage is truly a Gordian knot. But clearly something must be done, given excesses such as the granting of Pentagon office space to a private, proselytizing religious organization called the Christian Embassy, a clear case of blurring, if not erasing, the line between church and state. This sort of activity should not enjoy official sponsorship or even tacit military support. Yet it has, in large part because of the Christian ethos that has become such a major dimension of the military over the past four decades. As important as the spiritual domain is, it should be cultivated by the individual, not directed by officialdom. In the war against terrorists, the forces of our adversaries may be guided by one body of scripture, but our forces must not be officially directed by another.

How can problems of overt politicization, undue religious influence, and socio-economic segregation be mitigated? By restoring the draft, a process that would immediately end the notion that social elites are above military service. A draft would rekindle the sense that all Americans should be ready to accept an obligation to serve in the military when called upon to do so. In this way the return of the draft would remind all Americans of the implicit social contract that runs from citizen to government, and to one's compatriots.

Then, because of the wide-ranging pool of recruits from which a draft would draw—which ought to include young women as well, since there are so many places where they *can* serve—the politicization problem will slowly be mitigated. Some percentage of this diverse group will become career officers and remain in the service. The hope then would be that religious faith and values would not diminish, but rather that a more proper separation of church and a key state institution, the military, would reemerge, along with a variety of perspectives, in the wake of a troubling period when inappropriately large influence was wielded by one particular worldview.

Thus far only one congressional voice has been firmly raised in favor of restoring the draft: that of Representative Charles Rangel, himself a Korean War veteran. Congressman Rangel's declared position has been that American commitments and future contingencies cannot be met and mastered without a much larger force, and so a draft is needed. His critics have suggested that his initiative is really a political ploy, an indirect way of voicing criticism of the unpopular war in Iraq. But even if this were true, his suggestion should be evaluated on the merits. And on these terms, as Dr. John Williams, a retired military officer and expert on this subject at Loyola University in Chicago, has put it: "Rangel's bringing [the draft] up for political reasons, but . . . he's right. If we have some mechanism that links the military to civilian society in a way that spreads the burden around when you use the military, it's less likely to be used."

Thus a return of the draft would catalyze a powerful social transformation of the U.S. military. While virtually all Pentagon leaders, politicians, and the general public oppose conscription, they cannot ignore the fundamental issues of equity and the ability to mitigate politico-religious problems that undergird the argument for restoring the draft. It is time for a serious public debate about conscription, perhaps prompted by the findings of a new bipartisan commission, modeled along the lines of the 9/11 panel or the Iraq Study Group.

If none of the foregoing reasons to reconsider the draft seem compelling enough, the current plight of military reservists and some National Guard members should be carefully considered. They are already subject to an inequitable kind of hidden draft, in the form of "stop-loss" policies that can be used to keep them in the military well beyond their separation dates. Even though stop-loss orders are invoked because of the exigent circumstance of an ongoing conflict, there is much historical precedent—from the Revolution to Vietnam—to show that American military recruits have often left the service when their allotted time was up, even though war still raged. There is also a compelling ethical argument against stop-loss policies. As Bernard Rostker, a long-time RAND analyst and former under secretary of defense for personnel and readiness, has said of this practice: "It violates the spirit of the all-volunteer force and sets aside the terms of the contract that the service member . . . has with the government."

In considering a resumption of the draft, perhaps the words of Senator James Webb, which he wrote in 1980 (after his decorated service in Vietnam and before becoming Ronald Reagan's navy secretary), are especially worth recalling: "It is fundamentally wrong—and cowardly—in a democratic society to claim that those who stand between us and a potential enemy should be risking their lives merely because they are 'following the marketplace.' . . . Our greatest need is . . . to stop being afraid to ask the men of Harvard to stand alongside the men of Harlem, same uniform, same obligations, same country."

*

So far this chapter has concentrated on matters that relate to individual behavior, or to policies that aim at dealing with issues at the individual level. But the social character of the military extends beyond this to institutional matters. No discussion of social change in the U.S. military would be complete without a careful reconsideration of its overarching purpose. For much of our history, the military's reason for being has centered on self-defense. At the dawn of the Republic, this defense was provided primarily by the army against Native American raiders who preyed on settlers living on the rapidly expanding frontier. The navy aimed at securing seaborne commerce against blockade or seizure by other states' navies, and from attacks by commerce raiders like the Barbary pirates.

Throughout the nineteenth century, the U.S. military remained quite small, still limited mostly to actions against Native American tribes (but increasingly offensive in nature), with two important exceptions that saw us pitted against foreign adversaries, in each of which American territorial ambitions figured prominently. The first was a conflict with Britain (1812–1815) that had quite mixed results, including a failed invasion of Canada and a peace settlement that served for the most part to shore up the status quo ante. The second was a war with Mexico (1846–1848), where success in battle greatly expanded U.S. southwestern and Pacific Coast frontiers.

But by far the bloodiest conflict in American history, the Civil War, was also fought during this period. And while well over a million troops volunteered or were drafted to fight in that war, almost all were demobilized within just a few years of the final surrender of Confederate forces. The same was not true for the navy which, having built itself up in order to blockade the South during the war, remained a substantial service thereafter. This had been foreshadowed by the navy's role in transporting a military expedition to Mexico in the 1840s and by the use of a naval show of force in a coercive diplomatic effort to open Japan to American trade in the 1850s.

Still, the overarching purpose of the American military remained self-defense until the closing of the frontier in 1890. Thereafter our gaze shifted outward, and soon we fought a war with Spain (1898), ostensibly to put an end to its abusive rule of Cuba—the first hint of an emerging humanitarian agenda amidst territorial ambitions. This war ended with the United States in possession of a number of Spanish holdings, including the Philippine Islands, where a bitter insurgency erupted and some hard lessons of irregular warfare were learned and relearned by American troops.

During operations in the Philippines, the Boxer Rebellion erupted in China, and American troops soon joined a coalition of colonial powers in putting down this early "peoples' liberation" movement. Even with these two interventions, the U.S. Army and the Marine Corps remained small in size, though the navy continued to grow. The main point, though, is that this was the period in which a larger sense of social purpose—

making a better world via the use of force—was added to self-defense among the U.S. military's reasons for being.

This growing missionary zeal—one leading American historian describes our country as becoming a "crusader state"—was on full display as the twentieth century unfolded, beginning with intervention in the last two years of World War I in Europe (1917–1918); quickly followed by a disastrous military intervention against the infant Soviet Union; and continuing with our contribution to the defeat of fascism in World War II, a conflict we joined fully only in the wake of the December 1941 attack on Pearl Harbor. From a strictly military institutional perspective, the main difference between the world wars was that after the first the army was almost completely demobilized, while far greater numbers of troops were kept in uniform after the second.

For its part, the navy continued to maintain its size: demobilizing ships was more difficult, and security at sea was considered an ongoing, if not to say growing, concern. This was also a period in which airpower rose to prominence, and arguments similar to those advanced by naval advocates were used to keep a sizable standing air force. These years also featured a sharpening of American foreign policy, from the general notion of wanting to do good in the world to the more specific goal, first articulated by President Woodrow Wilson, of spreading democracy to all who wished to embrace this form of government.

In the wake of the world wars came the sustained challenge posed by communism, and a wide-ranging cold war for influence and control was soon being waged throughout the world, with Korea and Vietnam standing out as the two major conflagrations that drew in U.S. forces. The cold war lasted for forty years (1949–1989) and saw the American military evolve into its modern form as a large, standing force, ready to engage the enemy wherever the new "great game" demanded, on land, at sea, or in the air: from low-intensity proxy wars to the possibility of a major direct clash of armored forces in Central Europe, and on to notions of nuclear exchanges in which tens of millions of innocent noncombatants were deliberately held hostage in the deterrent stalemate known as "mutual assured destruction."

The practical threat to the American homeland was at best minimal during the cold war years, given the ultimate deterrent power of both sides' nuclear arsenals. But a broader vision of self-defense, rather than Wilsonian notions of spreading democracy or generally doing good in the world, nevertheless began to guide thinking about the purpose of American power. This hard-nosed extension of a self-interest-based national security strategy encouraged American leaders to enter into some uncomfortable alliances with dictators whose only merit was that they too professed an antipathy toward communism. American ideals, it seemed, gave way to a steely pragmatism.

Late in the cold war, however, in the 1980s, President Ronald Reagan began seriously to rekindle the notion of spreading democracy in the world—though for the most part he left the U.S. military out of this equation. The Reagan Doctrine that has come down to us specified that our purpose in the world was to help others free themselves, not to liberate them by direct force of American arms. For Reagan, the U.S. military's fundamental uses were to be limited for the most part to self-defense. His brief, problematic incursions into humanitarian realms were in Lebanon and Grenada in 1983, his only ventures into the murky waters of "regime change." In Lebanon, Reagan saw how ill-suited the U.S. military was to intervention and attempted peacemaking in someone else's civil war. In Grenada a clumsy victory of sorts was achieved, but the outsized costs and minimal returns diminished Reagan's appetite for such ventures. These interventions persuaded him to consider a broadly construed vision of self-defense.

Instead of pursuing humanitarian undertakings, Reagan emphasized investing heavily in rebuilding and modernizing the military, especially improving both the quantity and quality of precision-guided munitions that could be used at long range with high accuracy. The goal was to ensure that the U.S. armed forces would have all they needed—and more—to deal with any Soviet invasion of Europe by conventional means, without having to resort to the first use of nuclear weapons.

With the fall of the Berlin Wall in 1989 and the subsequent dissolution of the Soviet Union itself, Reagan's immediate successor, George H. W. Bush, crafted a hazy vision of a "new world order" in which the American military would serve to prevent the rise of any new threat (a foreshadowing of his son's doctrine of preemption?)* by applying preponderant U.S. military power—what Colin Powell would elucidate as a doctrine of "overwhelming force." The elder Bush soon had opportunities to practice democratic regime change (in Panama in 1989) and the imposition of international order (in the Persian Gulf region in 1990–1991). Both undertakings proved successful, but the American public, which had gone along with Operation Desert Storm against Saddam Hussein, proved reluctant to embrace the elder Bush's vision of a new world order, particularly if it meant using force to prevent the rise of other great powers. So once again the search for a new social purpose for our very large standing military forces grew complicated.

As the elder Bush was leaving office, the notion of using the American military in humanitarian fashion sprang to life once again, in this instance in Somalia, where tribal warlords were desolating their land and people. The rescue effort was neatly handed off in January 1993 to the incoming new president, Bill Clinton, who for the most part kept to his predecessor's

---

*Technically, the younger Bush has misused the term "preemption," which refers specifically to launching a spoiling attack in the face of an enemy's imminent attack. The notion of precluding the rise of another power, or striking at a threat before it grows too large, falls into the category of "preventive warfare." Preemption may be consistent with notions of self-defense; preventive war is harder to view as defensive.

course—though he too soon stumbled by adding to it an element of regime change. Clinton quickly found, as Reagan had in Lebanon and the younger Bush would in Iraq, that trying to play peacemaker between enraged parties in a civil war is a fraught business.

In the wake of an intense, bloody firefight between local militias and American units in Mogadishu in October 1993, U.S. forces were withdrawn from Somalia. The following year they would do nothing when nearly a million Rwandan Tutsis were hacked or shot to death by murderous armed bands of thugs. That same year, however, in a successful regime change in Haiti, the U.S. military played both a coercive diplomatic role in encouraging the dictator Raoul Cedras to flee, and helped, if only temporarily, to stabilize the small, impoverished nation during its transition to a kind of democracy.

Clinton's aversion to using force in humanitarian ways was on full display throughout the remainder of the 1990s, as the latter-day Balkan wars saw hundreds of thousands of Muslims killed in campaigns of "ethnic cleansing." When U.S. forces were finally employed, in conjunction with NATO allies, they were almost completely restricted to air strikes: the seventy-eight-day Kosovo War in 1999 was perhaps history's only case of a conflict conducted by one side entirely from the air.

Bill Clinton thus faced a serious question about the place and purpose of the U.S. military. His early reverse in Somalia had convinced him to refrain as much as possible from humanitarian interventions. And he was well aware that the American public had clearly expressed its doubts about the notion of using the armed forces to preempt or prevent new challenges to a U.S.-led new world order. Further, with the dissolution of the Soviet Union, Clinton had a hard time seeing a need to expand our capacities for self-defense, or even maintain those we had. And the rise of Muslim militants was a threat that did not require large field armies to counter. So Clinton settled for a rhetorical stance in favor of "democratic enlargement"—basically his version of the Reagan Doctrine—and complemented it by reducing military manpower by roughly a third, from about 2.1 million to 1.4 million service members. Still, the social purpose of the American military remained unclear.

This was the situation when George W. Bush took office in January 2001. His basic thrust in military matters was to continue to seek the kinds of efficiencies that Clinton had pursued, and to reject the humanitarian and nation-building goals that had fallen into disfavor with his predecessor. For the younger Bush and his hard-charging secretary of defense, Donald Rumsfeld, this policy took the form of seeking a "military transformation" designed to create nimbler, better-networked armed services. From the outset this goal was opposed by most senior military leaders—and still is today. But in the wake of the attacks on America in September 2001, all sense of seeking an efficiency-based, minimalist equilibrium in military affairs was lost, replaced with a vastly expanded sense of what appropriate mission profiles and social purposes might be.

Briefly, the response to terrorism provided an unusual opportunity to redefine self-defense (for example, see the Bush doctrine of preventive war) and to fold humanitarian and nation-building initiatives into the overall scheme of defeating terror by spreading democracy. But each of these three stated goals—self-defense, humanitarian relief, and nation-building—was undermined by the American invasion of Iraq, which appeared to the world to be offensive, not an act of self-defense. Further, the terrible suffering of Iraqis in the years after the invasion, at the hands of brutal insurgents—only a small fraction of whom were affiliated with al Qaeda—has made a mockery of American humanitarian intent. And the feebleness of the U.S.-supported, Iraqi-elected government exposed the fragility of the nation-building effort—just as continued American support for friendly authoritarians (such as the governing regimes in Pakistan, Saudi Arabia, and Egypt) exposed the inconsistent pursuit of the beloved "democracy project." In short, the social purpose of the military, as it has been traditionally understood over the course of American history, has come unglued as the nation's foreign policy has unraveled over the past five years.

It is time to rethink the U.S. military's social purpose as being driven principally by self-defense. There is no great existential threat to the United States, as was posed by the Soviet Union during the cold war. The People's Republic of China, a favorite future villain among many in the Pentagon, is many decades from mounting anything like a serious threat. The matter is further complicated by the fact that Sino-American trade is immense, with Beijing running a steady trade surplus of epic proportions. It's hard to see how a bitter war might be allowed to get in the way of this kind of economic benefit. As to terror networks, their numbers are so small and their ability to mount offensive strikes so limited that countering them need not require huge expenditures. No, institutional identity and a base military budget well over $1.5 billion per day cannot be based strictly on notions of self-defense.

It seems clear that the military's social purpose must move decisively in the direction of humanitarian assistance. Given the problematic nature of nation-building, and our inconsistency in applying the spread of democratic rule, these versions of humanitarianism will have to be jettisoned. But this still leaves the objective that lies at the heart of any vision of the humane use of force: saving lives. The U.S. military is highly advanced and able to move swiftly to any location in the world. What better force could be employed to deal with the catastrophes and conflicts that place millions of lives in peril? Given that the United States is a signatory of the 1948 Genocide Convention, we have, for the past sixty years, been obligated under international law to engage in military interventions for just such purposes.

There could not be a better time to begin living up to this responsibility. The world is filled with failing states, and few countries are ethnically homogeneous enough to be thought of as unitary "nations." Ethnic and religious hatreds abound, as can be seen most recently in both Iraq and Darfur. Territory and natural resources have continued to spark deadly conflicts, as in the case of diamonds, which did so much to catalyze the Congo War a decade ago, quickly leading to the deaths of nearly four million people, most of them innocent noncombatants. In the world's civil wars, defeat for one side can easily lead to the slaughter of those who surrender or who are no longer protected by their own forces.

This situation is a continuation of a deadly trend toward the increasing lethality of war throughout most of the world that has been going on for nearly two centuries. The trend began with the Taiping Rebellion in China (1850–1864), a conflagration ignited by a curious mix of religious zealotry and anti-colonial sentiment, which saw perhaps as many as thirty to forty million dead. Throughout the rest of the nineteenth century only one other conflict saw as many as a million dead: the Lopez War (1865–1870), in which more than three-fourths of Paraguayan males of military age were killed—all in a hopeless struggle against Argentina, Brazil, and Uruguay.

But in the first half of the twentieth century the pace quickened, with four conflicts surpassing the million-death level: the world wars and the Spanish and Chinese civil wars.* In the six decades since, "big kill" wars have proliferated, often in countries where the losses amounted to substantial proportions of the total national populations. There have been at least ten such conflicts since 1950, fought in Korea, Vietnam, Cambodia, Ethiopia, Sudan (the non-Darfur civil war, running since the 1960s), Mozambique, Biafra, Afghanistan (during the 1980s Soviet occupation), Rwanda, and the Congo. By official counts

---

*Some millions died in the forced collectivization of the Ukraine, and so one might think of including it—not because it was an actual "war" but because of the sheer scale of human suffering.

the Iran-Iraq War (1980–1988) did not produce more than a million dead, but the reality is murky, and this conflict may also be in the "club."

There is a crying need to protect the weak and the imperiled, and even a modicum of U.S. force could do great good. How much American firepower would be needed to hold off a Sudanese *janjaweed* raid on a Darfurian refugee camp? These terrorists have already killed about 300,000 innocents; there is no need to wait for their bloody tally to reach a million. And how hard would it have been to deploy small fire teams to stop Rwandan genocide in its tracks in 1994? On Rwanda, Bill Clinton has had second thoughts, noting that allowing the massacres there was his "greatest regret." With good reason. If we are willing to think in terms of stopping the slaughter of innocents, even in places where the numbers of dead are unlikely to reach the millions, we can do great good with even smaller detachments of our skilled service members.

In short, there is much good to be done in the world, and the U.S. military is uniquely positioned to do it. Engaging in these sorts of interventions would also habituate our forces to working in small, networked teams, to coordinating with allied militaries and nongovernmental organizations, and to making maximum tactical use of the swift movement of information, heading off attacks and tracking down the malefactors. This is not about overwhelming force or "shock and awe," or about taking sides in a civil war. It is about relying on basic soldiering skills and having the courage to respond quickly, with minimal mass but maximum purpose. The amount of force required to defend innocent civilians in peril from attack will almost always be relatively small; and a clearly protective rather than offensive posture should in most cases deter local factions from trying to drag us into their feuds.

Such a shift in the social role of the U.S. military offers all of us an opportunity to rekindle a sense that American purpose in the world is tied to being an unmistakable force for good. Spreading democracy, even chasing down terror cells—these goals pale next to the simple, powerful business of saving lives. For all our staggering defense spending, if we cannot bring ourselves to defend helpless innocents, we have truly lost our way.

CHAPTER NINE

Will the Military Embrace Change?

IN HIS landmark 1973 study *The American Way of War,* the historian Russell Weigley observed that our military leaders and the troops under their command have, at least since the Civil War, generally sought to win by annihilating opposing forces. Not by grinding them down by attrition, or by outfoxing them with clever maneuvers, but by destroying them in direct, decisive battle. Weigley saw this pattern emerge as the United States industrialized in the mid-nineteenth century, and repeat itself ever since. It was never more explicit than in the 1950s, when the nuclear doctrine of "massive retaliation" declared our intent to respond to any kind of aggression with an all-out atomic attack. And it was never more conspicuous than in the shift in the 1960s from an emphasis on special forces to the attempt to win with heavy firepower and big units in Vietnam, the conflict nearing its tragic end when Weigley was writing. The pattern he discerned was reaffirmed yet again in the wake of Vietnam, with the rise of the Powell Doctrine that called for the application of "overwhelming force" in any conflict—an attitude, not a strategic concept. This primal urge to annihilate was manifested yet again in recent years with the notion of pursuing victory via "shock and awe" aerial bombing. Viewed from a perspective informed by Weigley's argument, the course of events suggests that reforms to our military have almost always been limited to advancing the latest technologies and specific tactics; our essential strategic approach has remained constant.

Yet innovations even in the tactics of war may spark huge opportunities. An ability to think creatively about tactical engagements may encourage actions that have profound strategic consequences, spurring a fundamental reshaping of military organizations and their battle doctrines. Much historical evidence suggests that this "bottom-up" approach, one that begins with weapons and tactics, has been evident in American military culture—alongside the desire to mount massive attacks—since before the dawn of the Republic. In the Franco-British struggle for mastery in North America, colonial frontiersmen pioneered the practice of "ranging" far and wide in small strike teams. Although George Washington clung to traditional battle doctrines during the American Revolution, hit-and-run raiders in the South, operating in tandem with a small regular force, wore down the British. Later on, when sheer mass was more easily available, different sorts of new practices occasionally emerged—and not always pretty ones. Gen. William Tecumseh Sherman's famous march across Georgia during the Civil War was not undertaken by serried ranks of closely massed, well-ordered soldiers but by countless small, anarchic bands of "freebooters" swarming across a sixty-mile-wide swath of the state. Similarly innovative (and often just as ethically questionable) approaches may be seen in the "plains wars" against Native American tribes—who were themselves masterful irregular fighters—and in a wide range of colonial interventions in the late nineteenth and early twentieth centuries, ranging from the Philippines to Central America and the Caribbean. An aptitude for irregular warfare has been part of our military's DNA for a long time, and has co-existed, more and more uneasily, with our penchant for heavy hitting power.

Aside from our occasional receptiveness to unusual military practices, externally imposed constraints have sometimes conspired to foster great changes in our way of war. In naval affairs, for example, the attack on Pearl Harbor in 1941 put seven of our battleships—the heart of the Pacific Fleet—out of commission, forcing the navy to rely heavily on aircraft carrier operations. This turned out to be fortuitous, as the effective range of the best of our naval guns was only twenty-odd miles, while the dive- and torpedo-bomber aircraft of the day had an attacking radius ten times that of battleships. Thus we achieved a staggering increase in "reach." In the Battle of the Coral Sea five months after Pearl Harbor, conducted primarily with carriers on both sides, for the first time in history neither fleet saw the other. And at Midway the following month, a handful of aircraft carriers defeated the much larger Imperial Japanese Combined Fleet by sinking its carriers, changing the whole course of the Pacific War in a few minutes of furious aerial assaults.

Without air cover, surface fleets could no longer operate with any hope of victory. And so the U.S. Navy, which began World War II with just seven aircraft carriers—but seventeen battleships—soon cut production of the battleships and increased the pace of building flattops. At war's end it had made one hundred new carriers and launched just eight new battleships. This was a real technology-driven transformation, but it was catalyzed by the initial disaster at Pearl Harbor. If the navy had not lost most of them at Pearl, the battleships' preeminence at sea would likely have persisted—as it did for the Japanese, whose trust in the big ships was shattered only after their shocking defeat at Midway. Japan's strategic dilemma, however, lay beyond resolution, as the empire's production capacity could not compete in a new arms race to build aircraft carriers. So the Imperial Japanese Navy was relegated almost completely to a defensive strategy in the wake of Midway, dooming their cause a scant six months after achieving their remarkable *coup de main* at Pearl Harbor. The Americans had seen and seized an opportunity to transform the conduct of naval warfare by emphasizing *airpower* at sea. This was a true conceptual coup, but one that we have seldom matched in other aspects of our military affairs ever since.

*

Whether the product of having an inherent turn of mind toward irregular land warfare, or in response to rapidly shifting circumstances at sea, the U.S. military has sometimes been capable of making radical changes. Certainly the campaign against the Taliban and al Qaeda waged during the waning months of 2001 in Afghanistan is an example of this kind of strategic suppleness. In this instance small teams of American special forces, working with a few thousand indigenous allies—who were themselves greatly outnumbered by their opponents— won a remarkable series of engagements that hinted at the potential of the kind of nimble, networked military operations that Donald Rumsfeld and other reformers had envisioned. The result was enabled not by overwhelming force but rather by the skillful application of advanced information technology. Smart, precise employment of airpower was further enhanced by the introduction of innovative organizational forms based on networks, and a new battle doctrine employing "swarm tactics." Attack aircraft and small ground units were all linked via the "Tactical Web Page," which allowed them to move information to each other directly, without it having first to go up or down command "stovepipes." Targets were identified and struck swiftly, in a remarkable case of "waging war by minutes."

Despite the hidebound tradition of the U.S. military, the historical record is replete with evidence to suggest that major change has sometimes been embraced and even sustained. But Weigley was correct in seeing the debacle in Vietnam—in particular, the fatal shift to the "big-unit" war—as having grown out of a traditionalist mind-set that has become ever more dominant in American strategic thought. The "war on terror" has followed a somewhat similar—if more geographically extensive—path, with the successful small units employed in Afghanistan in 2001 giving way to a larger (and somewhat less successful) occupation force there, and to an even bigger conventional invasion force that was set loose upon Iraq in 2003, where massive strategic aerial bombing rounded out the Pentagon's preferred approach to the war. There was initially no way to get to Afghanistan quickly with large ground forces, so out of necessity we made do with small numbers of troops and a clever concept of operations. But in Iraq we had the fatal luxury of time: about six months to mass our forces. This led to a reassertion of conventional warfare and a concomitant neglect of the need to fight in a dispersed and highly networked manner against the terror networks.

Will we continue to ride the decaying orbit of the big-unit approach, as was done until nearly the end in Vietnam? Or will we begin to make the quantum shifts that are implied by the recent changes wrought in warfare? It is tempting, and all too comfortable, to say that the U.S. military bureaucracy will close ranks and quietly put an end to any thought of transformation. The debacle in Iraq has already been used to discredit Rumsfeld further and to argue that only a massive conventional invasion and occupation would have won through there. The fact that more than half a million troops on the ground, incessant aerial bombardment, and, ultimately, a tight naval blockade all failed to achieve victory in Vietnam will not be recalled as a cautionary analogy.

On top of these considerations, traditionalists are likely to contend that the reemergence of big, conventionally armed threats to our security and strategic interests will require us to retain a capacity for waging "good-old-fashioned war." They will point, with some justification, to the million-man North Korean army, poised to pounce in a way that makes a grim mockery of the so-called demilitarized zone between North and South. They will point to the possible conflict looming over Taiwan, which we may feel honor-bound to defend in the event of a mainland Chinese invasion. Such a war would be a major one. And they will argue that even a conflict with Iran would entail massive firepower and huge force requirements.

In sum, this perspective suggests that we must not become so distracted by demands of the struggle against al Qaeda that we fail to maintain a military capable of dealing with far more serious threats. Of course this point of view is good for the defense industry and intellectually reassuring to those who prefer a stable status quo to a future in which conflict may be utterly strange. But this approach will continue our primary focus on conventional war-fighting and prevent us from learning how to "fight the network" in our irregular wars; and it will guarantee that we remain wedded to a set of military tools and practices that are becoming ever more vulnerable to the innovations of opposing forces.

As I have argued throughout this book, there is good reason to believe that highly networked U.S. forces can defeat al Qaeda *and* make mincemeat of an old-style conventional opponent. While the need for what the military historian Bevin Alexander calls "broad preparation" for all types of wars is sensible, this does not demand two different kinds of forces. One new-style military can work in both arenas, in an efficient form of broad preparation. A bifurcated military, fatally divided between the two basic forms of war, will prove unable to prevail in either conventional or irregular conflicts.

It grows more evident each day that warfare has been moving into a new realm where very small combat formations can achieve high levels of destruction and disruption. The only question is whether we will explore this new landscape with new kinds of forces and weapons, or march our twentieth-century military off into a twenty-first-century wilderness, unchanged and unassisted. An interesting historical analogy here is the Anglo-American experience in the French and Indian

War (1754–1763). Early on, a British general named Braddock went off into the woods with a traditional massed army that was soon routed and very nearly massacred by an irregular force of Frenchmen and Native Americans. George Washington was one of Braddock's key aides in that campaign, yet somehow this experience never convinced Washington of the need to shift from conventional tactics and doctrine.

More than two centuries later, a new generation of Braddocks marched off to the jungles of Vietnam. Even in the wake of disaster there, they found little reason to reshape the military along lines that would improve its ability to wage irregular wars. Instead they refocused on the problems of conventional conflict that applied to defending Europe from the threat of an armored assault by Russian tanks. Such an attack never materialized. But, fortuitously for the traditionalists, just as the old Soviet Union was dissolving, a new conventional threat emerged in the form of Saddam Hussein. The gift he gave was his willingness to deploy hundreds of thousands of troops in open terrain suitable for tanks, and to do so while providing them no air cover. The result was a near slaughter of Iraq's army in 1991, a lopsided victory for the U.S. military that led the first President Bush to declare that the demons of Vietnam had been "exorcised."

Perhaps so. But a decade later these ghosts came back in the form of a network-styled irregular war that the Pentagon would soon try—with very mixed results—to force-fit into a conventional mold. While there have been hopeful signs of flexibility that mitigate the relentless drumbeat of traditionalism, there remains a palpable tension between those who defend the status quo and those determined to upend it. This divide is nowhere more apparent than in the contrast between the campaigns in Afghanistan and Iraq—the strategic yin and yang of our time—and their impact on the thinking of the commander-in-chief.

*

As dark as the overall picture sometimes seems to those of us who believe that major reforms to American military tactics, doctrine, organizational structure, and technology investments are needed now, there have been promising developments as well, most of them coming from Afghanistan. Beyond the initial campaign there in the fall of 2001, the troops have become accustomed to fighting in small units sprinkled liberally along the border with Pakistan. Although they have often been heavily outnumbered and outgunned by the insurgents, they have continually engaged the Taliban with great tactical success in firefights. The very smallness of our units of maneuver has often lured the Taliban into ill-advised attacks.

Our forces—and, increasingly, those of our allies—have won out again and again in these vicious firefights because they are superior at basic soldierly skills and employ innovative battle tactics. The combination of better muzzle discipline and clever new concepts of operations has proved to be a powerful mix. Allied counterinsurgent forces may never be able to deny the Taliban its haven across the border, because of political concerns that American or NATO military incursions into the tribal zone of Waziristan might spark an Islamist social revolution in Pakistan. But this limitation doesn't prevent our forces from routinely achieving highly favorable exchange ratios (the number of enemy killed in action divided by our own combat deaths)—in excess of 100 to 1—in firefights against Taliban formations. The fact that the overall numbers of American and NATO forces deployed to this theater have remained but a small fraction of the force sent to Iraq suggests the clear value of the strategy in Afghanistan.*

---

*About half of the international security assistance forces in Afghanistan are Americans—some under NATO command, some under the direct control of the U.S. Central Command. About four times as many troops have been deployed In Iraq, where the non-American coalition elements are much thinner, amounting to fewer than 10 percent of the occupation force.

The "Afghan lesson" has, for the most part, not been ab-
sorbed by those responsible for prosecuting the campaign in
Iraq. At the outset, in the months before the March 2003 invasion, the traditionalists wanted to invade Iraq with almost as
many U.S. troops as were used in Operation Desert Storm
(about 500,000). They thought in terms of massive armored pincer movements and a relentless, round-the-clock aerial bombing campaign. Opposing them were a small but significant
minority of reform-minded soldiers and civilian strategists—
some of whom opposed the very idea of war with Iraq but nevertheless worked on plans for the invasion—who argued that an
"Afghan approach" was preferable.

This would have consisted of just a few tens of thousands of
soldiers, a few hundred of them working with Kurdish *pesh
merga* fighters to liberate the northern part of the country. The
Shi'a would have been embraced in the south, again with small
forces, so that the liberation would have been conducted
mostly by the Iraqis themselves. Aerial bombing was to be generally limited to the close support of ground units. As to Iraq's
regular military, it was assumed that most of it would melt
away; so under this concept of operations emphasis was placed
on trying to "turn" these forces against Saddam via influence
operations—much as a large portion of the Italian army
switched sides against Mussolini and the Germans during
World War II.

Donald Rumsfeld initially favored an "Afghan approach."
But he faced sharp opposition from most of the Pentagon and
felt compelled to compromise. He did, however, reduce the expeditionary force to under 200,000, and did allow for an innovative approach in the north—where this was the only realistic
option, given that Turkey had prevented the United States from
staging an invasion from its territory. But Rumsfeld allowed a
major conventional armored campaign to be mounted from the
south, and unleashed a highly destructive air campaign that
caused much of the damage that has so greatly complicated
reconstruction efforts in Iraq. For the most part the Afghan

model was not followed, and the traditionalists won out. They remained dominant thereafter, calling for more and more U.S. troops as the principal means of coping with a relative handful of insurgents who were, for the most part, limited to sniping and setting booby traps. The few larger operations they tried failed miserably.

Ultimately the traditionalists were able to persuade President Bush to send a "surge" of some 20,000-plus troops to Iraq early in 2007—in addition to the 140,000 still there—which did little to tamp down the violence. But this was accompanied by a glimmer of innovation: a few American forces moved out of their city-sized operating bases, from which it had often taken them an hour to get to the scene of an attack, and redeployed to several dozen small outposts around Baghdad. From there the relatively tiny detachments were in position to respond in minutes to any violence—and wherever they were, these outposts deterred Iraqi death squads, and their small garrisons used skillful influence operations to enlist the support of local Iraqi tribal leaders in the fight against al Qaeda. Near the end of 2007, most U.S. forces remained laagered in on super-sized bases throughout the country; so not enough was done to reduce the carnage in what had become an Iraqi civil war. But even at this late date, a more pronounced shift toward the "outpost-and-outreach" concept might have salvaged the campaign.

More than anything else, fumbles in Iraq destroyed Rumsfeld's last, waning opportunity to effect a true military transformation on his watch. Absent the debacle there, he could have basked in the glow of success in Afghanistan, and might even have had sufficient political capital to carry through the radical changes that so dominated his agenda. But with the quagmire in Iraq he gave the traditionalists the means to pillory him and his program of reform. His compromise with the "big unit" lobby before the invasion both undermined his chances for success in Iraq and gave his opponents the ammunition they needed to claim that the invasion had failed because there were too few "boots on the ground." In this way the

Pentagon bureaucracy was able to turn the whole matter on its head, blaming Rumsfeld for a failure that was largely the result of their own insistence on fitting a conventional war model to a campaign that, to many of us, required a very different approach.

George W. Bush has shown little personal interest in the new ideas that might reform our military and perhaps retrieve the situation in Iraq. Instead his instinct was to consider creating a position of "war czar," and then to appoint one, army Lt. Gen. Douglas E. Lute, only after several distinguished retired officers had turned down the offer. This was a tacit admission, it seems, of President Bush's discomfort in becoming more directly involved with the strategic aspects of his duties as commander-in-chief.

How unlike Abraham Lincoln, who took such an active role in shaping Union strategy during the Civil War. Lincoln pushed for a "cordon offensive," to be conducted by a host of relatively small Union armies that were to be distributed around the Confederate states. He believed that the new transportation technology, railroads, could move substantial numbers of troops rapidly over great distances, allowing for multiple offensives against the outnumbered Confederate forces. Careful coordination of these far-flung efforts would be possible via the communications technology of the day, the telegraph. Despite stiff opposition from almost all his generals, who simply wanted to mass most of their troops at one "decisive point" and defeat the rebels there, Lincoln persisted in his quest for a different approach—and had no compunction about sacking recalcitrant generals. He prevailed, ultimately, because of his faith in the right idea and because he recognized that the favored Napoleonic concept of massing for a single decisive blow had repeatedly failed for both Union and Rebel generals. Lincoln's greatness as a strategist derived from his deep belief in the formative power of ideas, and his ability to identify the good and discard the bad. Further, he understood that his role as commander-in-chief included the responsibility to find and empower those military leaders—like Grant, Farragut, Sheridan, and Sherman—who could carry out his vision.

The Lincoln analogy reaffirms the importance of the commander-in-chief's role. To all those who believe that the Pentagon is simply too large and stodgy to be moved, I say, "Look at Lincoln." He faced stern resistance from the military and even from members of his own cabinet. Yet he won out. The Pentagon bureaucracy is much larger now, but the ranks of senior decision-makers in uniform are not much more numerous than during the Civil War, and the civilian bureaucracy in the Pentagon is replete with presidential appointees who are presumably loyal to the chief executive.

We need right now to identify and articulate ideas about new strategies and military reforms that can take us in the right direction—safely through a twenty-first century in which military affairs are being fundamentally reshaped by technological leaps, the rise of powerful networks, and the upending of most of the traditional principles of war. In the next section I outline a simple framework for structuring our thoughts around the set of ideas advanced in this book.

*

We have lost our national strategic consensus. Throughout the cold war, most Americans and their leaders agreed that our defense policy would be guided by the twin goals of deterring nuclear conflict and containing the spread of Soviet control or influence. There were occasional debates, sometimes sharp ones, over matters like nuclear weapons buildups and the war in Vietnam. But few seriously questioned these two goals. Containment and deterrence made up our "creed."

After the dissolution of the Soviet Union we were left with a large defense establishment that had little to do, at least in terms of the tasks that had occupied it for forty years. Our presidents began to articulate new visions to guide our purpose in the world: George H. W. Bush's "new world order"; Bill Clinton's new take on Ronald Reagan's ideas about spreading democracy by encouraging others to free themselves (though Clinton also showed a willingness to use force in coercive diplomatic ways, in Haiti and later the Balkans); George W. Bush's volatile strategic cocktail to both right the world system *and* spread democracy, if necessary through preventive war. With none of these worldviews were Americans entirely happy.

So the cold war consensus has not yet been rekindled. As a result, U.S. defense policy has been as confused as the American people and their elected leaders. Earlier I suggested an overarching purpose—to protect innocents at risk of genocide—that could serve as a new social construct around which to restructure the U.S. military in the twenty-first century. Noninterventionist sentiment could be mitigated by sharply limiting our involvements to those situations where we already have a legal obligation (under the 1948 Genocide Convention) to prevent mass murder. Beyond this finite humanitarian goal, which need not extend to nation-building or other quixotic schemes, the U.S. military would of course still provide us an incomparable capacity for self-defense in the face of overt aggression. An anti-genocide mission would help us rebuild a national consensus on strategic and military affairs while at the same time foster innovation. For to carry out such tasks our military would have to be able to deploy fast and far, in small numbers but in ways highly networked with others on or nearer the scene. And in the course of these kinds of operations, we would be retooling an instrument of national power— the U.S. military—to become, finally, effective in fighting terrorist networks too. As an added bonus, in its new form our military would grow even deadlier in its ability to defeat old-style traditional adversaries, further enhancing our self-defense capabilities.

In this way, by beginning with a determination to do good, we would end up doing well. The new consensus that must be forged should extend not only to the specific missions of the armed forces but to the manner in which they operate. In this area of "practices" there is also a great need to rebuild a broad national agreement. Over the past several years, considerable social anger and fear have begun to wear down the ethical health of our military. Because we suffered on 9/11, it seems that we have grown less sensitive to the suffering of others. Thus the cruel, inhumane, and degrading treatment of enemy combatants, evident in abuses at Abu Ghraib and elsewhere, has all too often been shrugged off. And the deaths of civilians as a result of our application of military "shock and awe"— which have run into many tens of thousands in Iraq alone— have been minimized by using the cool euphemism "collateral damage." Such abuses must stop. They are not only wrong but contrary to our character. And as a practical matter, brutality and bombing have not worked. They have only inflamed the re- sistance to our power and our policies, and reduced American influence in the world.

In addition to a new mission and a strict adherence to ethi- cal operations, the third important element in building a new national consensus is to spend less on the military. Without So- viet tank divisions, without a major Chinese threat, no external danger justifies our spending more than $1.75 billion per day on defense, as we now do. Terror networks are too small to war- rant grand expenditures; defeating them requires new opera- tional concepts rather than new weapons systems. Regional states like Iran and North Korea could also be handily defeated in battle with the kind of nimble, networked forces described in earlier chapters.

In every other era in American history when the external threat level has declined, so has defense spending. Why not now once again? Bill Clinton showed good instincts in this area, but his "peace dividend" proved illusory. Yes, the size of the total force was reduced by one-third during his presidency; but there was little or no organizational redesign or doctrinal innovation. Fewer troops were asked to continue doing the same things in the same old ways, putting greater strains—in operating tempo and distant deployments—upon them. Few of the Pentagon's costly weapons procurement programs were curtailed in the 1990s, so reductions in the defense budget were minimal at best. Thus we are still waiting for the changes implied by the end of the cold war almost twenty years ago. Considering the relatively minor external threats we have faced since then, we should now be asking ourselves how to go about the business of reducing defense spending sharply while retaining the ability to deal with terror networks and rogue states. There are several ways to do this.

One of the most important economizing initiatives would be to cut the size of the Marine Corps, putting an end to its standing as a "second army." The Marine Corps's federal mandate is to assist in the prosecution of naval campaigns. This includes, of course, the waging of amphibious warfare, which in the future might be pursued against either traditional nation-state foes or in a raiding fashion against terror networks. But neither of these types of missions requires a standing force of Marines at the current level in excess of 175,000. Indeed, just 30,000 Marines—about 10,000 in each of their statutorily authorized three divisions—would be quite enough for our needs. For more than two centuries, 10,000 has been a fairly steady number of troops for a division, even when new types of sub-units within divisions (like the squads and platoons that became so prevalent in the twentieth century) have arisen. Thirty thousand Marines in an active force would be more than sufficient for chasing terrorists or conducting the kind of "infiltration and exploitation" operations that are likely to be a large part of the future of amphibious warfare—and which are already being contemplated by the Marine Special Operations Command

and the Corps's emerging emphasis on "networked small-unit operations." It would also make sense to reduce the size of the Marine air component proportionate to the cuts made in the ground forces. The Marines could move to maintaining a somewhat larger force of reserves, to hedge against even the far-fetched possibility of a return to World War II–style conflicts.

For its part, the army can afford to cut its active force to about 100,000, down from the roughly 500,000 that serve today. This number would allow full manning of the existing ten divisions, with three brigades of about 2,500 soldiers each (slightly fewer than the number now in brigades). The other fourth of the soldiers in each division would serve, as is the case currently, in support functions. Of course the army could decide to organize around something other than the division, in which case that 100,000 number could fill out a far larger number of "units of action" (former army chief of staff Peter Schoomaker's preferred phrasing). Also, as noted earlier, the Eighty-second Airborne Division might simply go away, as the need for a whole division of parachutists seems to have diminished greatly since World War II, the last time we engaged in division-sized jumps.

As to the active-duty troops being demobilized, many would fit into the reserves, which would grow somewhat in size. This shift would allow large numbers of fine officers to remain more highly engaged in their profession, rather than simply be mustered out as most are because of the lack of higher-level promotion slots under the current system. For those with concerns about the return of old-style conventional warfare, the reserves could keep the flame alive by retaining the army's heavy tanks and artillery. But if the spirit of reform were truly to permeate the whole service, the reserves would equip and train themselves along the lines of the regulars and prepare to fight using more advanced concepts of operations. Either way, this is a system that would work well under the existing all-volunteer program or under a new draft in which, after their initial active service, conscripts would rotate into the reserves for several years. Finally, expansion of reserve components—not only in the army and Marine Corps but in the other services as well— would take some of the economic sting out of overall declines in defense spending. Increased investment in local reserve units would allow defense spending to be targeted at a broad range of local communities throughout the country.

What I suggest for the army and the Marines comes close to and draws much inspiration from former Senator Gary Hart's thoughtful notion of sharply downsizing our standing military and encouraging the cultivation of core competencies in counterterrorism and other irregular warfare missions. The army and the Marines would bear the brunt of these active-personnel reductions; but they would emerge from such a reorganization as the premier information-age fighting forces of the twenty-first century, as able to grapple with a terror network as to engage an old-style national army. Their new suppleness would also alleviate the growing pressure to expand special operations forces—the traditionalists' favored alternative that would allow them to keep most of our existing military intact while cultivating at least some new capacity for networked, small-unit actions.

This is a key concern, because the "grafting on" approach favored by the traditionalists would probably cripple us in the end. Overexpansion of special operations forces would simply water down quality and encourage the units to become more conventional, in the field and administratively. Thirty years ago the defense analyst Eliot Cohen argued compellingly along these lines, noting the value of keeping military elites small— that is, *elite*. He was right then, and his notion is perhaps even more salient today. We must not think in terms of trying to super-size our special operations forces. They should remain small, expert in their professional areas (such as hostage rescues, and training, advising, and fighting alongside friendly indigenous forces), and perhaps serve as what Cohen has called a "laboratory for military doctrine," passing on their best discoveries to the general-purpose forces. For example, the entire army need not be trained to the skill level of the "unconventional warfare"—that is, working with indigenous fighters—of the Green Berets. But large numbers of soldiers should have skills in training and leading friendly local units in far-off settings, as is the case with the army's military transition teams (MITTS). Thus a reformed U.S. military would not be one in which everyone is "special," as in some variant of Garrison Keillor's Lake Wobegon. Rather, it would be one in which many troops, perhaps most, throughout the services would be capable of doing things in ever more special ways. In this manner, ultimately, our capacity for unconventional warfare might be salvaged.

For the navy, the most important shift is in hardware. The super-carriers must be phased out—over a decade or so, not a century—to be replaced by many smaller, swifter vessels. Moving away from carriers and toward something lighter and more networked might actually give the Navy far more vessels than the 270 or so it now has, for about the same amount of money. Its submarine force should be retained, though a reduced need for nuclear ballistic missiles should encourage the conversion of some submarines to covert delivery vessels for SEAL and Marine combat teams. In terms of personnel, the navy too should reduce to roughly 100,000 sailors on active duty. This would still leave it with an average of 100 per vessel* if it were to have as many as 1,000 ships—a fleet goal that Adm. Michael Mullen, as chief of naval operations, elucidated only in the context of counting the fleets of close allies in addition to our own. Headquarters staffs would be sharply reduced, with much of the paperwork handled by reservists during their active-duty periods. For the air defense of surface ships we could rely on the cover provided by short- or vertical-takeoff-and-landing aircraft that

---

*This crew figure is in line with estimates of crew size for the coming generation of "littoral combat ships" (LCS). In a navy comprised of many more, and much smaller, vessels, there will be plenty of sailors to go around.

do not require large carriers. And these could be augmented by mounting smart defensive weapons on all ships, as well as by relying on allied aircraft or even in some instances U.S. Air Force squadrons.

The air force poses an intriguing problem. Among the services it may change least in its "tools"—though the many prospects for using airships should not be underestimated—but shift most in its practices. The strategic-bombardment paradigm simply must go away. A century of failures to break peoples' spirits with bombing should be enough, and our air force should concentrate almost exclusively on the close support of ground forces. The ambition of moving advanced weaponry into space—an outgrowth of the strategic-bombing mind-set—should also be abandoned. Our military would benefit more from the continued use of space assets to support land and naval operations than it would from any new ability to send tungsten "rods from God" hurtling down from space at Mach 10. For the sake of bureaucratic symmetry—and because so much can be done with such numbers—the air force too should reduce active personnel to 100,000. Like the navy and the other services, it could maintain strong reserve forces.

The idea of reducing active duty forces by about three-fourths during wartime is bound to be controversial. But if I have made a persuasive case that developments in military affairs—particularly the rise of networks—have empowered small, dispersed field units at the same time they have imperiled large, massed armies, the merits of such a shift should become apparent. Besides, reductions this sharp have been made several times in our history, in the wake of the Civil War and both world wars. Even at the height of the cold war in the early 1970s, when communism was still on the march and Vietnam was unraveling, the U.S. military's active force fell from 3.5 to 2.1 million, a 40 percent drop. At the end of the cold war, and in the wake of Desert Storm in 1991, the total declined to 1.4 million, a further decline of one-third. Given that the reductions I recommend in the active force have solid historical precedents, and that they can be offset to some extent by reenergizing reserve and Guard units, the opportunities presented by such a shift are more than likely to outweigh the risks.

Most important, force reductions will impel organizational redesign along networked lines. And if the new-style military performs well, change will be consolidated and a true transformation will have been realized. If for some reason effectiveness suffers, there will be time enough to return to the old ways. The risk of engaging in this experimentation now is low, given that our terrorist adversaries could mobilize every operative they have and still scarcely field a single division. The Russian military is in the midst of its own halting process of transformation, and remains a shadow of its cold war self. In Asia, China is decades away from having any real capacity for force projection beyond its borders or home waters, and the large North Korean army is already on the verge of technological obsolescence. Iran has little offensive capacity save for irregular warfare tactics that would not require large U.S. forces to counter. Besides the limited nature of all these potential threats, we also enjoy the continued security afforded by having many well-armed allies and the world's preeminent nuclear arsenal. If ever there were an ideal time for the radical restructuring of our armed forces, this is it.

What about the Pentagon, the world's largest office building? In my view, the networked future of our military has no room for such an emblem of hierarchy. The Pentagon was originally intended only to meet the military's management needs during World War II; the building was to be handed off for other use afterward, with conversion to a hospital or a national archive heading the list of possibilities. It is now long "afterward," high time for this amazing physical plant to be made available to others. By doing this, we would remove an institution that some senior officers believe poses the greatest obstacle to innovative change. The work of Pentagon staffs could be easily distributed to the various combatant commands, which could network together in ways that would move at light speed compared to the Pentagon's own pace of operations. Of all the reforms I have suggested in this book, getting the military out of the Pentagon is the one that would probably do the single greatest amount of good. That five-sided structure is the bastion of hierarchy, of old ways of thinking and acting. The practical and symbolic effects of moving away from it would be profound for our military.

Beyond encouraging a much needed network-building process, closing down the Pentagon—in a planned exodus over a few years—would solve the worst political problems that bedevil American defense policy. First, closure would virtually eliminate the influence of patronage at all levels below the secretariat. Sometimes political appointees have been knowledgeable and competent; all too often they have not. In an era of what appears to be perpetual warfare, it is essential that only those who merit appointment serve. A greatly trimmed defense bureaucracy, the product of the Pentagon's closure, would undoubtedly be accompanied by a rise in the quality of defense management.

Second, bureaucratic political squabbles within the U.S. military would be greatly eased. For example, there has been an assistant secretary for special operations and low-intensity conflict since 1986, but for twenty years not one man who has held the position has been able to wield significant influence. The reason is that the bureaucratic barons in the Pentagon have always sought to marginalize special operations forces in favor of conventional capabilities that require hundreds of billions of dollars to sustain. For its part, the Special Operations Command (SOCOM), located in Tampa, Florida, has preferred a weak assistant secretary so that it can maintain maximum independence. Removing this assistant secretariat—and eliminating much of the overall Pentagon hierarchy and dispersing the rest—would simultaneously empower SOCOM and make it more directly responsive to both the secretary of defense and the president. What holds for special operations applies to most other areas as well.

Diminishing the power of patronage and the effects of military turf fights are both worthy goals. But they pale next to the ultimate prize that would accrue from Pentagon closure: major defense spending cuts. Without the unending full-court press on Congress and the American people maintained by military leaders and their minions in the Pentagon, for whom this is something of a full-time job, it might be possible to think in terms of our government someday spending less on defense than the rest of the world combined. And the irony is that a much less expensive military is also likely to emerge as far more effective and innovative.

*

In the words of Murray Weidenbaum, one of Ronald Reagan's chief economic advisers, the post-cold-war world is one of "small wars and big defense." Weidenbaum was concerned with how a defense establishment geared to great wars and superpower rivalry would function in an era of brushfire insurgencies and other kinds of irregular conflicts. In a tour de force of crisp reasoning and logical analysis, he showed how the United States could move toward a downsized military and, of equal importance, a smaller military-industrial complex. The mechanics required to make the shift he describes are simple and straightforward. More complex is the matter of generating the political will necessary to make such changes. In this book I have argued that a whole new range of technological, organizational, and strategic possibilities lies before us, allowing us to make a fundamental shift toward an information-age military that is smaller, nimbler, and highly networked. Failing to make these changes will place us in the odd position of continuing to spend defense dollars at a frightening pace yet being unable to grapple with our current irregular foes—thus dooming ourselves to fight the next war with an increasingly outmoded set of heavy forces and old ideas.

It would be easy to blame a pork-addicted Congress or an avaricious military-industrial complex for our situation. But both are only symptoms of the military malaise that bedevils our defense community. Yes, members of Congress will always try to benefit their constituents by bringing programs to their states and districts. But our elected representatives have almost always strived—in a consistently bipartisan way—to give the military what it asks for. Defense contractors, though surely driven by the search for profit, are exceptionally—even unhealthily—"customer-oriented," which, according to the great scholar of business innovation, Clayton Christensen, is a key obstacle to creativity. The real problem lies not with Congress or corporations but with the military, whose professional expertise is trusted by both these sets of actors, as well as by the American people and the president. The military has not used its bully pulpit well. Congress, defense contractors, the commander-in-chief, and the public all wait for and rely upon the military's stated judgments about its needs. But these judgments have become far more the result of bureaucratic pulling and hauling than of sharply reasoned debates about the future of conflict. For our country's—and the world's—sake, this state of affairs must change.

Notes

Chapter 1. Stability, Change, and the Art of War

page

6 "with the weapons of the 1950s": Richard Overy, *Why the Allies Won* (New York, 1996), p. 243.

7 "Mobility plus firepower equals attrition": Cited in Michael Maclear, *The Ten Thousand Day War* (New York, 1981), p. 183.

9 "have seen no war": Will and Ariel Durant, *The Lessons of History* (New York, 1968), p. 81.

10 "overwhelmed the naked and trembling legions": Edward Gibbon, *The History of the Decline and Fall of the Roman Empire*, ed. by J. B. Bury (New York, 1946), vol. II, p. 853.

11 "duel between the legion and the phalanx!": Lynn Montross, *War Through the Ages* (New York, 3rd edition 1960), pp. 744–745. Emphasis in the original. On the rise of German small-group infiltration tactics, see Bruce Gudmundsson, *Stormtroop Tactics: Innovation in the German Army, 1914–1918* (Westport, Conn., 1995).

12 the rise of the West: The far-reaching consequences of the Athenian shift to sea power are thoughtfully chronicled in Barry Strauss, *Salamis: The Naval Encounter That Saved Greece—and Western Civilization* (New York, 2004).

12 outbreak of World War I in 1914: On the diffusion of Mahan's ideas, see W. D. Puleston, *Mahan: The Life and Work of Captain Alfred Thayer Mahan, USN* (New Haven, 1939). The best account of the naval arms race between Britain and Germany may be found in Paul Kennedy, *The Rise of the Anglo-German Antagonism* (London, 1980). On Mahan's influence on Japanese strategic thought, see Sadao Asada, *From Mahan to Pearl Harbor* (Annapolis, 2006).

13 "could only cruise in home waters": Alfred von Tirpitz, *My Memoirs* (New York, 1919), vol. I, pp. 179–180.

13 reluctant to risk in battle: On these themes, see Jonathan Steinberg, *Yesterday's Deterrent: Tirpitz and the Birth of the German Battle Fleet* (London, 1965), and Holger Herwig, *"Luxury Fleet": The Imperial German Navy, 1888–1918* (London, 1980).

15 board the enemy vessel: On the *corvus* and other Roman innovations, see William Ledyard Rodgers, *Greek and Roman Naval Warfare* (Annapolis, 1937).

16 an exceptional new keenness: See Michael Roberts, *The Military Revolution* (Oxford, 1956), and his *Essays in Swedish History* (London, 1967).

16 "recruited from the lowest ranks of society": William H. McNeill, *The Pursuit of Power: Technology, Armed Force, and Society Since A.D. 1000* (Chicago, 1982), p. 117.

16 "embed information" in their military organization: This is an important theme in McNeill's work.

16 Britain's New Model Army: See Christopher Hill, *God's Englishman: Oliver Cromwell and the English Revolution* (New York, 1970).

16 "Fighting Instructions": For a good analysis of these developments, see G. J. Marcus, *A Naval History of England*, vol. I, *The Formative Centuries* (Boston, 1961), pp. 348–350.

17 massed, drill-driven armies: See Jean de Bloch, *Is War Now Impossible?* (Boston, 1899).

18 "Our adversary will not stand": Charles Ardant du Picq, *Battle Studies (Etudes sur le combat)*, translated by John N. Greely and Robert C. Cotton (Harrisburg, Pa., 1946), pp. 126–127.

18 overcome even the deadliest fire: For a more detailed analysis of the impact of French military thought during this period, see Azar Gat, *The Development of Military Thought: The Nineteenth Century* (Oxford, 1992). The attractiveness of du Picq's ideas to others may be seen in David Woodward, *Armies of the World, 1854–1914* (New York, 1978).

18 in the face of artillery and machine guns: On this point regarding selective learning in the years before World War I, see Sir Michael Howard's remarkable Oxford lecture, "Men Against Fire," contained in his *The Lessons of History* (New Haven, 1991), pp. 97–112.

19 obliterated the Russian fleet at Tsushima: One of the most insightful accounts of the destruction of the Russian fleet at Tsushima may be found in Richard Hough, *The Fleet That Had to Die* (New York, 1958).

19 strategic thought about aerial bombardment: An outstanding overview of this era is provided by Williamson Murray and Allan R. Millett, eds., *Military Innovation in the Interwar Period* (New York, 1996).

21 roots in irregular warfare: Two seminal studies of guerrilla warfare framed the debate about the efficacy of this mode of conflict. The ar-

gument that guerrillas had the edge, and would continue to triumph, was advanced in Robert Taber's *War of the Flea* (New York, 1970). A dissenting view was well articulated by Lewis Gann in his *Guerrillas in History* (Stanford, 1971), which pointed out that, over the past centuries, guerrillas were often defeated—and could be beaten in the future too.

22   smart weapons guidance packages: For an overview of his remarkable vision, see William Owens and Ed Offley, *Lifting the Fog of War* (New York, 2000).

23   that feature more offensive punch: See George and Meredith Friedman, *The Future of War* (New York, 1996).

23   allocated for defensive purposes: The Friedmans put it this way: "Modern aircraft carriers have between twenty-four and thirty-six strike aircraft on board—more in specialized cases. Some sixty other planes, a cruiser, one or two destroyers, and one or two nuclear attack submarines, along with supply vessels, shore facilities, and so forth, all exist so that the handful of aircraft can each drop eight to twelve tons of ordnance at a time. As threats against the aircraft carrier rise and the cost of keeping it operational soars, its offensive capability will tend toward zero." Ibid., p. 27.

28   militaries have failed to appreciate: Martin van Creveld, *The Transformation of War* (New York, 1991).

Chapter 2. The Once and Future Army

29   muskets that were far less accurate: The mixture of irregular tactics and advanced weaponry used in this confrontation is skillfully depicted in Robert Remini, *The Battle of New Orleans* (New York, 1999), and Winston Groom, *Patriotic Fire: Andrew Jackson and Jean Lafitte at the Battle of New Orleans* (New York, 2006).

29   in the form of needless casualties: An especially trenchant analysis of this problem, particularly in terms of how it bedeviled Southern strategy, may be found in Grady McWhiney and Perry D. Jamieson, *Attack and Die: Civil War Military Tactics and the Southern Heritage* (Tuscaloosa, Ala., 1982).

30   counterinsurgent campaign in the Philippines: American skill at irregular warfare was also displayed at times in these wars. Two of the best studies of them are by Jerome A. Greene, *Yellowstone Command: Colonel Nelson A. Miles and the Great Sioux War, 1876–1877* (Lincoln, Nebr., 1991), and Brian McAllister Linn, *The U.S. Army and Counterinsurgency in the Philippine War, 1899–1902* (Chapel Hill, 1989).

30   never more than 10 to 15 percent mechanized: On this point, see Overy, *Why the Allies Won*, especially Chapter 7, "A War of Engines."

33   the first decade of the cold war: For an overview of the complexities of trying to blend traditional ways of war with weapons of mass de-

struction, see Otto Heilbrunn, *Conventional Warfare in the Nuclear Age* (London, 1965).

33 "in decline from the moment it was enunciated": Thomas Schelling, *Arms and Influence* (New Haven, 1966), p. 190.

34 "uncertain trumpet": See Maxwell Taylor, *The Uncertain Trumpet* (New York, 1959), which both critiques the New Look and makes the case for flexible response.

36 the air assault paradigm: An outstanding chronicle of the improvements that were made to the American concept of operations is Lewis Sorley, *A Better War* (New York, 1999).

38 "dumb iron bombs": Citation from Richard Hallion, *Storm over Iraq* (Washington, D.C., 1992), p. 188.

40 welded together both knowledge and force: See our *In Athena's Camp: Preparing for Conflict in the Information Age* (Santa Monica, 1997).

40 "generals put their heads down on their desks in despair": Bob Woodward, *Bush at War* (New York, 2002), p. 247.

41 insist that virtually nothing new had happened in Afghanistan: The most articulate exposition of this point of view may be found in Stephen Biddle, *Afghanistan and the Future of Warfare* (Carlisle Barracks, Pa., 2002). His assessment is that the campaign was "much closer to a typical 20th-century mid-intensity conflict" (p. vii) than it was to something reflective of revolutionary change.

42 midway between the two camps' preferences: For an excellent summary of the prewar debate, see Nina Bernstein, "Strategists Fight a War about the War," *New York Times*, April 6, 2003.

42 considered the whole matter of the missing Iraqis something of a "mystery": John Keegan, *The Iraq War* (New York, 2004), Chapter 1, "A Mysterious War."

45 "few and the large": I am building on phrasing introduced by Martin C. Libicki in his *The Mesh and the Net: Speculations on Armed Conflict in a Time of Free Silicon* (Washington, D.C., 1994).

48 out of their country: On this point about the Chechens' concept of small-unit operations, see John Arquilla and Theodore Karasik, "Chechnya: A Glimpse of Future Conflict?" *Studies in Conflict and Terrorism*, vol. 22 (1999), pp. 207–226. An excellent general history of this war may be found in Carlotta Gall and Thomas de Waal, *Chechnya: Calamity in the Caucasus* (New York, 1998).

49 a profoundly dislocating effect on their adversaries: On this point, see S. L. A. Marshall, *Night Drop: The American Airborne Invasion of Normandy* (Boston, 1962).

49 and overcome a large garrison: See the memoir of this attack by its leader, Lt. Gen. E. M. Flanagan, Jr., *Corregidor: The Rock Force Assault, 1945* (Novato, Calif., 1988).

Chapter 3. War at Sea . . . and from the Sea

57   "castles of steel": The phrase is from the historian Robert K. Massie. For a comprehensive history of battleships before and during World War I, see both his *Dreadnought* (New York, 1991) and *Castles of Steel* (New York, 2003).

59   never make visual contact with each other: This first happened in the Battle of the Coral Sea, in May 1942, was repeated at Midway the following month, and became the norm for most major fleet actions throughout the rest of the Pacific war. When surface combat ships did come within gun range of each other, as in the several naval battles off Guadalcanal, it was usually at night, when attack aircraft could not threaten them.

60   the Red Navy ended up deploying several hundred submarines: See Gorshkov's *The Sea Power of the State* (New York, 1982).

61   six of these ships were sunk and a dozen others suffered varying degrees of damage: See Sandy Woodward, *One Hundred Days: The Memoirs of the Falklands Battle Group Commander* (Annapolis, 1992), a remarkably insightful analysis of this conflict from the perspective of the British naval commander who conducted the campaign. Another thoughtful account may be found in Max Hastings and Simon Jenkins, *The Battle for the Falklands* (New York, 1983). The most comprehensive history of these events is Lawrence Freedman's *Official History of the Falklands Campaign,* 2 vols. (London, 2007).

61   "The era of the submarine as the predominant weapon of power at sea must there be recognized as having begun": John Keegan, *The Price of Admiralty* (New York, 1989), p. 274.

62   Russia's ironically named *Gorshkov:* The *Gorshkov* is slated to be renamed the *Vikramaditya,* after an ancient Indian ruler. Aside from this acquisition, India has also been developing a carrier of its own design, scheduled for completion in 2012.

63   a big fleet of expensive ships: Two of the seminal studies of the directions that Chinese sea power might take, written by Chinese naval officers, are: Shen Zhongchang, Zhang Haiyin, and Zhou Xinsheng, "21st Century Naval Warfare," *China Military Science* (Spring 1995), and another article of theirs, "The Military Revolution in Naval Warfare," in *China Military Science 1* (1996). Both studies emphasize the importance of "remote warfare," and both are included in a remarkable volume about Chinese strategic thought compiled, edited and analyzed by Michael Pillsbury, *Chinese Views of Future Warfare* (Washington, D.C., 1997). Pillsbury presciently suggests that the Chinese approach to "remote grappling" at sea even contemplates the need for a space warfare capability as well (pp. xxxvii–xxxviii).

64   "few and the large": For a thoughtful exposition of French concepts of naval operations, written at the time by a principal advocate of the

Jeune École, see Gabriel Charmes, *Naval Reform* (London, 1887). A modern historical analysis may be found in Theodore Ropp, *The Development of a Modern Navy: French Naval Policy 1871–1904* (Annapolis, 1987).

64 driving Britain and France into closer alliance: See Kennedy, *The Rise of the Anglo-German Antagonism*.

66 empower naval strike forces in fundamentally new ways: See Arthur Cebrowski and John Garstka, "Network-Centric Warfare," U.S. Naval Institute *Proceedings* (January 1998). For the system-of-systems approach, see Owens and Offley, *Lifting the Fog of War*.

67 dismantled by an explosive ordnance disposal team: See *"USS Carl Vinson* Returns from Deployment," CVN 70 Press Releases, July 31, 2005. The experience of the *Vinson* may have been extreme, but further research into the attacks conducted by several other carriers—that have not publicized such matters and so cannot be named—finds that they averaged about 150 bomb drops during their six-month deployments. While much more than the *Vinson*, these numbers would not match a single day's activities of an aircraft carrier during the Vietnam War, much less six months.

69 "valid enough as far as it goes": See his *American Carrier Air Power at the Dawn of a New Century* (Santa Monica, 2005), p. 102.

69 "portends a revolutionary improvement": Ibid., p. 79.

69 electronic rather than chemical explosives as triggers: The "rails" that define this gun are two metal rods that conduct huge streams of electricity—positively charged on one rail, negatively on the other—that repel each other and redirect the energy at an angle perpendicular to the rails. The rail-gun concept has been around since the 1970s but has made little progress because of the huge power requirements and the amount of damage done to the "rails" by each shot. Nevertheless the navy is devoting considerable resources to this system, which would be much cheaper than using cruise missiles and holds out the promise of returning naval gunfire to prominence. Given that a rail gun's nonexplosive ammunition (the gun relies on kinetic energy to kill) takes about six minutes to cover a two-hundred-mile shot, it is not hard to imagine that a smart opponent will engage with cruise missiles and, on defense, zigzag to avoid being hit.

71 the range of activities from raids to invasions: Bernard Brodie, *A Layman's Guide to Naval Strategy* (Princeton, 1944), especially Chapter 6.

72 "by none of the oceanic powers before": John Keegan, *The Second World War* (New York, 1989), p. 561.

75 "infiltration and exploitation": See Allan R. Millett, "Assault from the Sea," in Murray and Millett, eds., *Military Innovation in the Interwar Period*, especially pp. 64–70.

75 "the worst disaster and largest capitulation of British history": Winston S. Churchill, *The Second World War*, vol. 4, *The Hinge of Fate*

(Boston, 1950), p. 92. For an exceptionally detailed narrative of the campaign, see James Leasor, *Singapore: The Battle That Changed the World* (Garden City, N.Y., 1968).

76 driving them away from coastal communities throughout South Vietnam: On these campaigns, see Edwin H. Simmons, "Marine Corps Operations in Vietnam, 1965–66," in Frank Uhlig, ed., *Vietnam: The Naval Story* (Annapolis, 1986). For an account of Navy/Marine/SEAL riverine operations in Vietnam, see Thomas J. Cutler, *Brown Water, Black Berets* (Annapolis, 1988).

77 they killed some four hundred Allied troops in a single raid: Douglas Reeman, a British veteran of service in motor-torpedo boats during World War II, gave perhaps the finest account of the bitterness and intensity of the fighting between opposing light coastal forces in his novel *A Prayer for the Ship*.

77 "remote-controlled explosive motor boats were employed with some effect": Samuel Eliot Morison, *The Two-Ocean War: A Short History of the United States Navy in the Second World War* (Boston, 1963), p. 406.

78 better for the Russians during the cold war: On the Soviet navy's development and use of midget submarines during the cold war, see Gordon McCormick, *Stranger Than Fiction: Soviet Subs in Swedish Waters* (Santa Monica, 1990).

Chapter 4. Airpower in the Information Age

82 destructiveness of air-delivered munitions: On the poor results of strategic air campaigns, see Robert A. Pape, *Bombing to Win: Air Power and Coercion in War* (Ithaca, N.Y., 1996).

83 firebombings of Hamburg and Dresden: Hans Rumpf, the Third Reich's inspector general for fire prevention, wrote a wrenching firsthand account of these events, *The Bombing of Germany* (New York, 1963).

83 the amount of force needed to make aerial bombardment work: The seminal, influential study that made this point is by Harlan Ullman, James P. Wade, and L. A. Edney, *Shock and Awe: Achieving Rapid Dominance* (Washington, D.C., 1996).

84 "the mutual fear of big weapons": Kenneth N. Waltz, *Man, the State and War* (New York, 1959), p. 236.

84 "belief in 'victory through air power' was put to the test and found wanting": Max Hastings, *The Korean War* (New York, 1987), p. 268.

85 in clever new ways: The most highly regarded restatement of orthodox thinking about strategic bombing, which went on to suggest sophisticated new techniques, was John Warden's *The Air Campaign: Planning for Combat* (London, 1989).

86 after eleven weeks of air attacks: See Ivo Daalder and Michael O'Hanlon, *Winning Ugly: NATO's War to Save Kosovo* (Washington, D.C., 2000), and Benjamin S. Lambeth, *NATO's Air War for Kosovo: A Strategic and Operational Assessment* (Santa Monica, 2001).

87   had shown tremendous potency: On this point, see Charles Briscoe, Richard Kiper, James Schroeder, and Kalev Sepp, *Weapon of Choice: U.S. Army Special Operations Forces in Afghanistan* (Fort Leavenworth, Kans., 2003), especially Chapter 3. The most comprehensive study of the integrated air-ground campaign in Afghanistan is Benjamin Lambeth's *Air Power Against Terror: America's Conduct of Operation Enduring Freedom* (Santa Monica, 2005).

87   helped overcome German resistance: See Biddle, *Afghanistan and the Future of Warfare.*

89   proponents of this approach: On the prewar debate, see Bernstein, "Strategists Fight a War About the War." For more on the debate about the number of ground forces needed for an invasion of Iraq, see the discussion of this matter in Chapter 2.

92   networks of human spies to wither in the late 1970s: On the great confidence placed in satellites, and the history of their use, during these years, see William E. Burrows, *Deep Black: Space Espionage and National Security* (New York, 1986).

95   to strike at with nuclear warheads: The definitive study of these early efforts to think through the problems associated with attacking or defending satellites is James Canan, *War in Space* (New York, 1982).

96   collision with a satellite target: Ibid., pp. 20–21.

99   "air-going people": William Mitchell, *Winged Defense* (New York, 1925), p. 5.

101   because they lacked air cover: On the rise of close air support, and its crucial impact on the fighting in World War II, see Richard Muller, "Close Air Support," in Murray and Millett, eds., *Military Innovation in the Interwar Period.*

101   operations in Malaya and Kenya in the 1950s: A thoughtful discussion of the British experience may be found in Bruce Hoffman, *British Air Power in Peripheral Warfare, 1919–1976* (Santa Monica, 1989).

103   showed the feasibility and utility of this approach again and again: Over the past five years the school's "surveillance and target acquisition network" (STAN) and its "tactical network topology" (TNT) programs have repeatedly demonstrated the superior function and cost effectiveness of this approach, under the most rigorous conditions, to high-level Pentagon officials. Support for adopting these concepts is growing, but slowly, since there is already some emphasis on developing lighter-than-air platforms that can linger in "near space" for weeks on end, relaying data and facilitating command and control. See William B. Scott, "The Fringe of Space," *Aviation Week & Space Technology,* January 30, 2006.

104   23 percent before the relief effort, 50 percent after: A good summary of the air force's growing involvement in humanitarian relief operations and the positive effects of this trend may be found in Richard Whittle, "Built for War, Air Force Units Reap Peace," *Christian Science Monitor,* December 1, 2006, p. 3.

104   humanitarian responses to natural disasters: A good overview of the potential of airships today may be found in Jeff Wise, "Just Don't Call It a Blimp," *Popular Mechanics*, October 2006, pp. 60–65.

104   "return of the Zeppelins": The first airship was created and launched in July 1900 by the German Count Ferdinand von Zeppelin. During World War I, Zeppelins were used, unsuccessfully, in a strategic aerial bombing campaign against Great Britain.

105   short takeoff and landing capability: The perceived need for this capability drives development and production costs for the fighter sky high.

105   "pointing" still matters: On the emergence of air combat tactics, see Quentin Reynolds's classic account of the aerial aspects of World War I, *They Fought for the Sky* (New York, 1957).

Chapter 5. Thinking About Nonlethal Weapons

113   sorted out among crowds of mostly innocent people: For a thorough discussion of these NLW—and a wide range of other types—see John Alexander, *Future War: Non-Lethal Weapons in Twenty-First Century Warfare* (New York, 1999).

114   do damage far from the site of their initial deployment: Ibid., pp. 82–83.

115   the gas killed 129 of the hostages: For an analysis of just what type of "knockout weapon" was used, see Valeria Korchagina, "U.S. Says Gas Used Was Opiate," *Moscow Times*, October 29, 2002.

115   they swarmed out and freed everyone: For an excellent account of this rescue, see the reportage of *El Comercio*, assembled in their book on this crisis, *Base Tokio: El Verano Sangriente* (Lima, Peru, 1997). Also the memoir of the Peruvian military officer who commanded in this action is quite powerful. See General de Ejército Nicolás de Bari Hermoza Ríos, *Operación Chavin de Huantar: Rescate en la residencia de la Embajada del Japón* (Lima, 1997).

117   briefly knocking out power all over the world: In the film version of the story, power was out for half an hour, but in the original tale by Harry Bates, "Farewell to the Master," the outage was for just three minutes. See also the later novelization by Arthur Tofte, *The Day the Earth Stood Still* (New York, 1976), p. 113.

119   driven theorists of air power to distraction for the better part of a century: See the discussion in the preceding chapter. For more on the analogy between air power and cyberspace-based operations, see Greg Rattray, *Strategic Warfare in Cyberspace* (Cambridge, Mass., 2001).

119   a point of view held by most experts in the field: See Alexander, *Future War*, especially Chapter 10, "Information Warfare."

120   take command of a particular machine much as its legitimate owner would: On this point see Lara Jakes Jordan, "Hackers Control Millions of Computers," Associated Press, June 14, 2007.

120   envisioned this new arena of conflict: See Martin Libicki, *What Is Information Warfare?* (Washington, D.C., 1995), pp. 81–83. Gibson's pioneering novel is *Neuromancer* (New York, 1984).

122   by as much as several days or weeks: The RAND Corporation's Glenn Buchan led some of the early research into this problem. See in particular his *Information War and the Air Force* (Santa Monica, 1996). For a more general view of early military perceptions of vulnerability to cyber attack, see Neil Munro, "The Pentagon's New Nightmare: An Electronic Pearl Harbor," *Washington Post*, July 16, 1995.

123   undermine the ability of the Pacific Fleet to perform in the war game at hand: A very good discussion of Eligible Receiver may be found in Dan Verton, *Black Ice: The Invisible Threat of Cyber-Terrorism* (New York, 2005), pp. 31–34.

127   pushed to make crypto available: Steven Levy, *Crypto: How the Code Rebels Beat the Government—Saving Privacy in the Digital Age* (New York, 2001).

128   keeping crises from mushrooming into conflicts: James Adams provided an example of how cyber attack might be used preemptively in his thoughtful *The Next World War: Computers Are the Weapons and the Front Line Is Everywhere* (New York, 1998), pp. 21–34. Dan Verton does something very similar in his *Black Ice*, pp. 1–16.

131   money movement and many other functions: For a comprehensive survey of terrorist use of cyberspace, see Gabriel Weimann, *Terror on the Internet: The New Arena, the New Challenges* (Washington, D.C., 2006).

Chapter 6. The Rise of Influence Operations

135   out of sheer rhetorical verve: On the more ethically questionable aspects of this practice, see John Mueller, *Overblown: How Politicians and the Terrorism Industry Inflate National Security Threats, and Why We Believe Them* (New York, 2006).

135   "they will believe the good, if we tell them the bad also": From a letter Jefferson wrote to James Monroe dated January 1, 1815. See Paul Leicester Ford, ed., *The Writings of Thomas Jefferson* (New York, 1898).

136   the new office might engage in deceptions: It is widely believed that senior leaders in the military "public affairs" community—those most directly involved in informing the media of ongoing service matters, in peace and war—raised awareness of the OSI's intended purpose because they were outraged at the notion of deceiving the public in any way.

137   "we cannot make policy concessions": There were also Pentagon officials in attendance, including an assistant secretary of defense responsible for this aspect of our information strategy, his principal deputy, and a number of the serving military officers charged with developing our influence operations. The serving officers were the most

outraged at the idea that we might ever consider making concessions based on feedback.

137 "an opportunity to dialogue with terrorists": Russell D. Howard, "Preemptive Military Doctrine," in Howard and Reid L. Sawyer, eds., *Defeating Terrorism: Shaping the New Security Environment* (Guilford, Conn., 2002), p. 121.

140 Rumsfeld chose to accede, in large part, to their preferred plan: He did not give in to the traditionalists' desire for an expeditionary force of nearly 500,000 troops, but he did agree to send around 200,000 and authorized the full-scale aerial bombing campaign. The most thorough account of these debates may be found in Bob Woodward's *Plan of Attack* (New York, 2004).

141 favored a rapid end to the occupation: The Kurds, who amount to about one-fifth of the population of Iraq, and harbor separatist dreams of their own, accounted for most of those who expressed a willingness to countenance a continued occupation. The polling was done under the combined sponsorship of *USA Today*, the BBC, ABC News, and the German television network, ARD. For a good summary of the results, see Jesse Nunes, "Polls Show Iraqis Live Surrounded by Violence, Distrust US," *Christian Science Monitor*, March 20, 2007.

141 "the battle of ideas that's taking place in the world today": The speech was given at the Carlisle Barracks, Pennsylvania, on March 27, 2006, some seven-plus months before President Bush announced his intention to dismiss Rumsfeld as defense secretary.

142 accomplished their higher education in non-Muslim countries: See Marc Sageman, *Understanding Terror Networks* (Philadelphia, 2004), pp. 74–77.

144 notions of waging war in a just fashion: Fighting ethically is referred to as *jus in bello*, and includes using force in a proportionate rather than in an overwhelming manner. Going to war justly, *jus ad bellum*, requires demonstrating "right purpose" (e.g., self-defense), due authorization, and exhausting diplomatic options so that conflict is pursued only as a last resort. The great modern scholar of just war theory is Michael Walzer. See his *Just and Unjust Wars* (New York, 1977).

144 air attacks on suspected insurgent safe houses: Aerial attacks on suspected safe houses are allowed, if not preferred, because of the desire to mitigate the risks faced by our ground forces. It is far less dangerous to call in an air strike on a home than to kick in the doors and either be involved in a firefight with those inside or have to confront a jihadi willing to blow himself up rather than be captured. This is a principal reason why Abu Musab al Zarqawi was killed by an air attack on his safe house rather than given the chance to kill Americans in a bloody last stand.

146 one of the most basic human impulses: On the use of these techniques during the Korean War, see Edgar Schein, "The Chinese Indoctrination Program for Prisoners of War: A Study of Attempted

'Brainwashing,'" *Psychiatry,* 19:149–172 (1956). On the principle of commitment and consistency, see Robert Cialdini, *Influence: The Psychology of Persuasion* (New York, 1996), especially Chapter 3.

148   the ANO was never itself again: This counterterror coup against the ANO remains a highly classified matter, but there has been some mention of it in the open record. See, for example, Faye Bowers, "A Lesson in Defeating a Terrorist," *Christian Science Monitor,* November 15, 2002; and David Tucker, *Skirmishes at the Edge of Empire: The United States and International Terrorism* (London, 1997), pp. 40–42.

149   the real target was Sicily: See Ewen Montagu, *The Man Who Never Was* (Philadelphia, 1954).

150   achieved very high returns: See Barton Whaley, "The 1% Solution: Costs and Benefits of Military Deception," in John Arquilla and Douglas Borer, eds., *Information Strategy and Warfare: A Guide to Theory and Practice* (London, 2007).

152   or to escalate the war: The Mueller quote is from his "American Public Opinion and the Gulf War," in Stanley A. Renshon, ed., *The Political Psychology of the Gulf War: Leaders, Publics, and the Process of Conflict* (Pittsburgh, 1993), pp. 210–211. See also Eric Larson's *Casualties and Consensus: The Historical Role of Casualties in Domestic Support for U.S. Military Operations* (Santa Monica, 1996), especially p. 89 on opinion during the Vietnam War. On this last point, John Mueller's seminal *War, Presidents, and Public Opinion* (New York, 1973) also provides important insights.

152   illusory but powerful belief in the media's anti-war biases: Study after study has confirmed the balanced nature of journalists' reporting—both in print and visual media—including official surveys by the Department of Defense's own Center for Military History. Perhaps the most telling study of the limited influence of television reporting may be found in Johanna Neuman, *Lights, Cameras, War: Is Media Technology Driving International Politics?* (New York, 1996).

153   "the winning of the clash of wills": Gen. Rupert Smith, *The Utility of Force: The Art of War in the Modern World* (New York, 2007), p. 410. Emphasis added.

155   warned so eloquently: See Andrew Bacevich, *The New American Militarism* (London, 2005).

155   what the scholar John Prados calls its "seductiveness": See John Prados, *Safe for Democracy: The Secret Wars of the CIA* (Chicago, 2006), especially p. 645; and Tim Weiner, *Legacy of Ashes: The History of the CIA* (New York, 2007).

Chapter 7. A New Course of Study: "Netwar 101"

158   we first fielded this concept for the Department of Defense: Although we discussed netwar briefly in a paper in 1993, our first major

study of this topic may be found in John Arquilla and David Ronfeldt, *The Advent of Netwar* (Santa Monica, 1996).

158   killing or capture of the leaders of the Medellín and Cali cartels: On the "counter-leadership" campaign against the major cartels, see Mark Bowden, *Killing Pablo: The Hunt for the World's Greatest Outlaw* (New York, 2001).

160   defeated one of the world's great militaries in direct battle: Two important accounts of this conflict are Anatol Lieven, *Chechnya: Tombstone of Russian Power* (New Haven, 1998), and Gall and de Waal, *Chechnya: Calamity in the Caucasus*. For analysis of the networked aspects of this conflict, see Arquilla and Karasik, "Chechnya: A Glimpse of Future Conflict?," pp. 207–229.

161   a protracted contest against the better-armed Americans for control of Iraq: In the already voluminous literature on the Iraq War, Loretta Napoleoni stands out in terms of having an especially keen appreciation of the networked aspects of the uprising. See her *Insurgent Iraq* (New York, 2005).

161   "command and control systems of traditional insurgent organizations": Letter from James Thomson to Donald Rumsfeld, February 7, 2005.

161   "between vulnerable and hardened systems": Donald Rumsfeld, "Transforming the Military," *Foreign Affairs* (May–June 2002), p. 28.

161   "communicate and operate seamlessly on the battlefield": Ibid., p. 31.

162   "be straight with the American people. Tell them the truth": Ibid., p. 32.

162   closely coordinated with military actions in the field: See the detailed discussion of influence operations in the preceding chapter.

165   withstood the Israeli occupation of southern Lebanon for years: The first Israeli invasion of Lebanon, which sparked the rise of Hezbollah, is thoughtfully chronicled in Ze'ev Schiff and Ehud Ya'ari, *Israel's Lebanon War* (New York, 1984).

166   the vast majority of fighting for the past half-millennium took place between recognizable nations: For an excellent overview of the past five hundred years in military affairs, see Max Boot, *War Made New: Technology, Warfare, and the Course of History, 1500 to Today* (New York, 2006).

167   the underlying dynamic driving conflict since the 1950s has been internal: An early awareness of the increasing salience of civil wars and revolutions may be seen in Harry Eckstein, ed., *Internal War* (New York, 1964), a volume to which many of the leading social scientists of the day contributed. Eerily, most of what they had to say then still seems quite relevant.

169   "ought to be waged in a revolutionary manner": Russell Weigley, "American Strategy from Its Beginnings Through the First World

War," in Peter Paret, ed., *Makers of Modern Strategy* (Princeton, 1986), p. 410.

170   "one of the ablest military critics and historians of this or any other day": Preface to Antoine Henri de Jomini, *The Art of War* (Philadelphia, 1862), p. 7.

170   in search of a single decisive battle: Lincoln's struggles against Jominian orthodoxy are nicely recounted in T. H. Williams, "The Military Leadership of North and South," in David Donald, ed., *Why the North Won the Civil War* (New York, 1962).

171   soon all went awry, with tragic end results: This is a theme in Andrew F. Krepinevich, Jr., *The Army and Vietnam* (Baltimore, 1986).

172   "surprisingly orthodox": See his *Afghanistan and the Future of Warfare: Implications for Army and Defense Policy* (Carlisle, Pa., 2002), p. iv.

173   "leadership needed to intercede in specific targeting decisions": Michael E. O'Hanlon, "A Flawed Masterpiece," *Foreign Affairs* (May–June 2002), pp. 57, 59.

173   his initial idea about the major shift in the nature of war: See Martin van Creveld, *The Changing Face of War: Lessons of Combat from the Marne to Iraq* (New York, 2006).

174   Over the past several years, I have attempted: In my capacity as director of an information operations "center for excellence" established by former Deputy Secretary of Defense Paul Wolfowitz in September 2004.

176   classical strategists have not been ignored: The most comprehensive survey of classical thought about the principles of war may be found in John I. Alger, *The Quest for Victory* (Westport, Conn., 1982). Col. Harry Summers, *On Strategy: A Critical Analysis of the Vietnam War* (Novato, Calif., 1995 reissue), looks at Vietnam through the specific lens provided by the principles of war I have been describing.

177   the modest investment of nineteen fighters and perhaps $300,000: An important critique of the classical principles of war, written pre-9/11 but having a distinct post-9/11 sensibility, may be found in Robert R. Leonhard, *The Principles of War for the Information Age* (Novato, Calif., 1998). A thoughtful blending of some old principles in the context of a new kind of warfare is featured in Bevin Alexander, *How Wars Are Won: The Thirteen Rules of War from Ancient Greece to the War on Terror* (New York, 2002).

178   "light on the ability to find and fix": From a speech given at the Council on Foreign Relations, February 17, 2006.

179   achieved much at low cost: The most comprehensive study of our more networked approach in this campaign may be found in Charles H. Briscoe, Richard L. Kiper, James A Schroder, and Kalev I. Sepp, *Weapon of Choice: U.S. Army Special Forces in Afghanistan* (Fort Leavenworth, Kans., 2003).

180   "swarm tactics": See John Robb, *Brave New War: The Next Stage of Terrorism and the End of Globalization* (New York, 2007).
180   "dynamic, decentralized resilience": Ibid., especially pp. 164–183.
180   share sensitive information in timely, targeted ways: See Gary Hart, *The Shield and the Cloak: The Security of the Commons* (Oxford, 2006).
180   "focus the intellectual capital of our people": Thomas X. Hammes, *The Sling and the Stone: On War in the 21st Century* (St. Paul, Minn., 2004), pp. 5, 226.

Chapter 8. Social Change and the Armed Forces

183   the military seems to have gotten things right: In coming to grips with black/white relations, this success was apparent at least twenty years ago. See, for example, the analysis of the eminent military sociologist Charles C. Moskos in his seminal article, "Success Story: Blacks in the Military," *Atlantic Monthly* (May 1986), pp. 64–72.
183   routinely go in harm's way: A thorough history of the military's relationship with women may be found in Jeanne Holm, *Women in the Military: An Unfinished Revolution* (Novato, Calif., 1992). A sharp critique of the notion of allowing women into combat is articulated in Stephanie Gutmann, *The Kinder, Gentler Military: Can America's Gender-Neutral Fighting Force Still Win Wars?* (New York, 2000).
185   the number of evangelicals in the overall American population is only 14 percent: The term evangelical refers to those with a very strong belief—often literal—in Scripture, and a clearly felt sense of having been "born again to Christ." A significant subset of this group (a bit less than half) falls into the Pentecostal category, which features an emphasis on the deep individual connection with the Holy Spirit, sometimes manifested in the form of speaking in tongues or in acts of faith healing. Catholics and mainline Protestants who embrace such practices are generally considered "charismatics." They are not included in the overall tally of evangelicals. Sources: Center for the Study of Global Christianity; The Pew Forum on Religion and Public Life.
185   the military social environment is a forbidding one for gays: Source: Department of Defense. See also Jeff Brady, "Evangelical Chaplains Test Bounds of Faith in Military," National Public Radio, January 6, 2007.
185   continue to trump notions of social equity: Interestingly, Colin Powell's successor as chairman of the joint chiefs, John Shalikashvili, has recently taken the position that gays can and eventually will be openly accepted in the service. See his "Second Thoughts on Gays in the Military," *New York Times*, January 2, 2007. But this view was more than offset soon after by Gen. Peter Pace, the chairman who stepped down in mid-2007, who publicly called homosexuality "immoral." See Dan Ephron, "General Comment," *Newsweek*, March 26, 2007. Pace was

made to recant, but the fact that a chairman would stir up this hornets' nest in such a manner is troubling.

186   the claim of homosexual orientation: I am grateful to my colleague Kalev Sepp, a retired army lieutenant colonel and currently a deputy assistant secretary of defense for special operations, for first drawing this matter to my attention.

187   pursuing the recruitment of more Muslims: See Richard Whittle, "Uncle Sam Wants U.S. Muslims to Serve," *Christian Science Monitor,* December 27, 2006.

189   only nine entered the military, of roughly 1,100 men and women: Statistics cited from Brad Knickerbocker, "Behind Talk of a New Draft: Equity," *Christian Science Monitor,* November 22, 2006.

189   the shared experience of military service: On this point, see Thomas Ricks, "The Widening Gap Between the Military and Society," *Atlantic Monthly,* July 1997.

189   "no tradition of a draft, absent an ongoing war, hot or cold": Bernard Rostker, *I Want You! The Evolution of the All-Volunteer Force* (Santa Monica, 2006), p. 3.

189   larger reserve was first argued for by former Senator Gary Hart before 9/11: See Gary Hart, *The Minuteman: Restoring an Army of the People* (New York, 1998).

190   disparaging comments about the performance of conscripts: See Vernon Loeb, "Rumsfeld Apologizes for Remarks on Draftees," *Washington Post,* January 22, 2003.

191   from burger flipping to trigger pulling: For details of the more combat-oriented tasks undertaken by contractors in Iraq—and elsewhere, see Jeremy Scahill, *Blackwater: The Rise of the World's Most Powerful Mercenary Army* (New York, 2007).

192   competent, ethically healthy, and politically neutral standing national force: For balanced, thoughtful discussions of this issue, see Robert Mandel, "Fighting Fire with Fire: Privatizing Counterterrorism," in R. D. Howard and R. L. Sawyer, *Defeating Terrorism* (Guilford, Conn., 2004), and John P. Sullivan, "Terrorism, Crime and Private Armies," in Robert Bunker, *Networks, Terrorism and Global Insurgency* (London, 2005).

192   enlisted personnel and noncommissioned officers: The best overview of this development is provided by Lance Betros, a military historian on the faculty at West Point. See his "Political Partisanship and the Military Ethic in America," *Armed Forces & Society,* vol. 27, no. 4 (2001), pp. 501–523.

193   "or in any way lend his name or support to politicians seeking office": Forrest C. Pogue, *Education of a General* (New York, 1963), p. 280.

196   "it's less likely to be used": Cited in Knickerbocker, "Behind Talk of a New Draft: Equity."

197   "sets aside the terms of the contract that the service member . . . has with the government": See Rostker, *I Want You!*, p. 695.

197   "ask the men of Harvard to stand alongside the men of Harlem, same uniform, same obligations, same country": James Webb, "The Draft: Why the Army Needs It," *Atlantic Monthly*, April 1980, pp. 34–44. Note that Webb's mention of "men" implies his opposition at that time to conscription of women. My hope is that his support for a draft has not waned but that his opposition to the inclusion of women in the selective service process has.

198   battle greatly expanded U.S. southwestern and Pacific Coast frontiers: On the poor results achieved in the first war, see William Hickey, *The War of 1812: A Forgotten Conflict* (Chicago, 1989). The classic account of our great success in the latter conflict is Bernard de Voto's *Year of Decision* (Boston, 1950). Also excellent is Otis Singletary's *The Mexican War* (Chicago, 1960).

199   "crusader state": On this point, see Walter McDougall, *Promised Land, Crusader State: The American Encounter with the World Since 1776* (Boston, 1997).

Chapter 9. Will the Military Embrace Change?

210   out of commission: Five were later refloated and restored. All served with distinction in supporting amphibious operations. But in all of the Pacific war, the U.S. Navy would fight only one battleship-on-battleship action, off Guadalcanal in November 1942. On this episode, see Ivan Musicant, *Battleship at War* (New York, 1986).

210   launched just eight new battleships: Production details on aircraft carriers and battleships are in Samuel Eliot Morison, *History of U.S. Naval Operations in World War Two*, vol. 15, *Supplement and General Index* (Boston, 1962), pp. 29–35.

210   the battleships' preeminence at sea would likely have persisted: On the stubbornness with which serving naval leaders of all the great powers clung to their battleships—and the candidness with which retired admirals in the 1920s and 1930s sometimes spoke about their battleships' vulnerability to air and torpedo attack—see Richard Hough, *Death of the Battleship* (New York, 1963), especially Chapters 3–4.

211   "war by minutes": I am paraphrasing from the title of Robert Leonhard's thoughtful study, *Fighting by Minutes: Time and the Art of War* (New York, 1994).

212   until nearly the end in Vietnam: An important argument that some positive changes were made during the last years of our intervention in Vietnam may be found in Sorley's *A Better War*. But it is important to note that little of what Sorley has to say affirms the validity of the big-unit approach, which was surgically dissected in Krepinevich's magisterial *The Army and Vietnam*.

213 "broad preparation": See Bevin Alexander, *The Future of Warfare* (New York, 1995), especially p. 51.
214 assault by Russian tanks: For an in-depth account of the birth of the "AirLand Battle" doctrine that came out of the ashes of Vietnam, see Alvin and Heidi Toffler, *War and Anti-War: Survival at the Dawn of the 21st Century* (Boston, 1993), especially pp. 54–55 and 134–140.
218 several distinguished retired officers had turned down the offer: See Peter Baker and Thomas E. Ricks, "In White House Plan, War 'Czar' Would Cut Through Bureaucracy," *Washington Post,* April 13, 2007.
218 communications technology of the day, the telegraph: See John E. Clark, Jr., *Railroads in the Civil War* (Baton Rouge, La., 2001), and George Edgar Turner's classic *Victory Rode the Rails* (New York, 1953). On Lincoln's personal level of involvement in keeping track of events with near-daily visits to the central telegraph office, see the memoir of one of the operators, David Homer Bates, *Lincoln in the Telegraph Office: Recollections of the United States Military Telegraph During the Civil War* (New York, 1907).
219 resistance from the military and even from members of his own cabinet: See Doris Kearns Goodwin's remarkable *Team of Rivals: The Political Genius of Abraham Lincoln* (New York, 2005).
220 With none of these worldviews were Americans entirely happy: The danger posed by this increased emphasis on the use of force in our statecraft is the subject of Gabriel Kolko's *Another Century of War?* (New York, 2002), a thoughtful meditation on our strategic "drift."
224 competencies in counterterrorism and other irregular warfare missions: For a full examination of his policy recommendations, see Hart, *The Minuteman.*
224 keeping military elites small—that is, "elite": See Eliot Cohen, *Commandos and Politicians: Elite Military Units in Modern Democracies* (Cambridge, Mass., 1978), especially Chapter 5.
225 "laboratory for military doctrine": Ibid., pp. 31–32.
225 unconventional warfare might be salvaged: On the parlous state of our capacities in this area of endeavor, see Hy S. Rothstein, *Afghanistan and the Troubled Future of Unconventional Warfare* (Annapolis, 2006).
227 a national archive heading the list of possibilities: For an outstanding overview of the Pentagon's place in American military affairs, see Steve Vogel, *The Pentagon: A History* (New York, 2007).
229 a smaller military-industrial complex: See Murray Weidenbaum, *Small Wars, Big Defense: Paying for the Military After the Cold War* (Oxford, 1992).
230 a key obstacle to creativity: See his *The Innovator's Dilemma: When New Technologies Cause Great Firms to Fail* (Boston, 1997).

Index

A NOTE ON THE AUTHOR

John Arquilla is professor of defense analysis at the
United States Naval Postgraduate School in Monterey,
California. Born in Oak Park, Illinois, he received
M.A. and Ph.D. degrees from Stanford University. As
a policy analyst at the RAND Corporation, he consulted
to General Norman Schwarzkopf during the first Gulf
War, and to the deputy secretary of defense during the
Kosovo War. His other books include *The Reagan Im-
print*, *From Troy to Entebbe*, *In Athena's Camp*, and
Networks and Netwars. He is married with two chil-
dren and lives in Monterey, California.